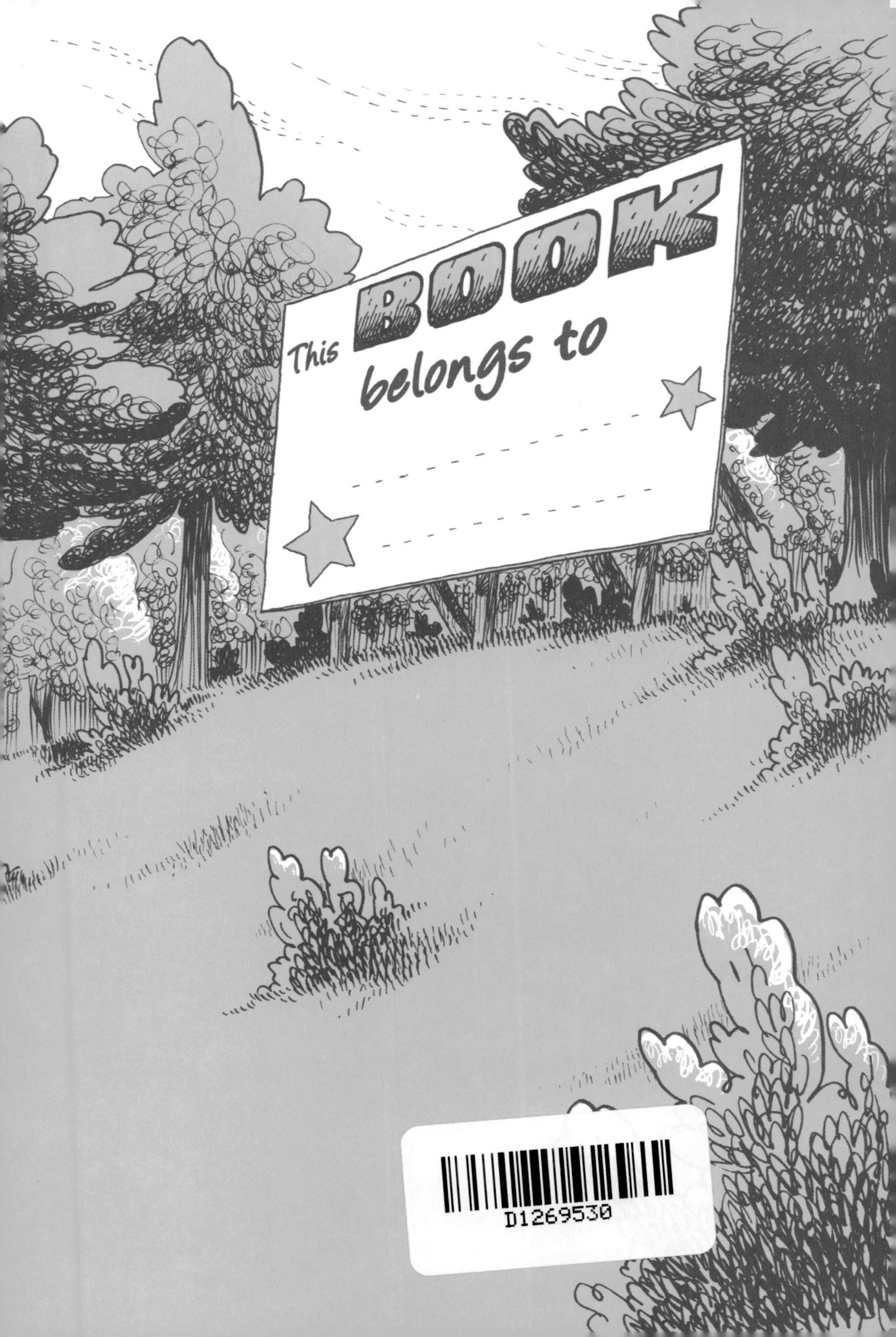
This BOOK belongs to

Written by Sibylline and Capucine
Illustrated by Jérôme d'Aviau

Translation by Edward Gauvin
Editing, localization, and layout by Mike Kennedy

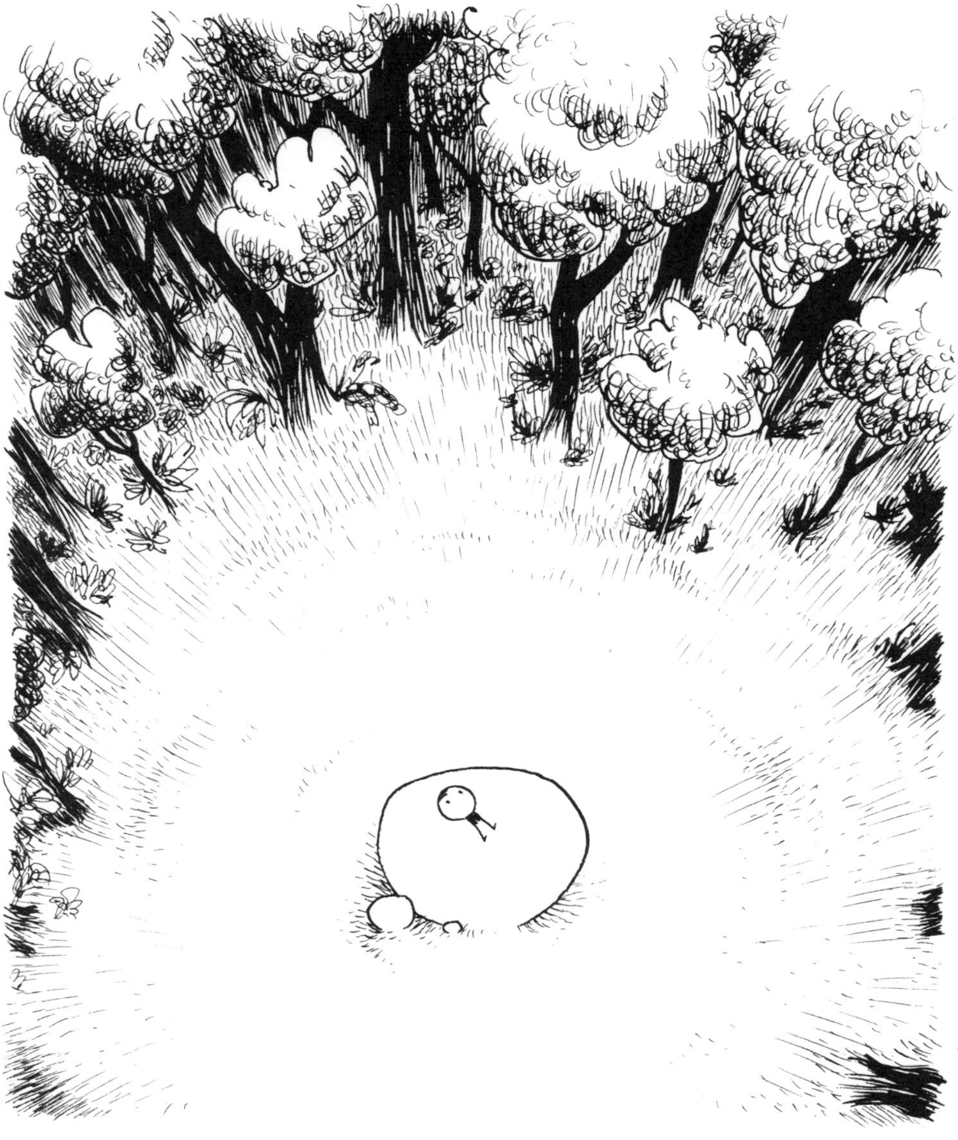

Once upon a time, early one morning...

In the middle of a quiet, not-so-special clearing in the woods, a wee tiny whatsit woke up without any memory at all.

He couldn't remember what he was doing there, or what he wanted, or that he had even been sleeping in the first place.

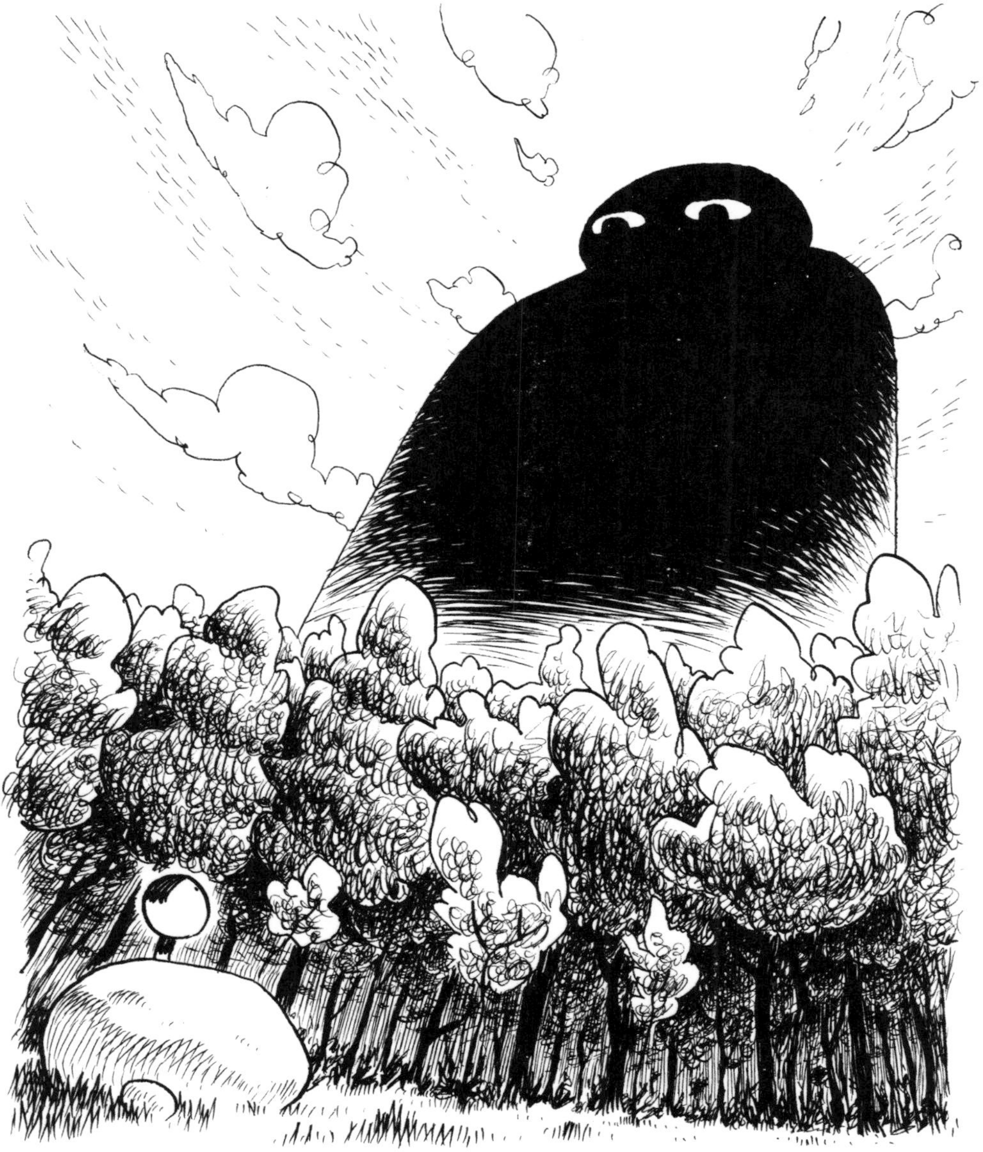

"Who am I? What am I doing here?"

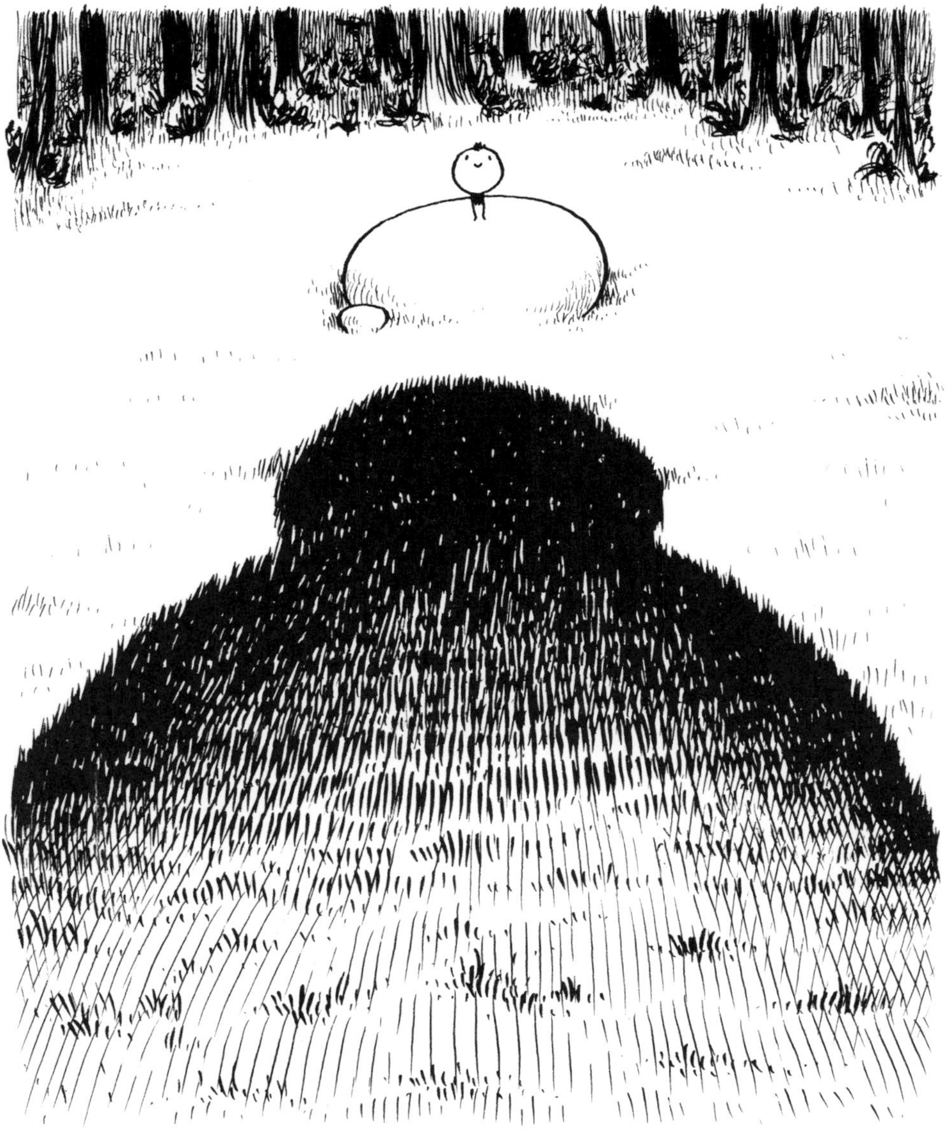

"You were born from the recent rain. I watched you grow, and you were cute. I named you Alphonse Tabouret. It suits you, now that you know how to speak."

"Alphonse Tabouret? Neat. I like that name."

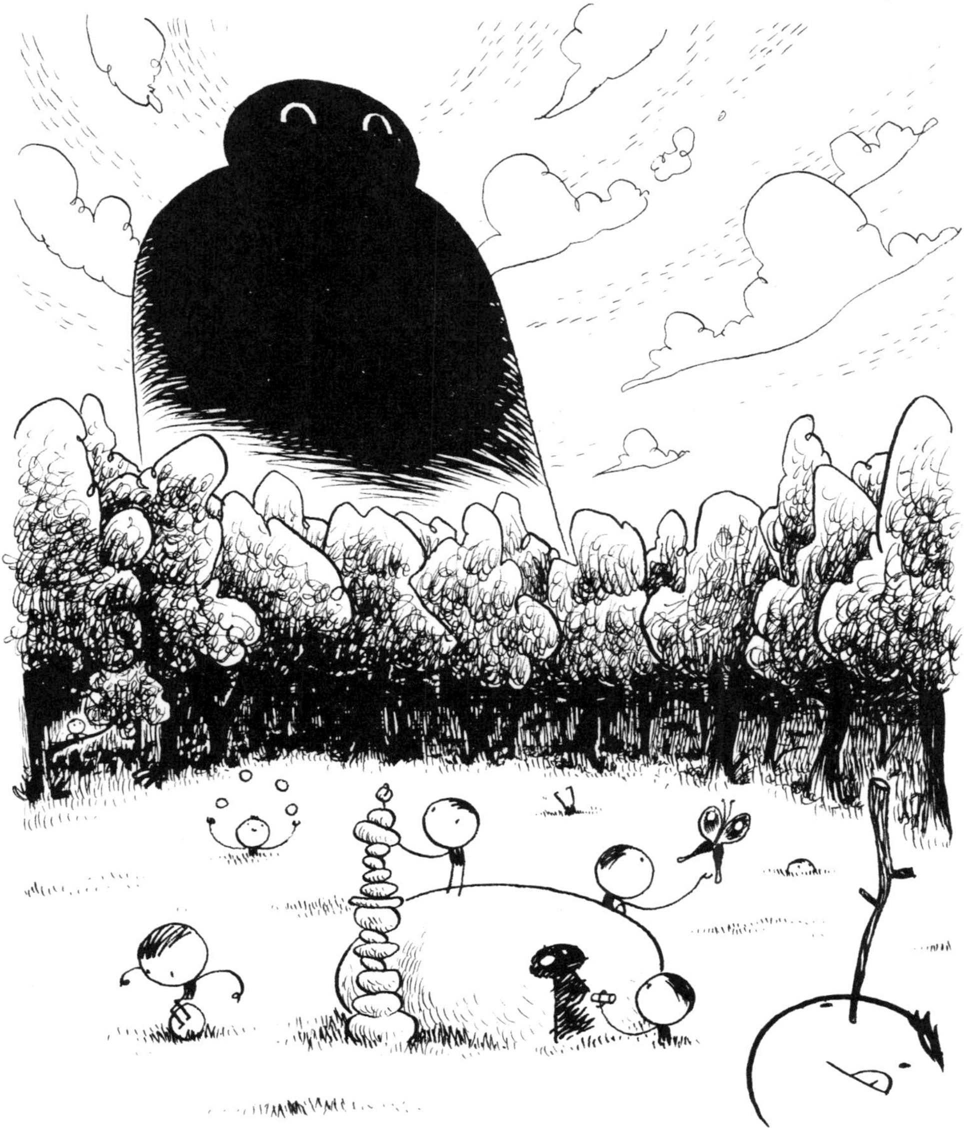

The Big Man then taught him a lot of other very essential things.

 "Well, I hope I haven't been wasting my time on you. What do you have to share?"

"Share? What does that mean?"

"It means you give me things, and I give you things back."

"But I don't have anything to give! What do I do?"

"Come up with something. Even a word can be a gift. But if you don't come up with something, it means you don't want to share. And that makes you selfish."

"Whoa! Hang on, I just got here!"

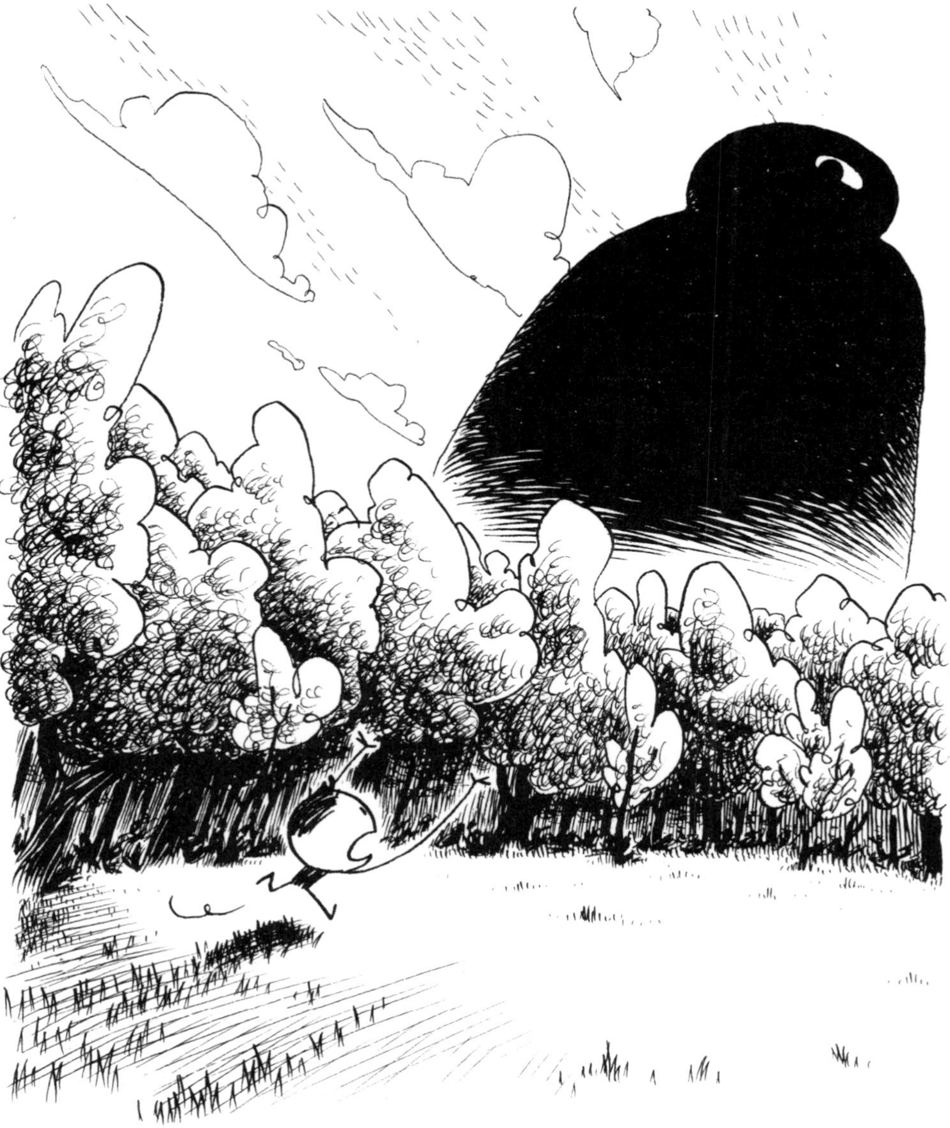

"Wow, who taught you manners? If that's how you're going to be, I'm leaving."

"Wait!"

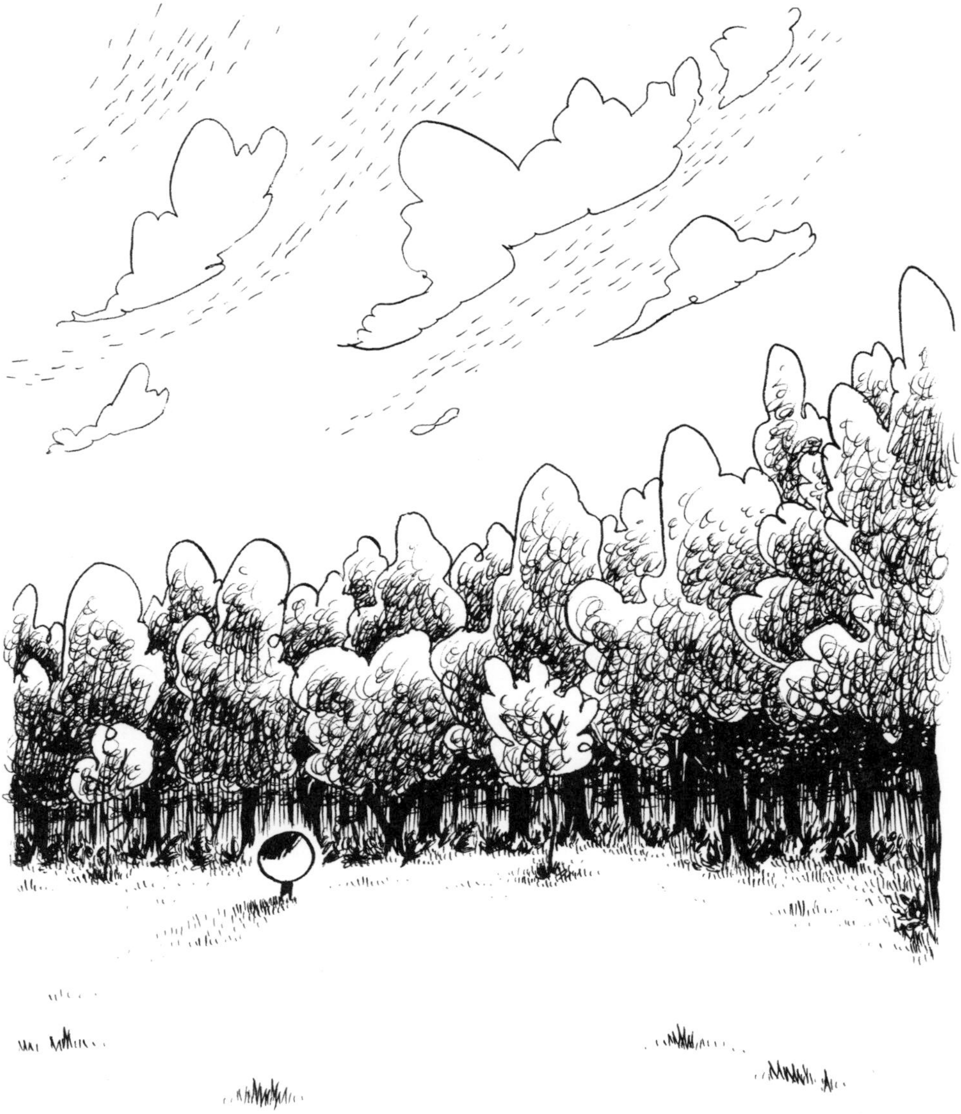

But it was too late.

The Big Man was gone.

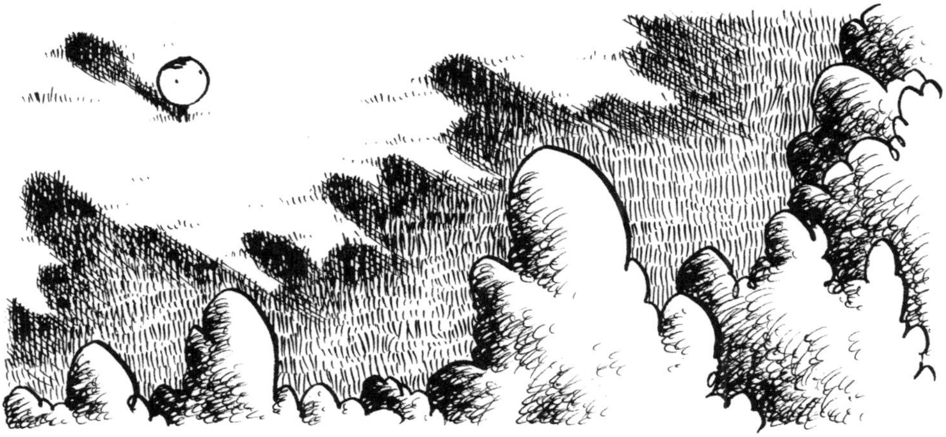

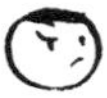
"Ah, he's just playing around. He'll be back. I mean, he's been around for my whole life so far!"

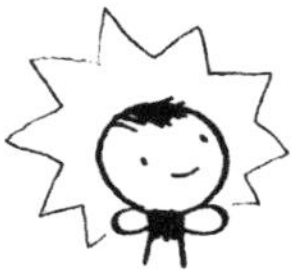
"Now that I'm alone, I'm gonna have some fun!"

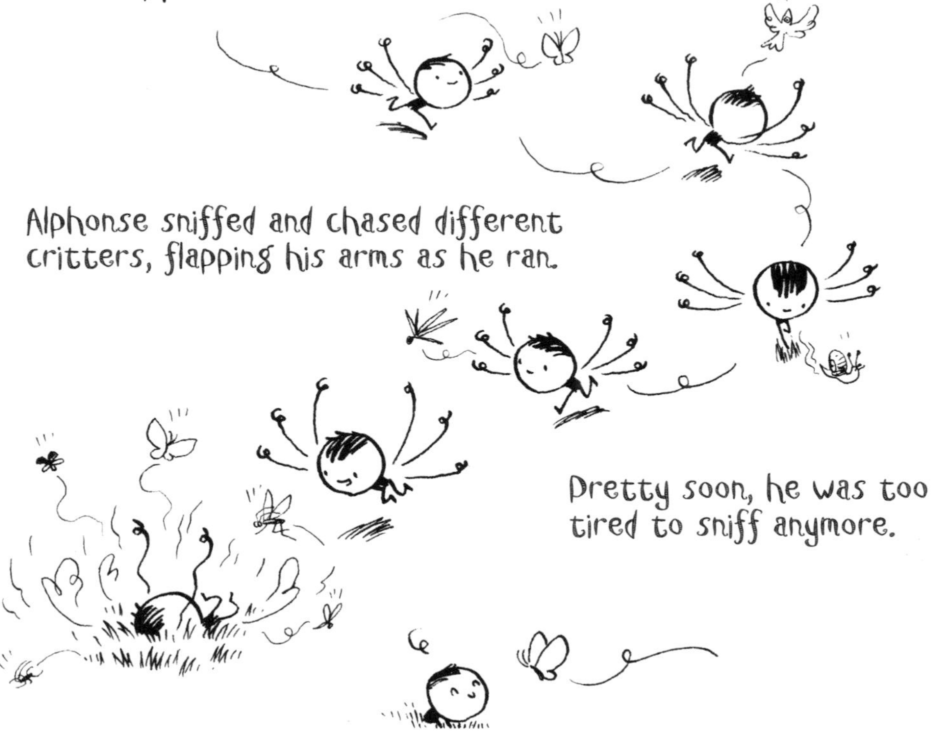
Alphonse sniffed and chased different critters, flapping his arms as he ran.
Pretty soon, he was too tired to sniff anymore.

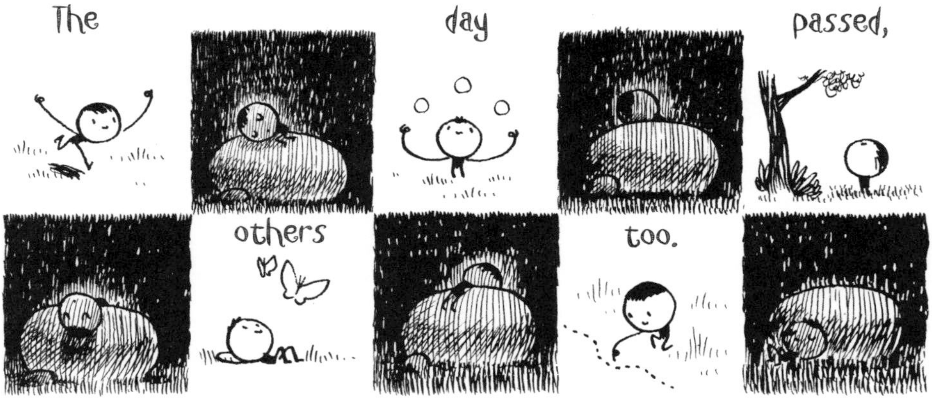
The
day
passed,
others
too.

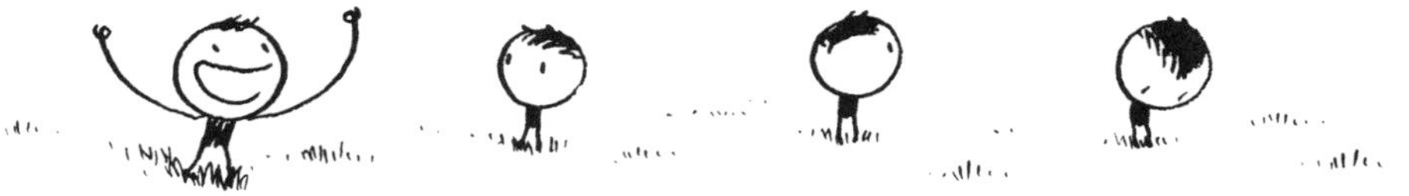

Then, one day, Alphonse felt like telling someone about how he'd spent his day.

But he had no one to talk to.

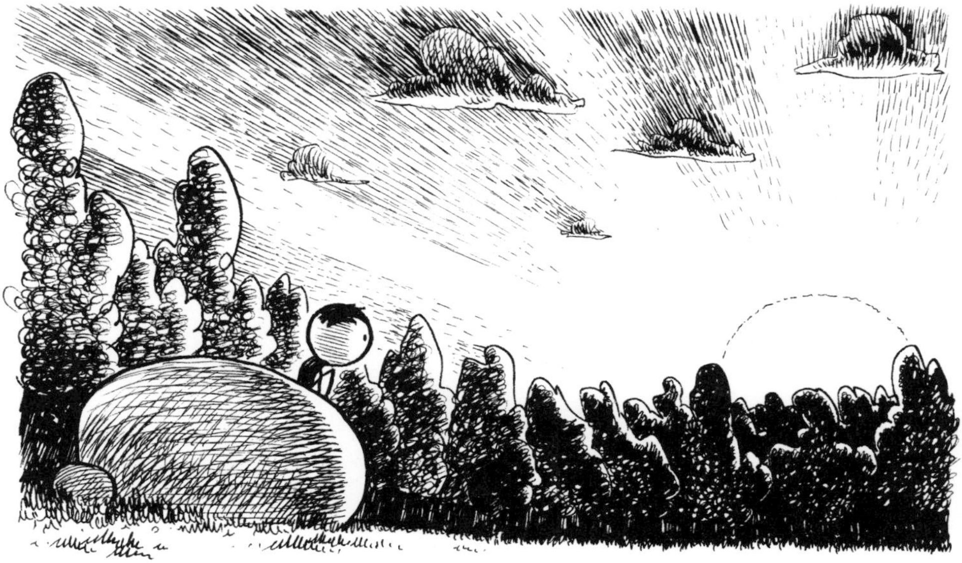

He was happy but a bit less so with each passing day.

He wanted to see the Big Man again.
He wanted to show him how he was putting
everything he learned to good use.

But the Big Man wasn't there.

"Well, then... I guess I'll just have to go find him!"

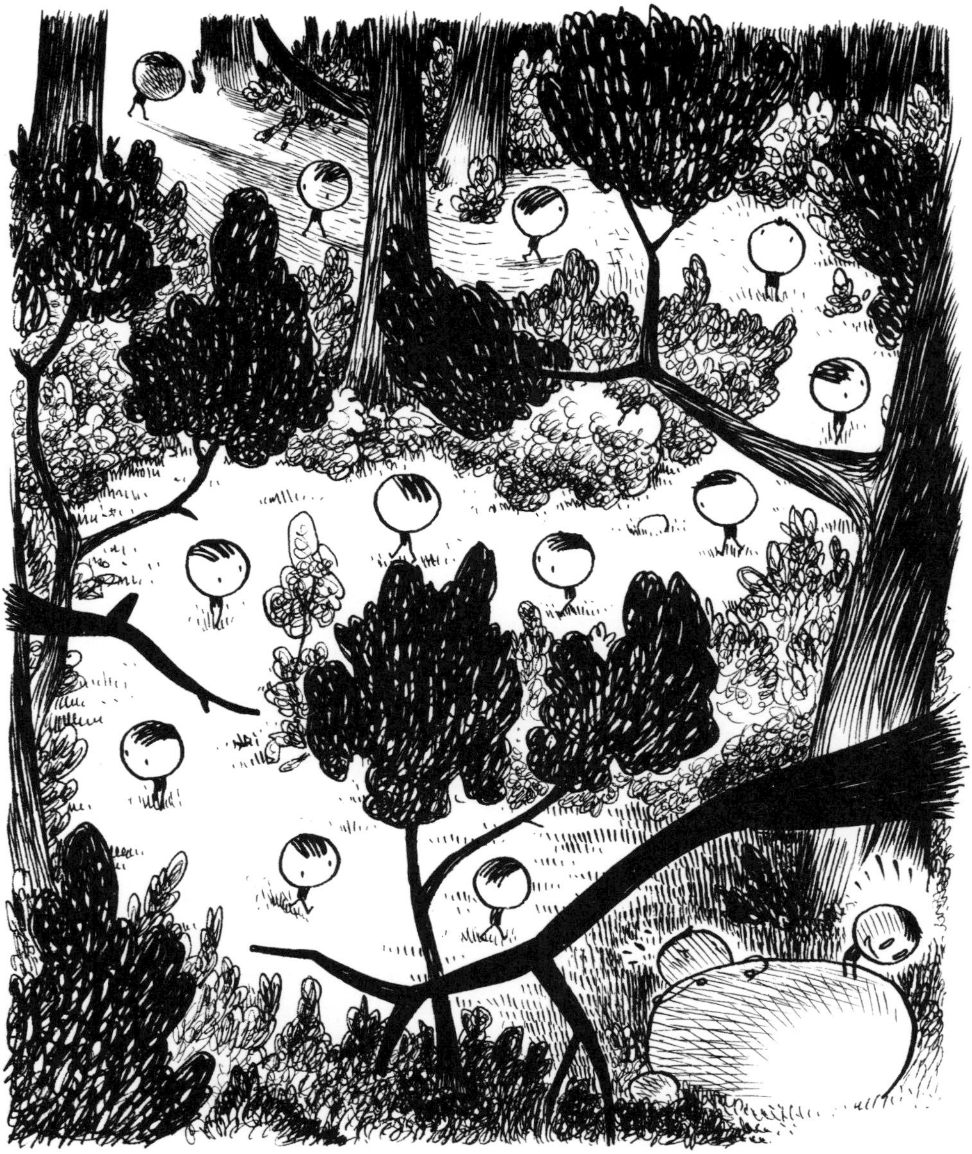

For a long time, Alphonse wandered through the woods. He listened to the sighing of the wind and let the plants tickle his knees, which made him laugh.

When he was all worn out, he sat down on a rock and looked down at the ground.

At long last, someone else was there!

"Hi there!"

"Hi there!"

"I'm so happy to see you!"

"I'm so happy to see you!"

"Wow, I think you and
I were made to see
eye to eye!"

"Wow, I think you and
I were made to see
eye to eye!"

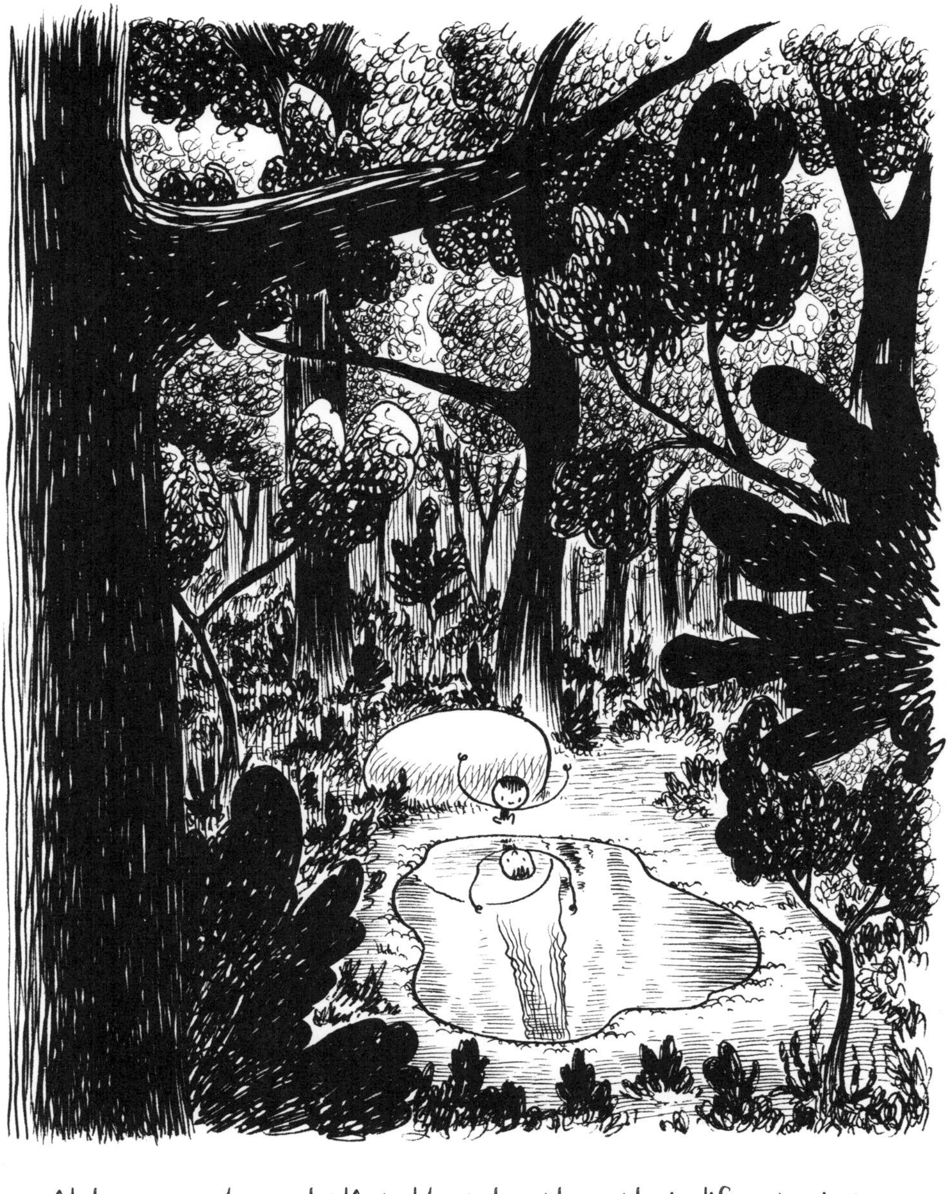

Alphonse and esnohplA told each other their life stories, sometimes laughing with joy, sometimes crying real tears, which made esnohplA shake a little.

Alphonse was touched that his new friend could be so compassionate.

"You're a good listener. But I'm getting kinda hungry. I'm going to go pick some growy things. Stay here, I'll be right back!"

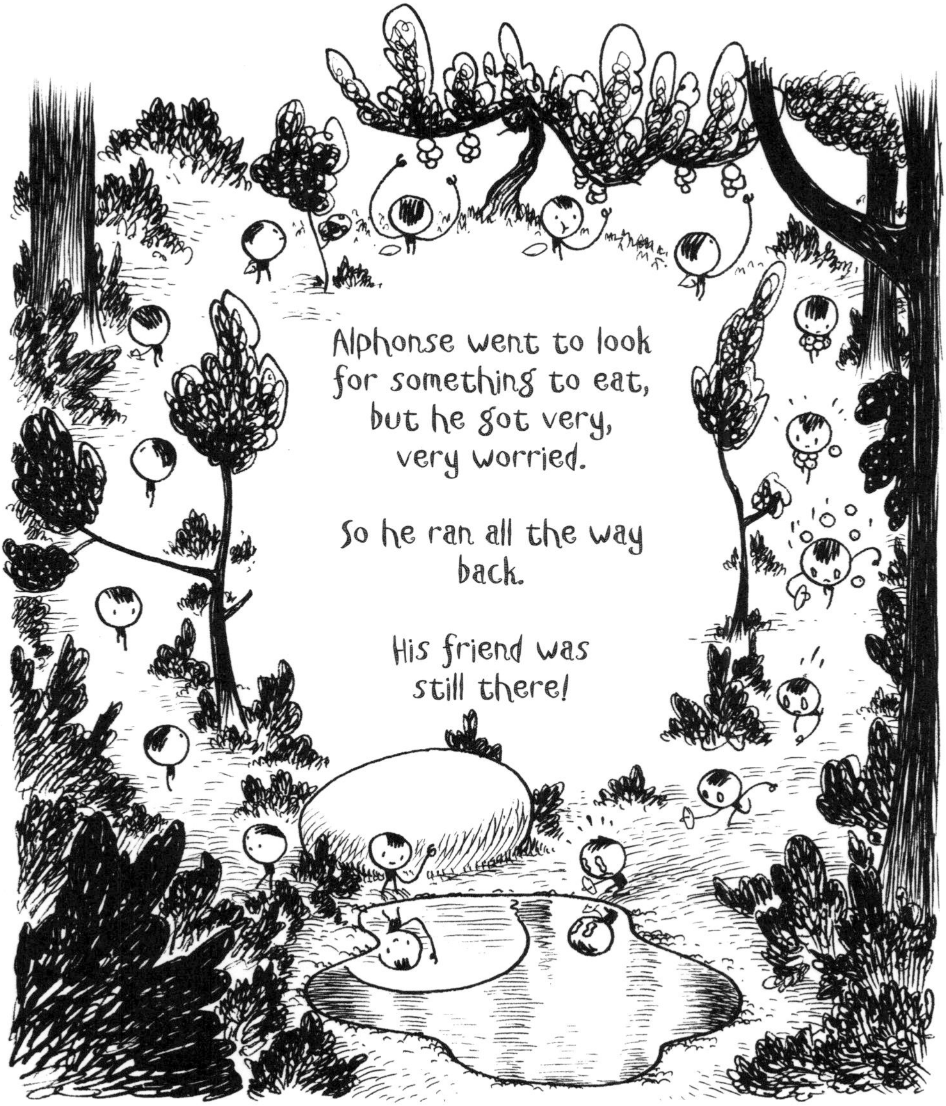
Alphonse went to look for something to eat, but he got very, very worried.
So he ran all the way back.
His friend was still there!

"I brought back an endive! We should live right here by this rock. It'll be our home, and I promise never to wander too far away, and I'll always come back!"

"I know."

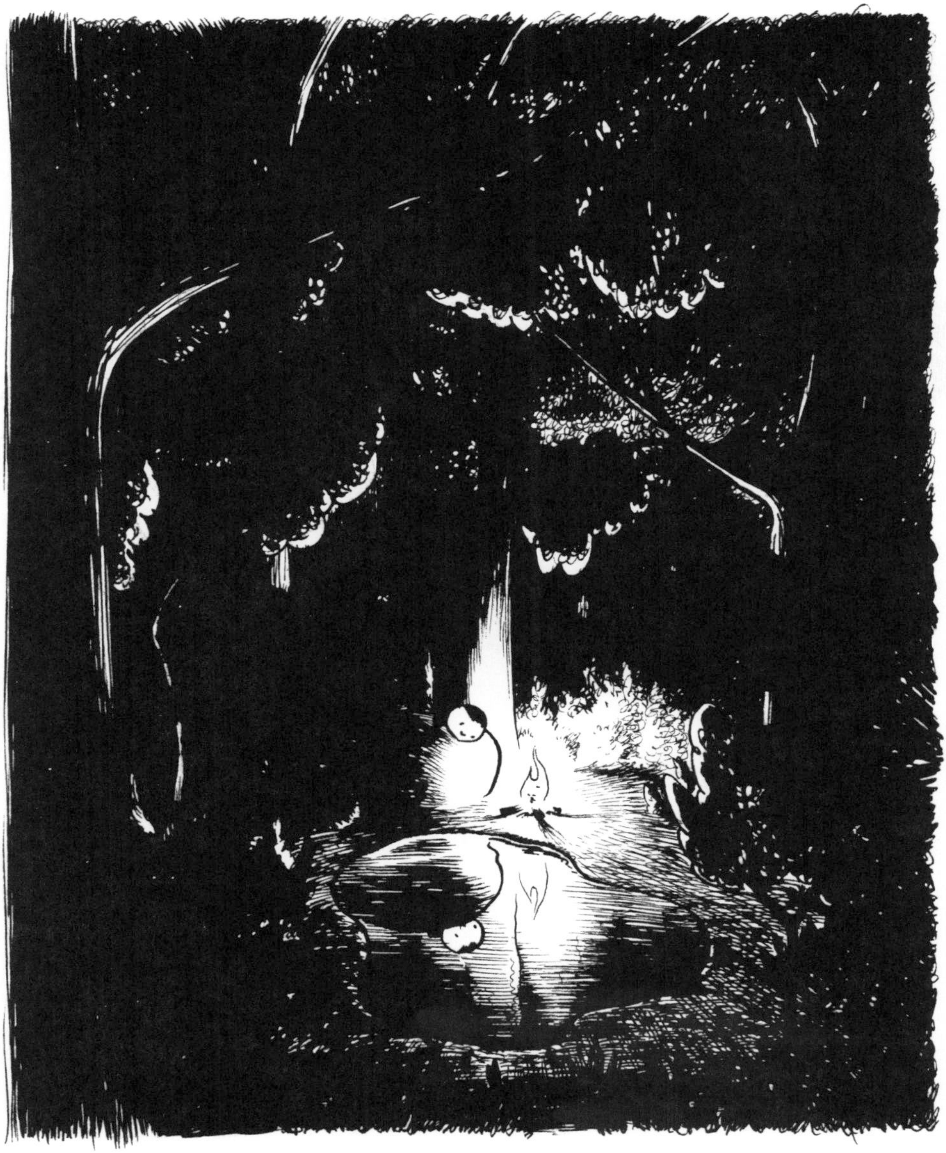

The days passed, and they continued to share each other's mood.

Whenever he felt angry, Alphonse tried really hard to smile instead. He could tell that esnohplA was kind of fragile, emotionally speaking.

And it's important to take care of your friends' feelings.

Alphonse wanted to thank him for always being
there, so one day he set off in search of a gift.

He wanted to find something very special, so he
decided to go a little farther than usual, which
took a little longer than usual.

A bit too long.

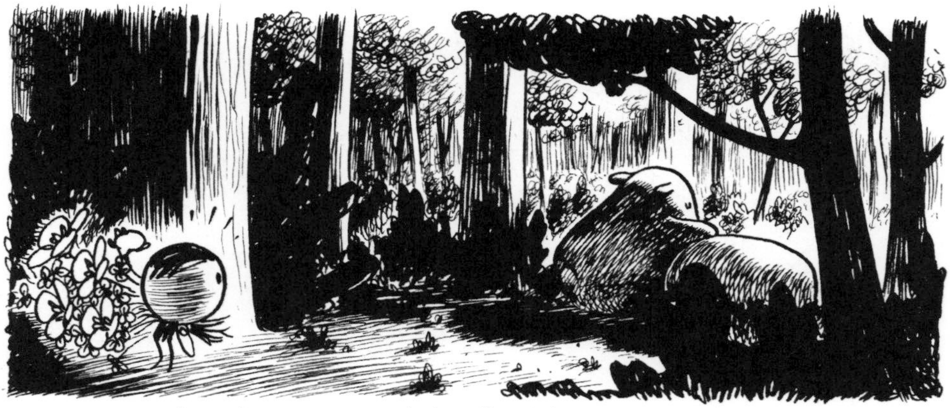

When he returned, he found someone else sitting by the rock.

"Maybe that funny-looking person is telling esnohplA his secrets! That'll give us more to talk about! Brand new stories! Hee hee!"

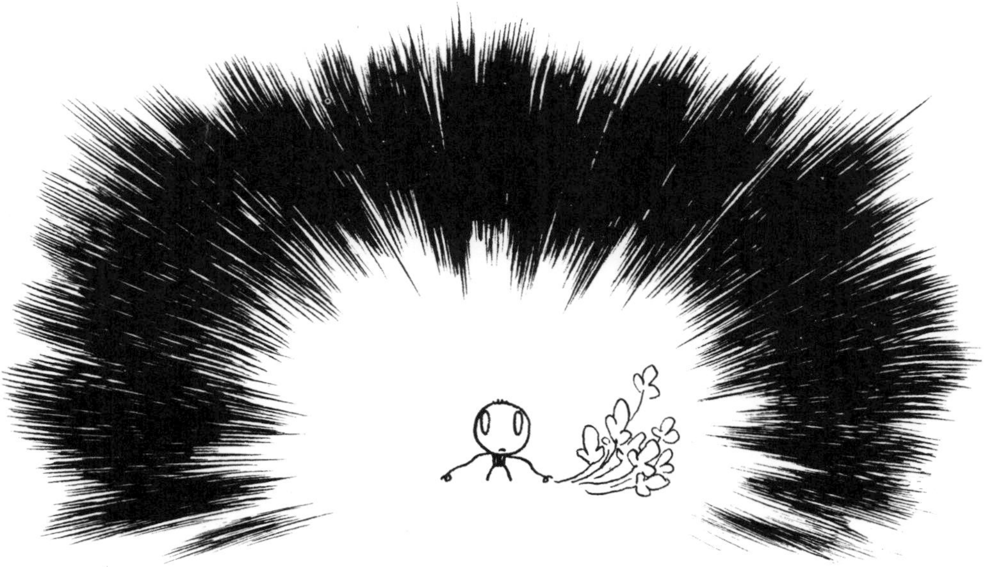

When Alphonse drew closer, however, he stopped hee-heeing.

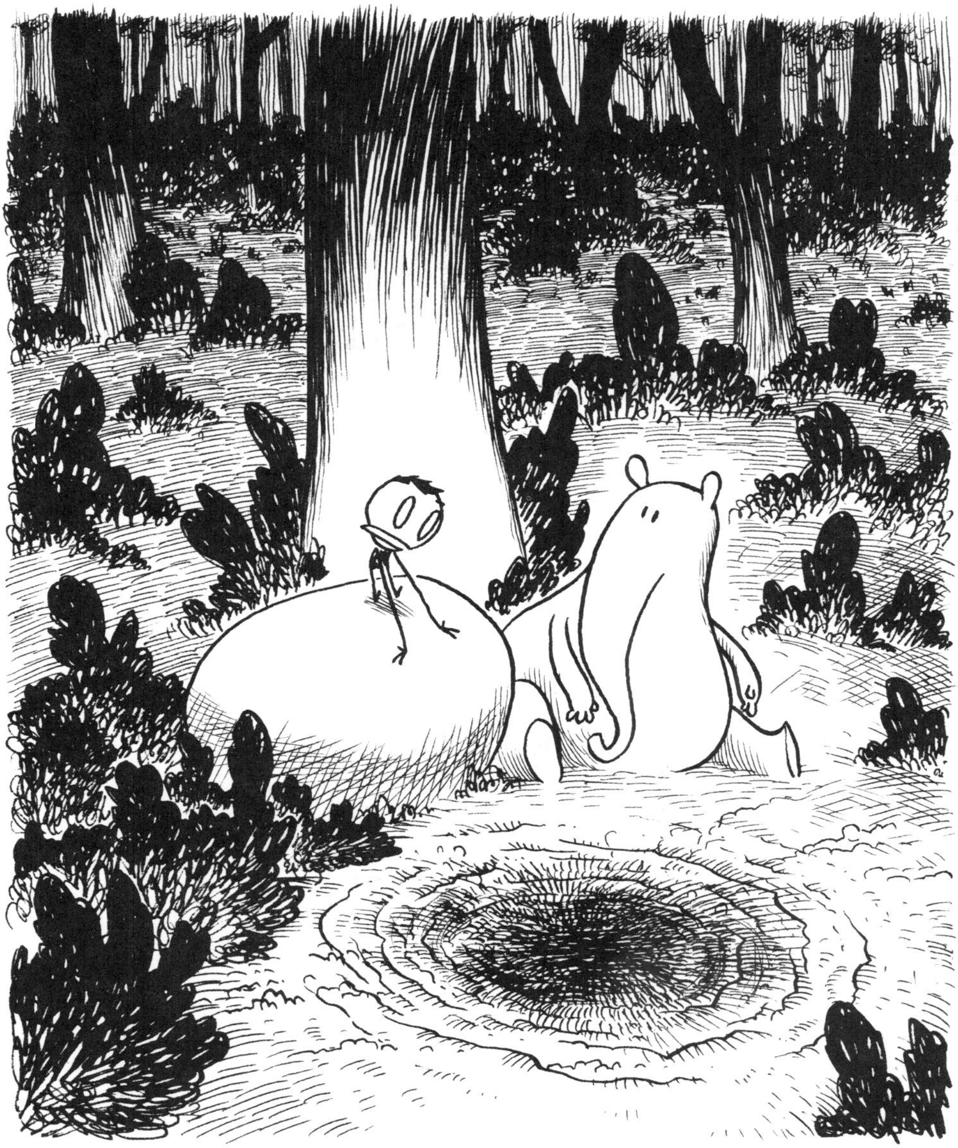

"You... YOU ATE MY FRIEND!"

"Huh? No, I was just having a drink."

"YOU DRANK HIM?! That's horrifying!"

"I can assure you, I didn't eat or drink anybody. How big was your friend?"

"...about this big."

"Mm-hmm. And what did he look like? Just in case, you know... maybe I've seen him."

"His head was round, and he had tiny eyes, and he had stick arms, and his hair looked kinda like mine. And he was all flat, and very damp, too. I tried to kiss him once and my nose got wet."

"I see."

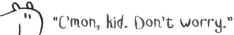 "So you saw him?! You didn't drink him?"

"Follow me, let me show you something."

"But I can't leave. What if he comes back? He's my friend. I really need him a lot..."

"C'mon, kid. Don't worry."

So Alphonse followed the stranger.

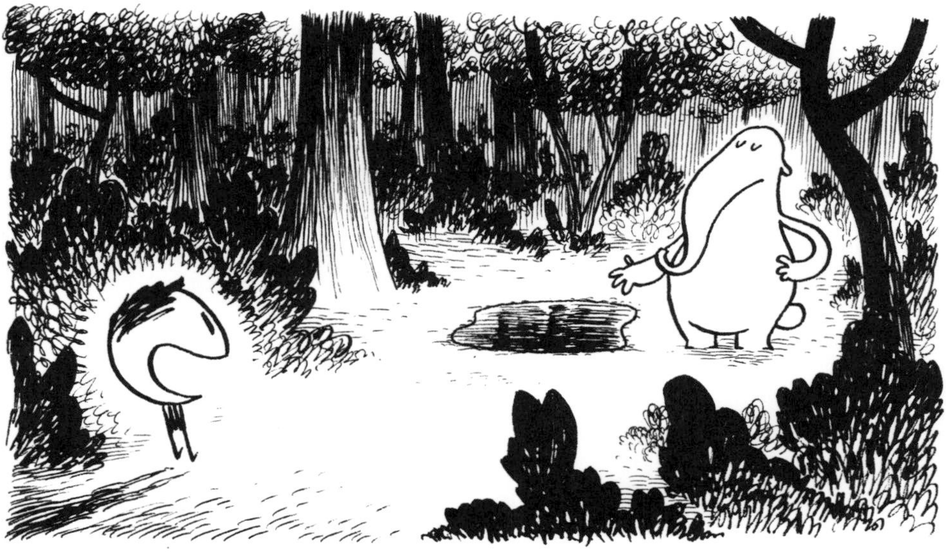

"Look."

"You found him! THANK YOU, THANK YOU, THANK YOU!"

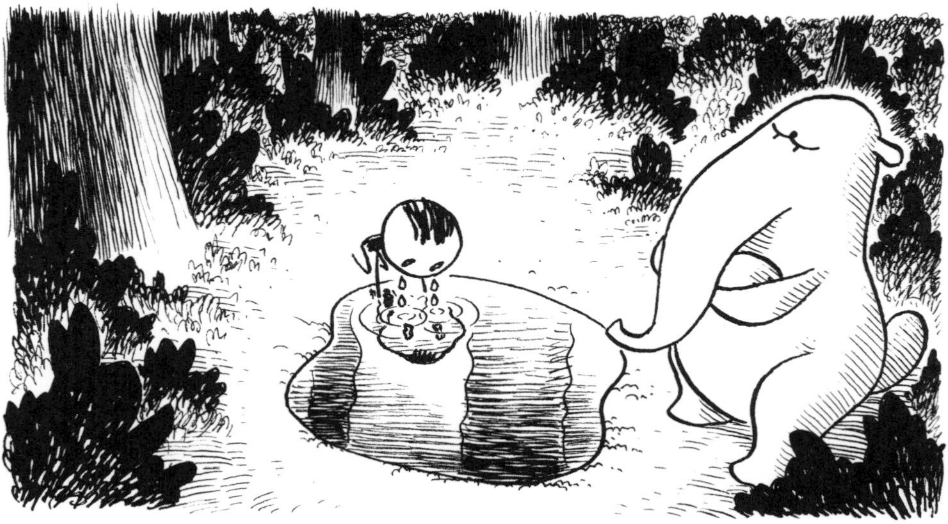

"Hey, you! Why'd you leave without saying anything?"

"Here, let me show you something else..."

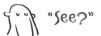 "See?"

"Cool! You have a flat friend, too!"

"Er, no, not exactly. Watch. If I move, he moves, too."

"And he looks just like you, too! You two make a perfect match!"

"But that's not actually another person. That's just my own reflection. And that's your reflection."

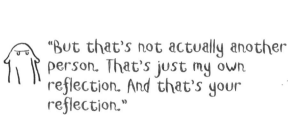

 "Wait... you mean that...?"

"Yup."

Alphonse Tabouret leaned over the pond and realized...

 "Oh. That's just me."

 "Yup."

 "I feel like a dummy."

 "Understandable."

 "Thanks anyway."

 "You should find something else to fill your time."

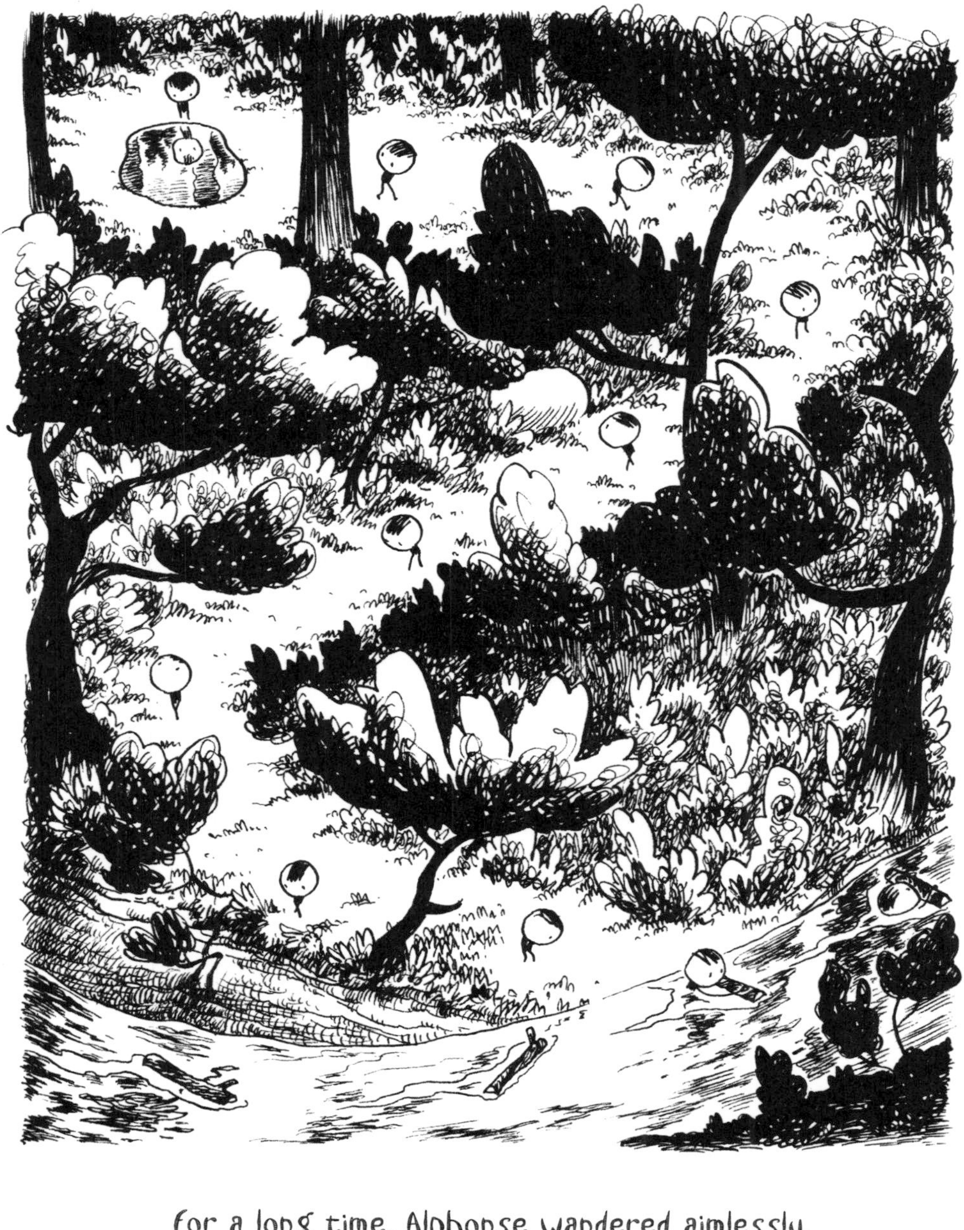

for a long time, Alphonse wandered aimlessly,
wondering what to do with his life.

Life wasn't exactly filled with signposts
to lead the way.

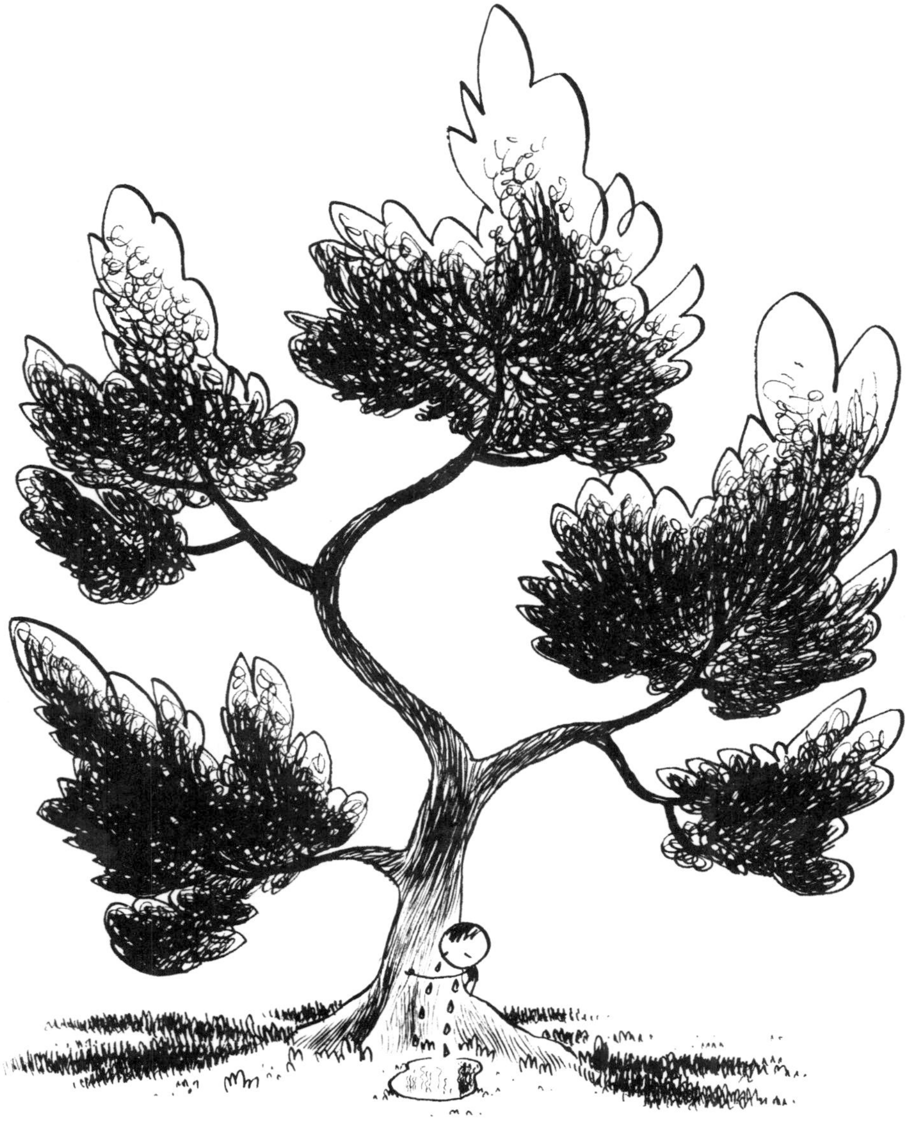

for a long time, he cried.

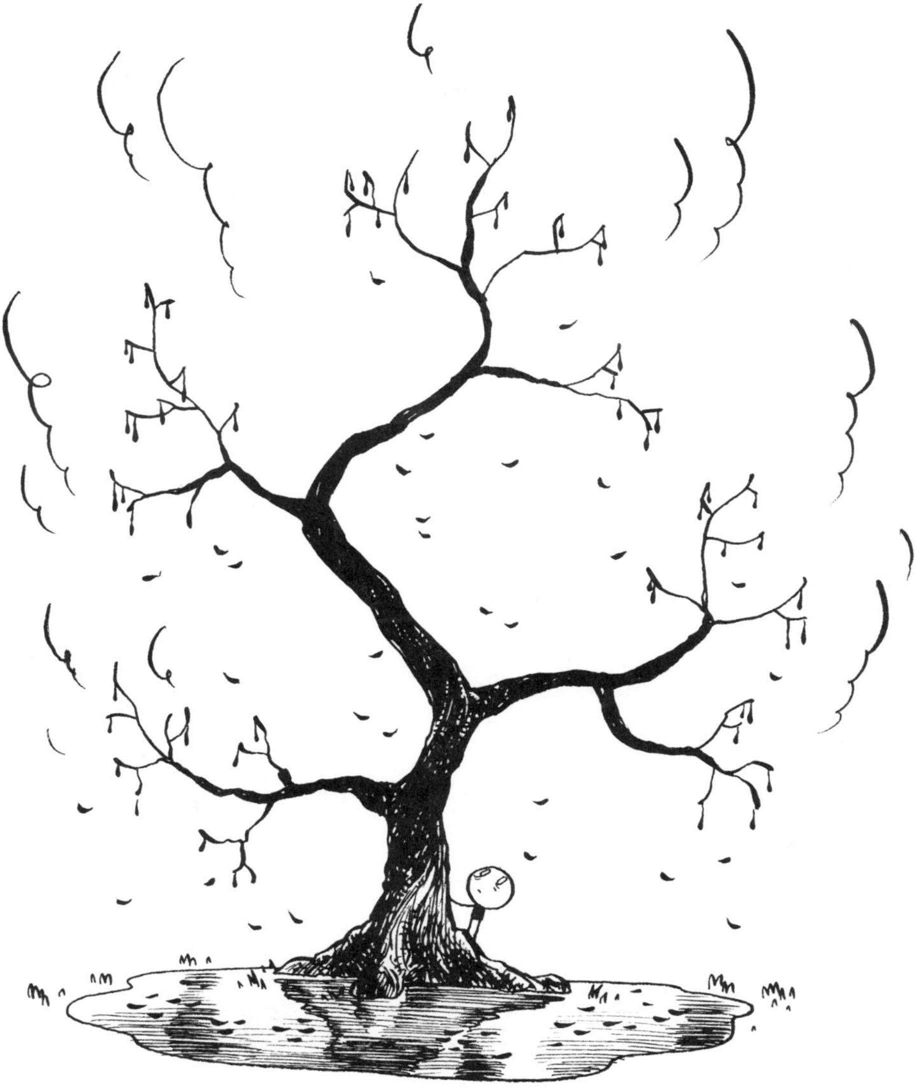

A very long time.

"Sorry."

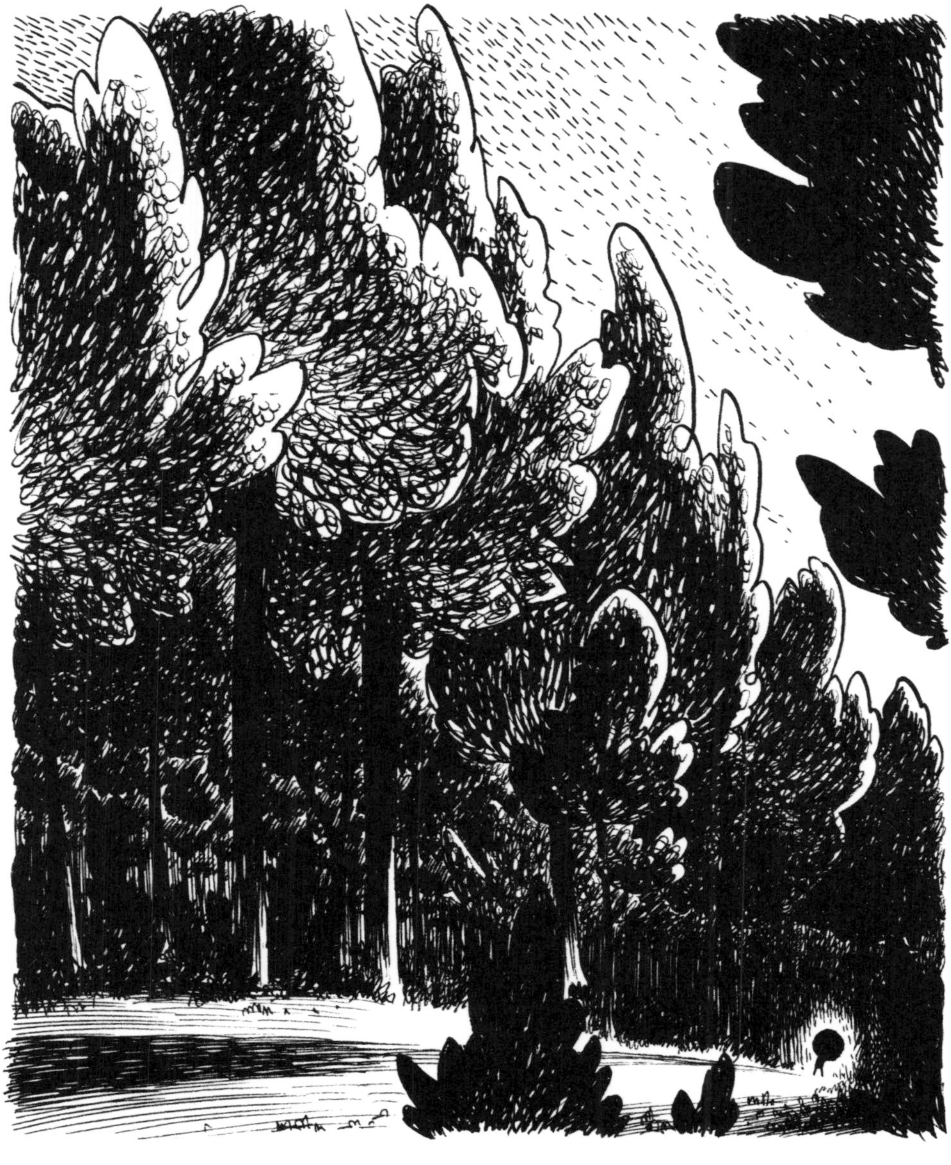

Because his sorrow emptied out his insides,
he was inconsolable.

Particularly because there was no one else around.

Which was what he needed the most: someone else.

But he didn't realize that at the time.

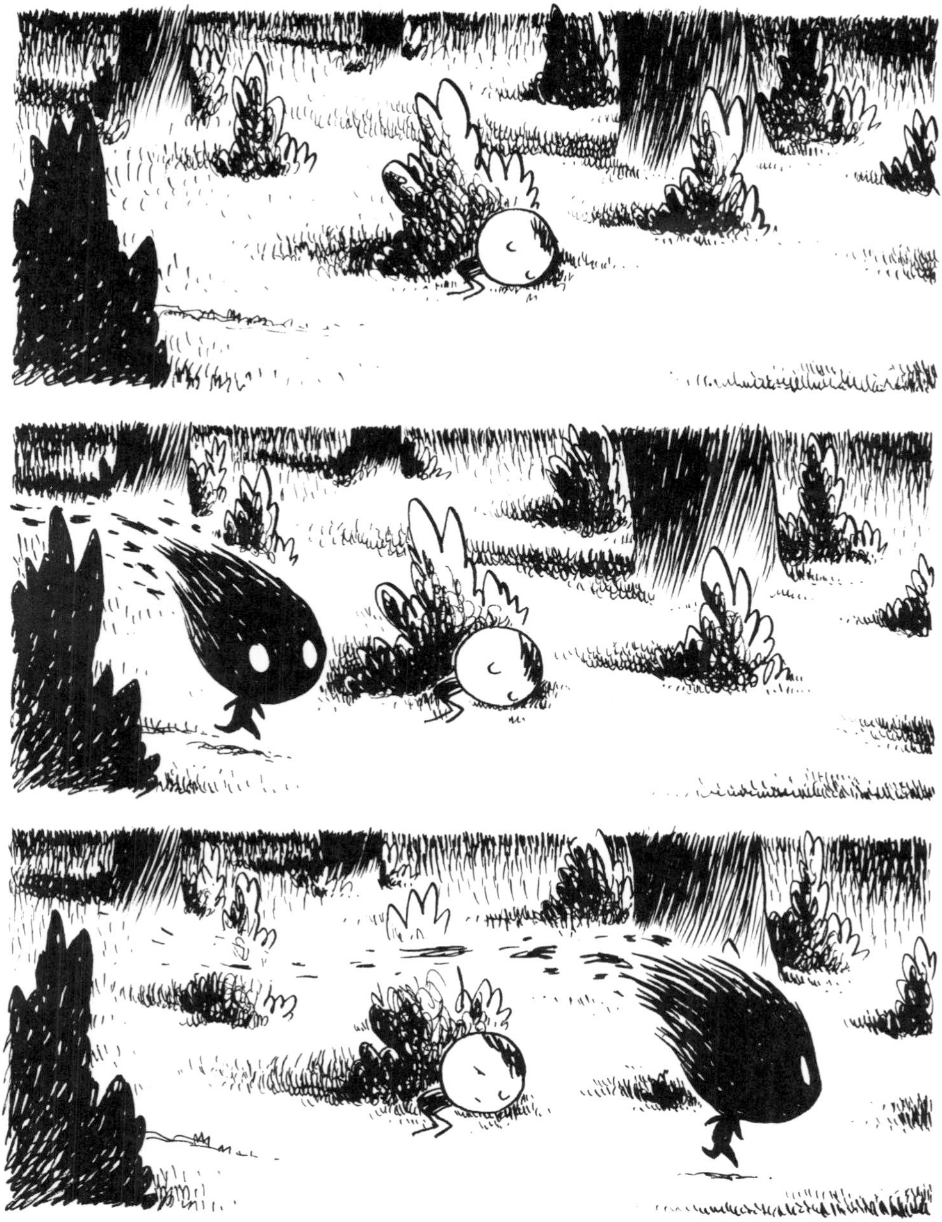
"Hey!"

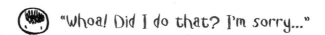 "Whoa! Did I do that? I'm sorry..."

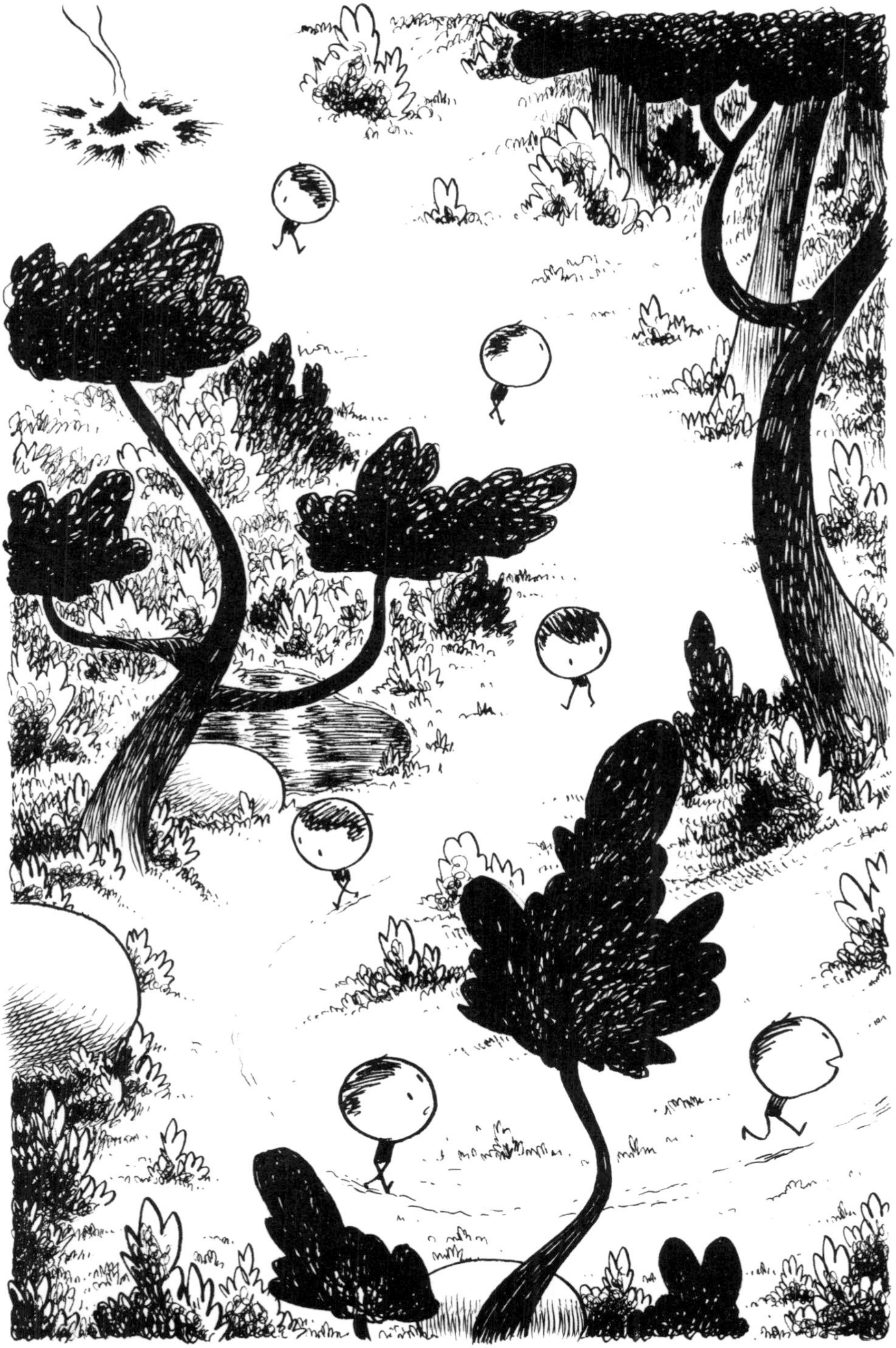

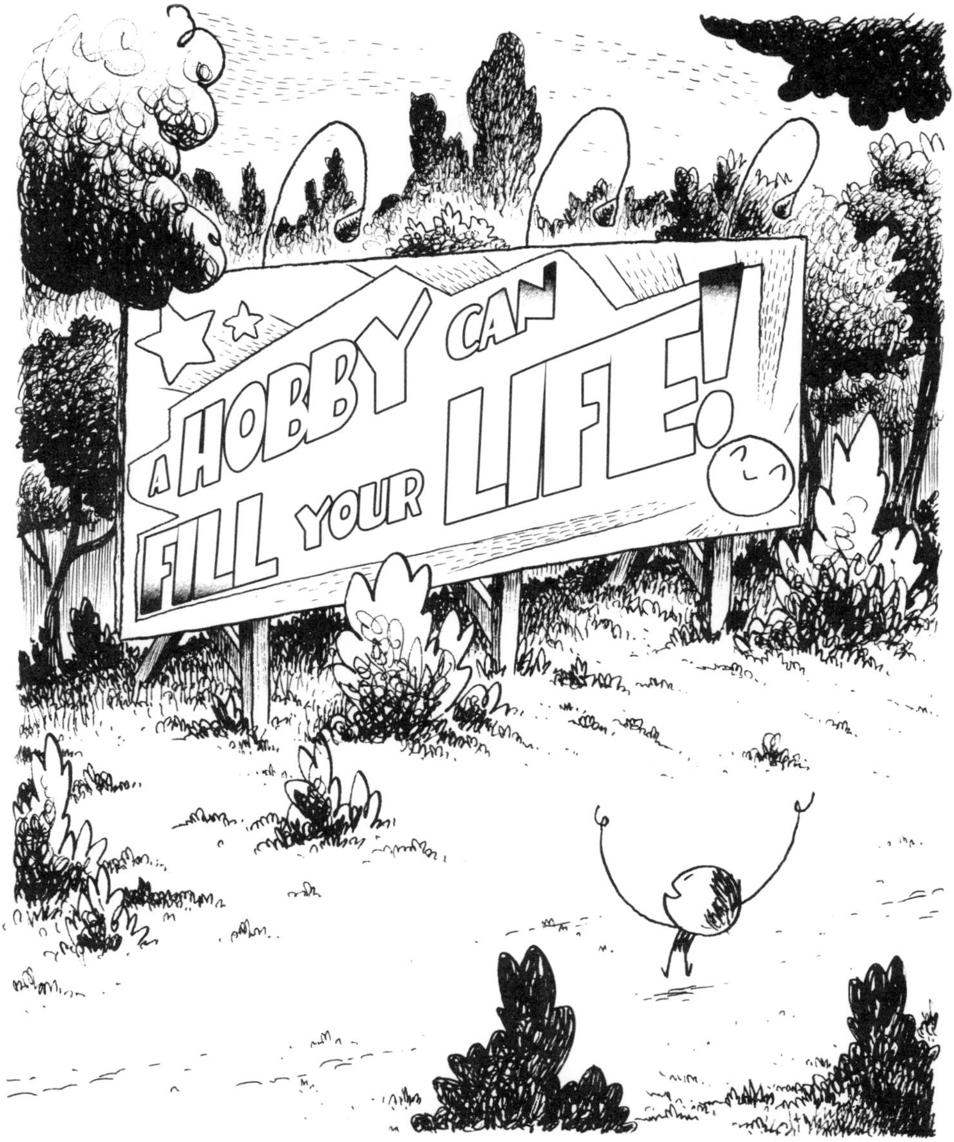
A HOBBY CAN FILL YOUR LIFE!

"Wow! That looks wonderful!
I gotta get me one of those!
I need a hobby!
A hobby sounds terrific!
I want a hobby!"

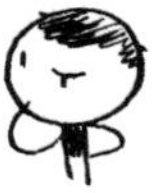

 "...but where in the world can I find a hobby?"

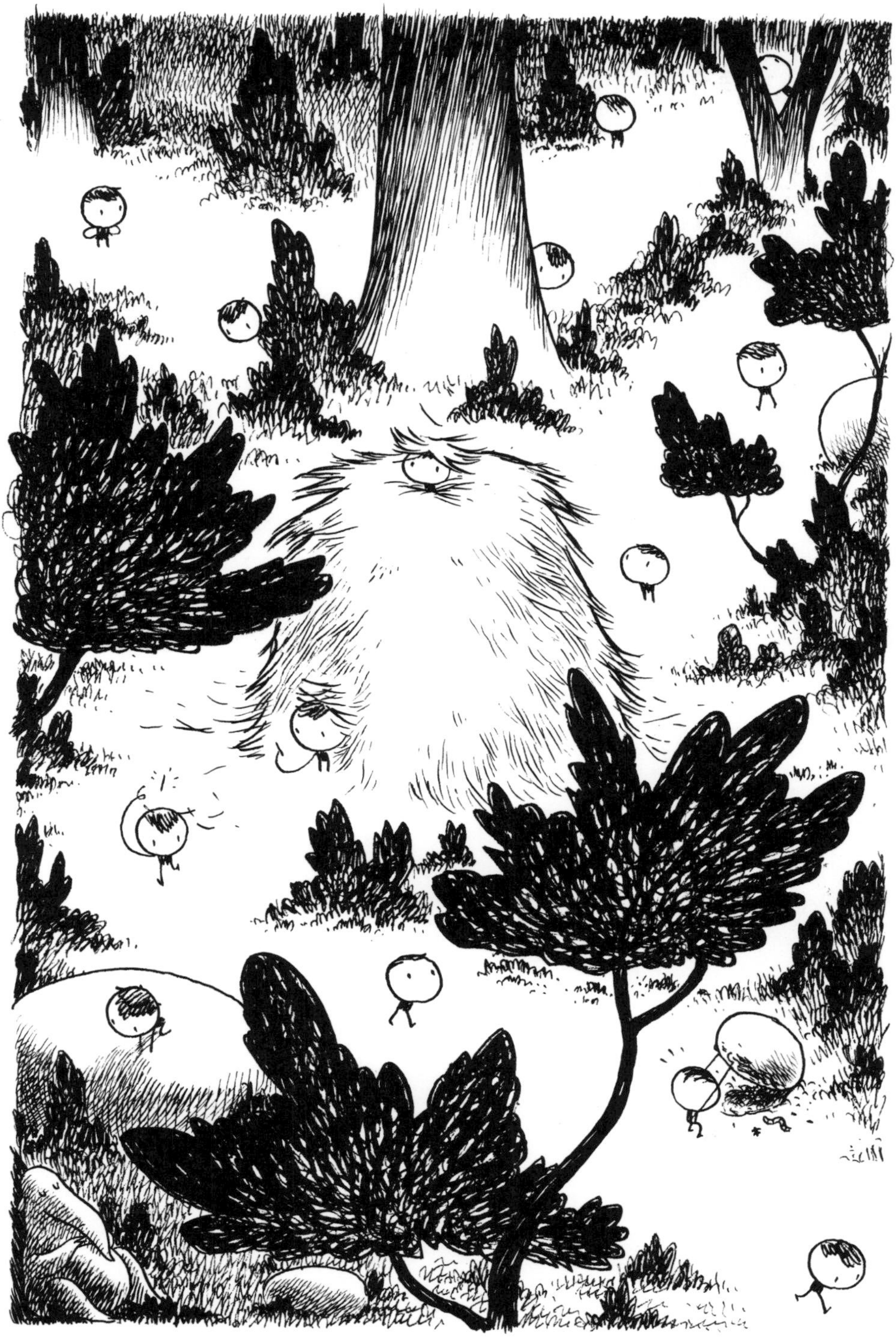

KnickKnack
SHOP
OPEN
Noon
TO
2PM

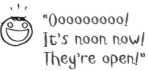

"Ooooooooo!
It's noon now!
They're open!"

 "Hey, Mr. Tambourine man!"

 "You know who I am?"

 "Huh? No, I just said that as a joke."

 "Good one!"

 "So, what can I do for you today?"

 "I'm looking for a hobby!"

 "Ah, I prefer ping-pong, personally."

 "Oh, yeah?"

 "Wanna try a quick game?"

 "Uh... sure."

Alphonse played ping-pong with the knickknack Man...

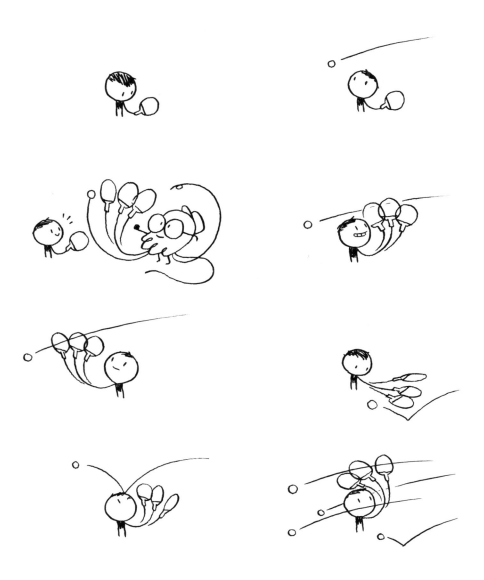

...but it was really more as a favor to him.

 "So what kind of hobby do you have for me?"

 "Well, you tell me! You gotta tell me what you like to do. I can't decide that for you, you have to tell me, get it?"

 "No, you don't understand, I'm looking for a hobby to fill my life. The billboard said it would."

 "I see, I see."

 "Your eyes are weirding me out."

 "I see, I see. Stay right there, Mr. Toblerone Man..."

 "Spud! Hey, Spud!"

 "...what?"

 "Help me find this kid a hobby."

 "You didn't have to wake him up."

 "Eh, Spud wasn't really sleeping. He's just a couch potato."

 "Then why was he stuffed in a drawer?"

 "C'mon, Spud, my faithful assistant! Let's get to work!"

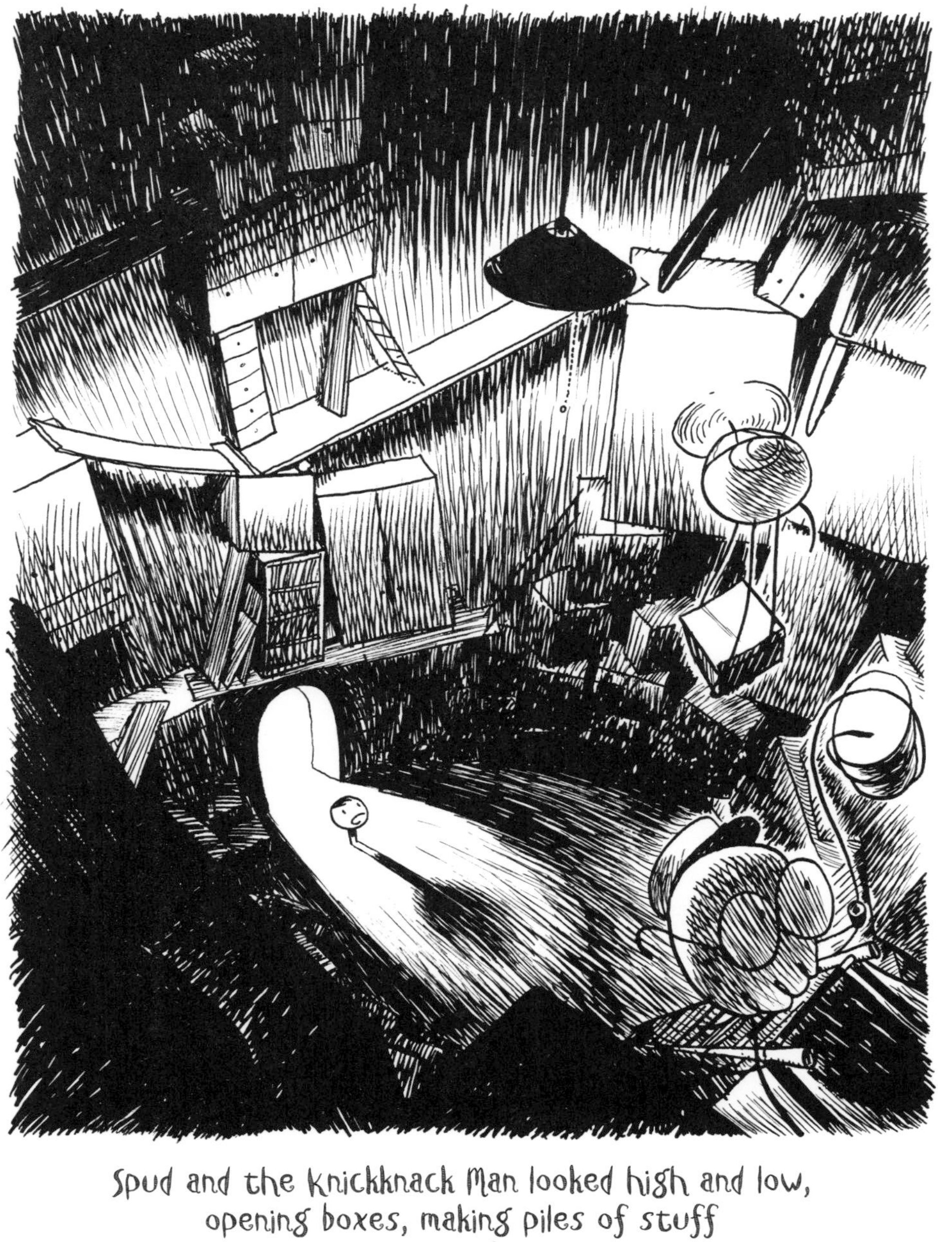

Spud and the Knickknack Man looked high and low,
opening boxes, making piles of stuff
and a lot of noise.

Then, all of a sudden,
they returned victorious.

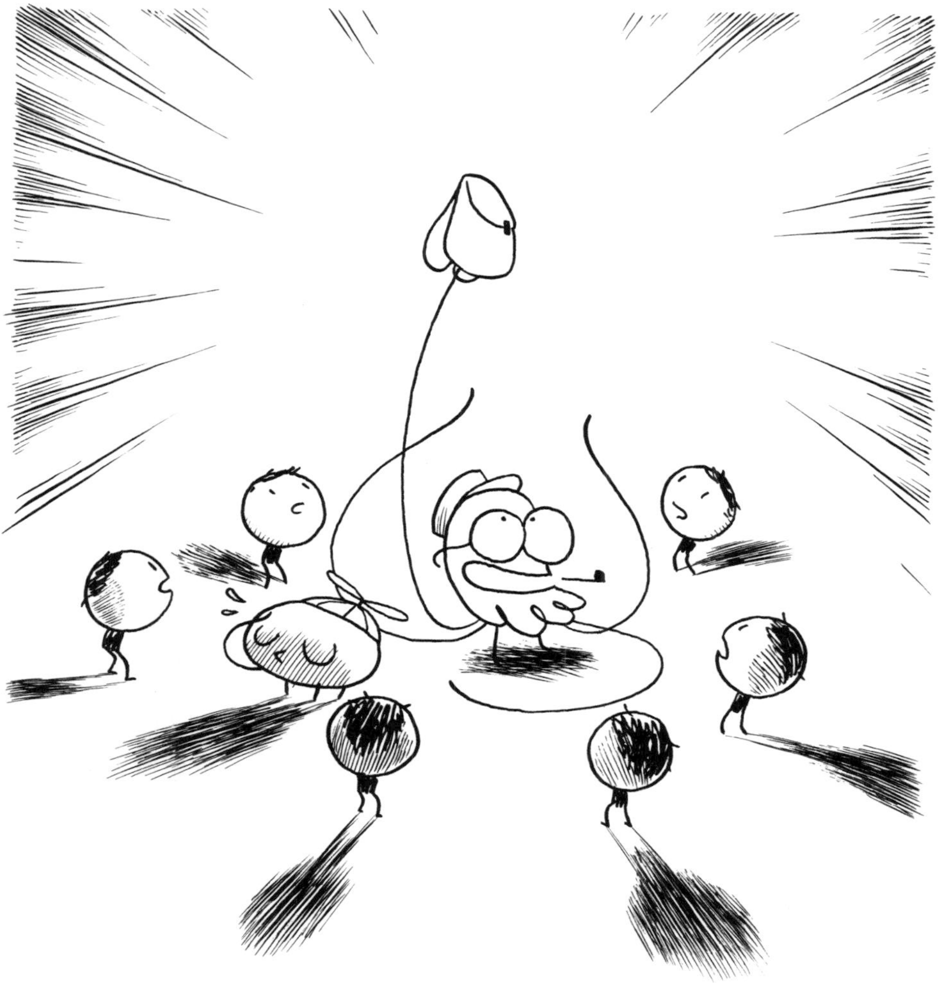

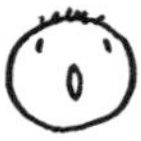

"Oooooooooooooooooo! What is it?"

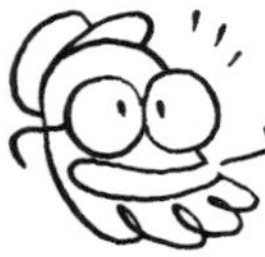

"A BACKPACK!"

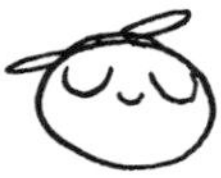

"..."

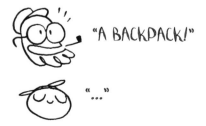

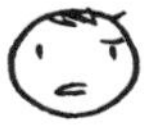

"No offense, but that's not what I asked for. I asked for a hobby."

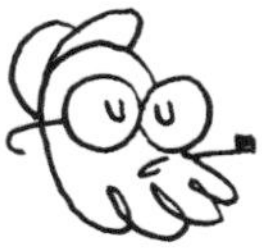

"Listen, kid. If you're looking to fill something, nothing beats a backpack."

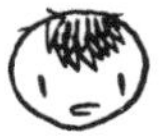

"So is that my hobby?"

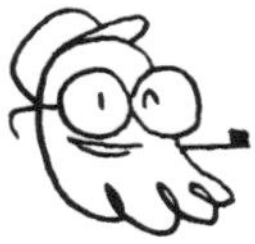

"Sure, why not?"

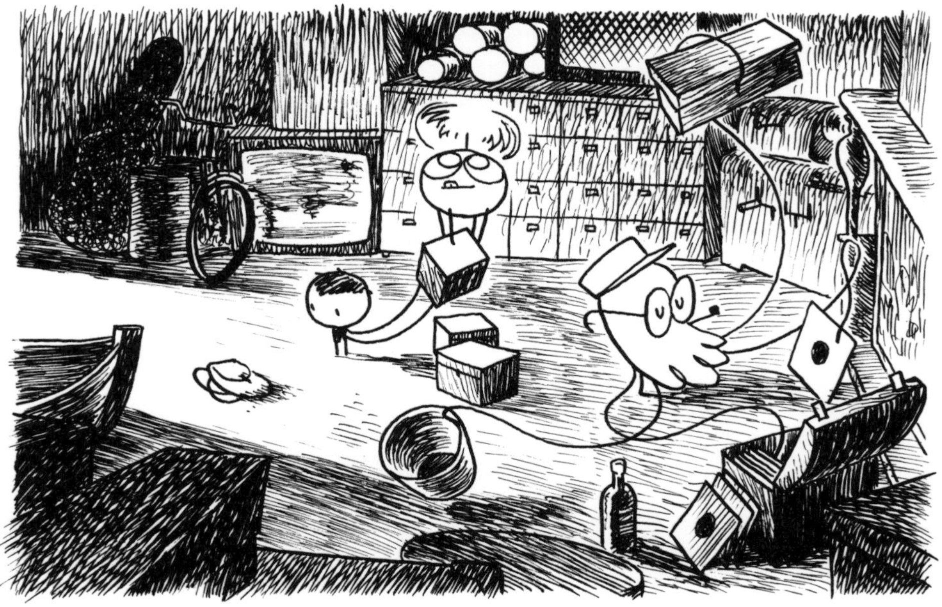

Confused, Alphonse said "thank you" and helped clean up the mess they made.

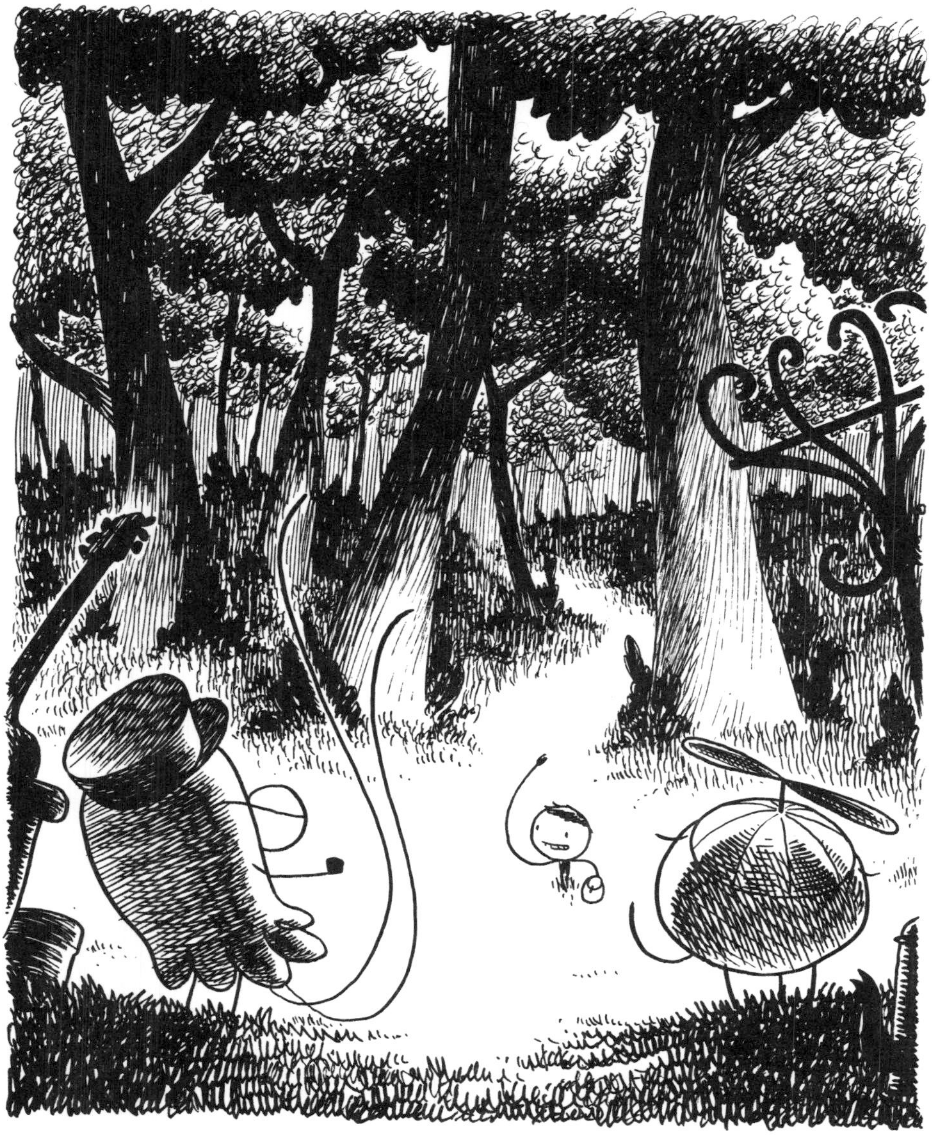

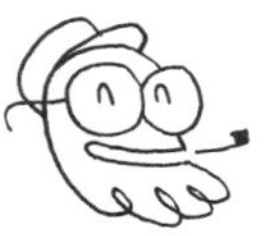

"So long, Taboo Rainman!"

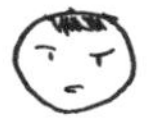

"...that guy's weird."

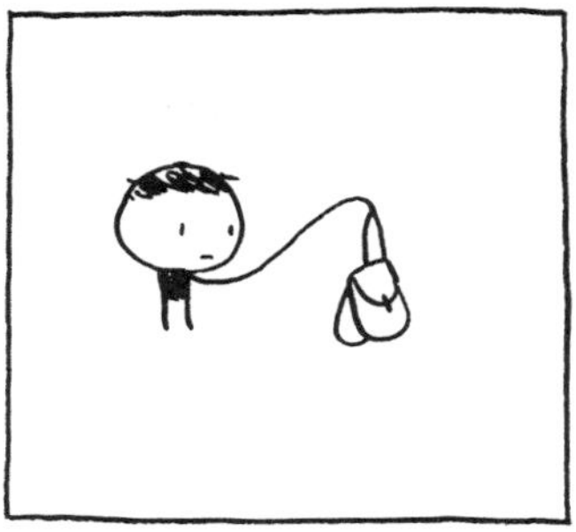

"Hmm, this thing's not so special.
How do I even use it?"

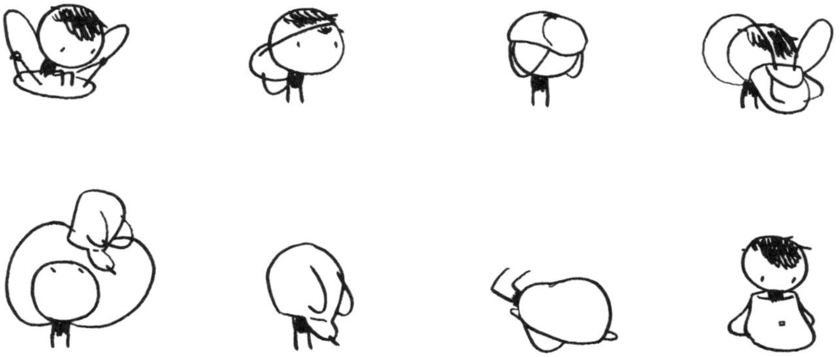

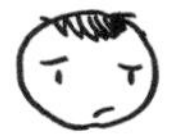

"Not exactly what I was hoping for...
And it makes it harder to get around."

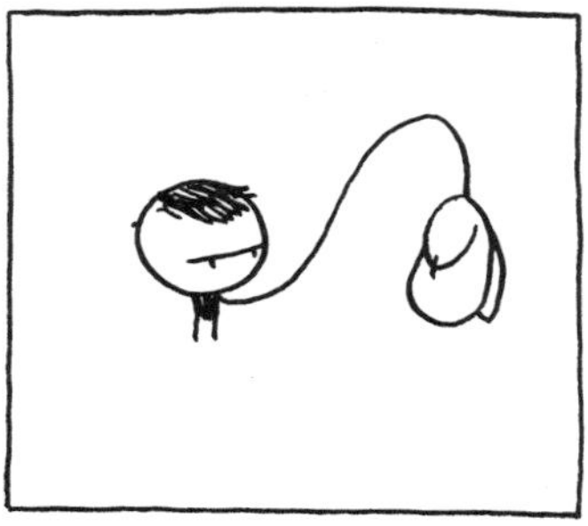

Alphonse stared at the backpack,
wondering if he'd been had.

 "Whoa! Awesome backpack! Can I look inside?"

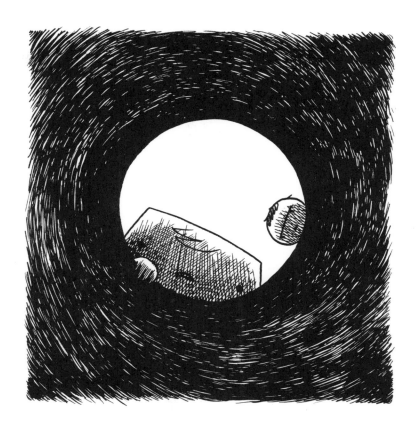

 "It's empty."

 "Well, it wasn't just a minute ago, when I was inside of it. But that wasn't so great."

 "Yeah... and as you get older, there won't be much left to keep in there."

 "Wow, you're pretty wise!"

 "Tell ya what, here's a key ring. You can have it. I've got two."

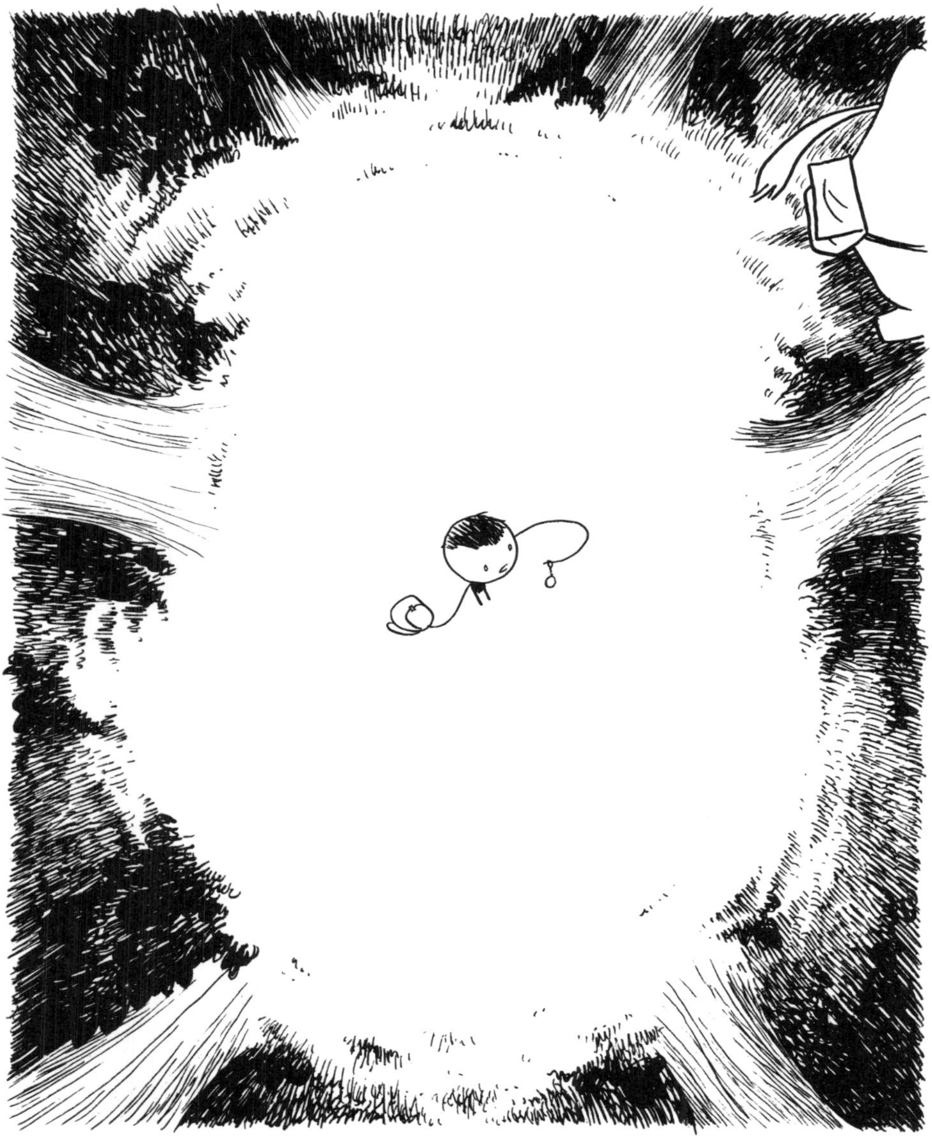

Alphonse didn't even notice the who-knows-what leave.
He was too mesmerized.

Alphonse was sorta happy with the backpack,
but it was just okay.

The key ring, however, was amazing!

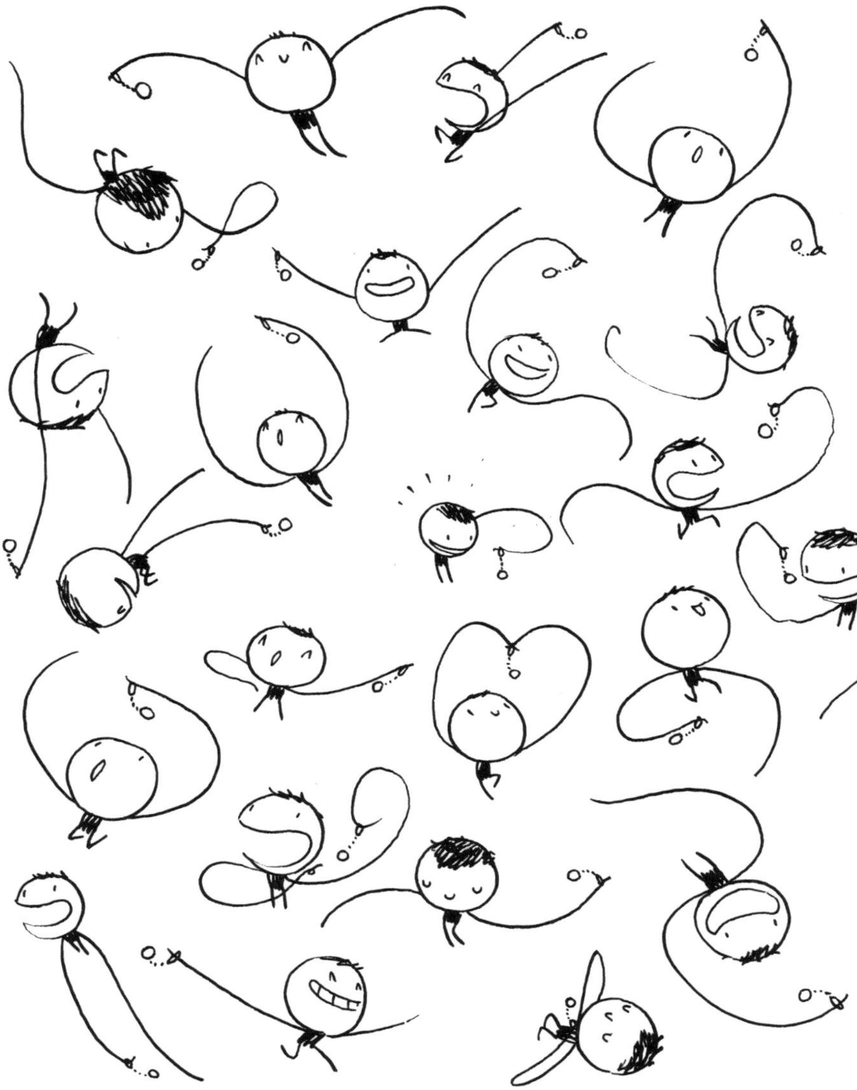

He launched into a wild dance of excitement.

"I need other thing-rings! Lots of 'em!"

Alphonse spent days looking for things that held other things together.

"Awesome! A leaf-ring!"

"Excellent! A time-ring!"

"A feather-ring! I love it!"

"A ring for wood AND nails!"

And so his collection began.

He collected things and more things.

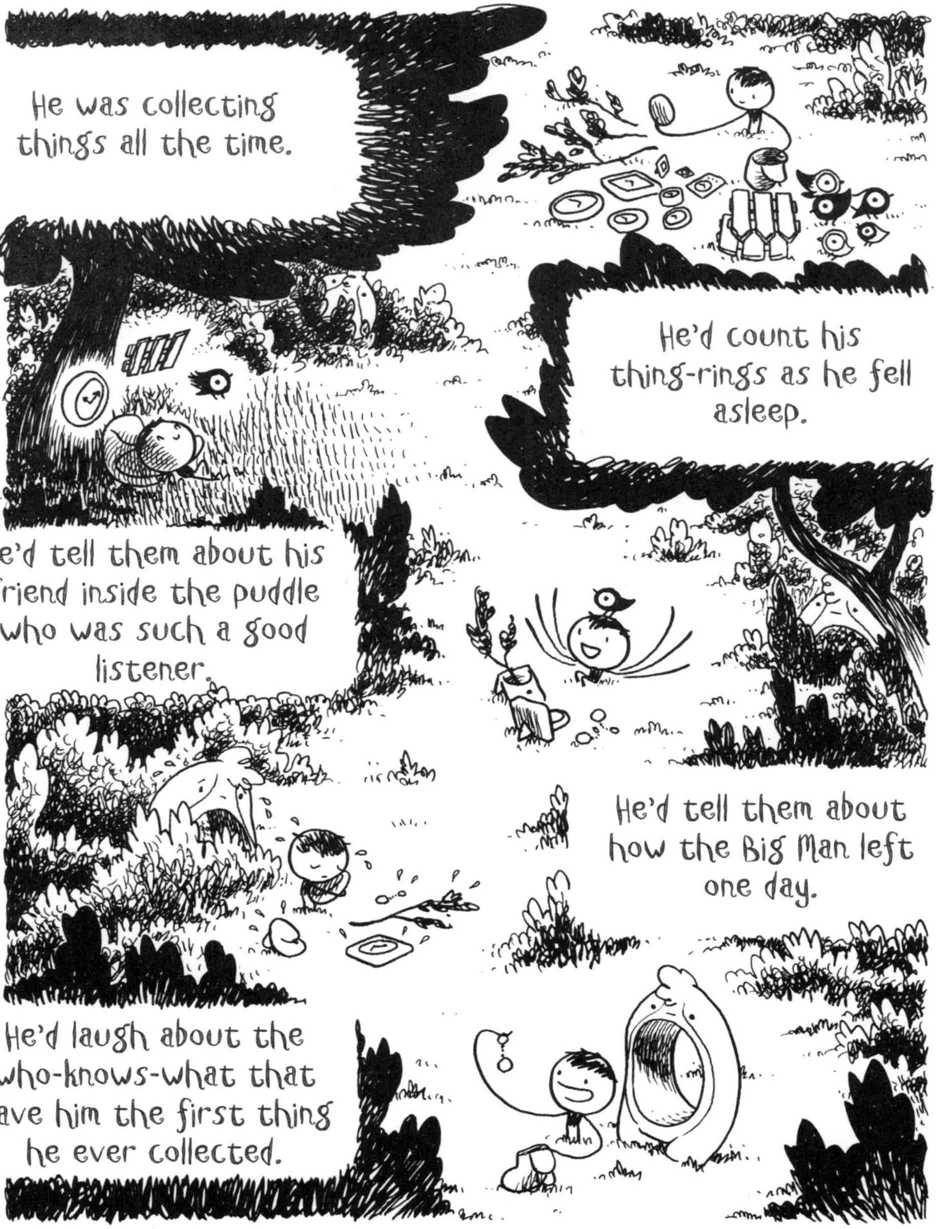
He was collecting things all the time.
He'd count his thing-rings as he fell asleep.
He'd tell them about his friend inside the puddle who was such a good listener.
He'd tell them about how the Big Man left one day.
He'd laugh about the who-knows-what that gave him the first thing he ever collected.

He talked out loud a lot.

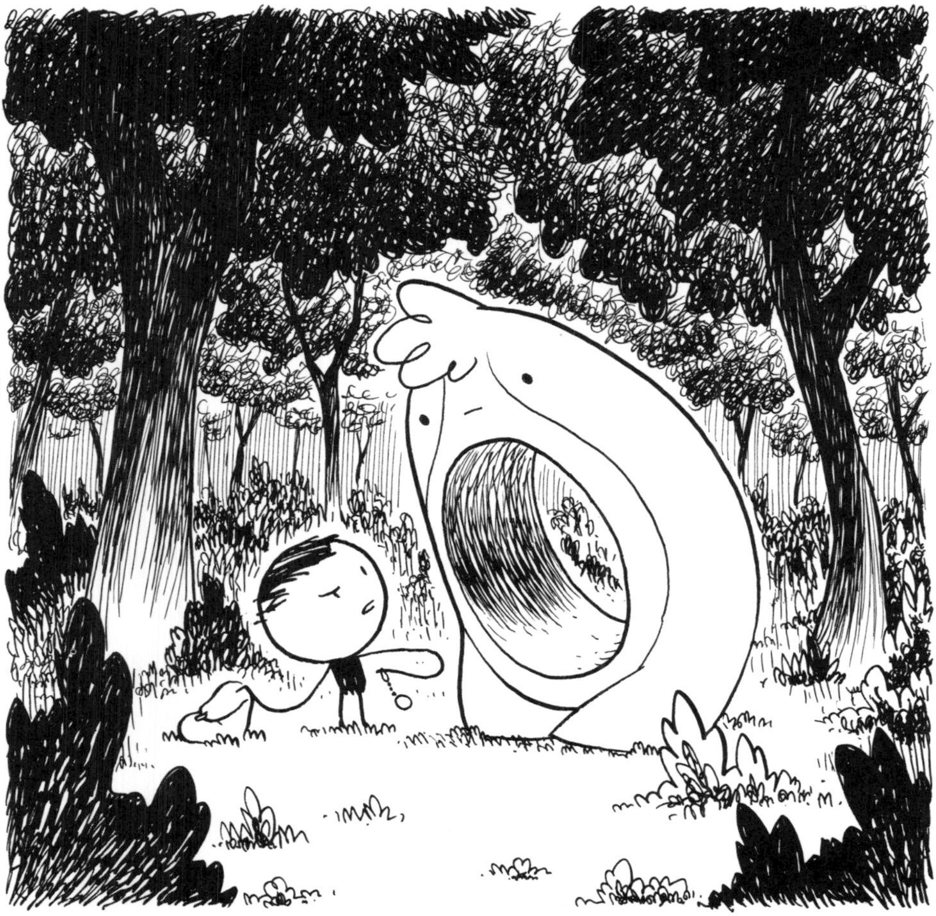

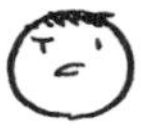 "What do you want?"

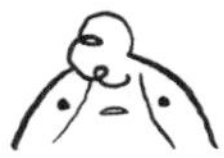 "Nothing. I'm Hole."

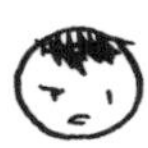 "Well, you're standing kinda close."

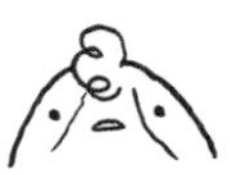 "Really? This is the first time I've ever been close to anyone."

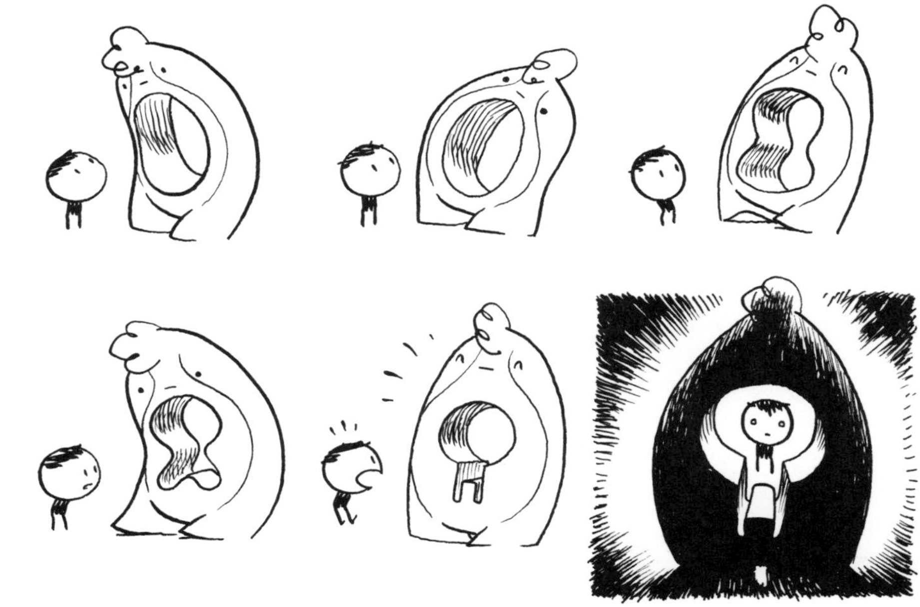

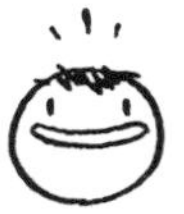

"Ha ha! I can see right through the me-shaped hole in your belly!"

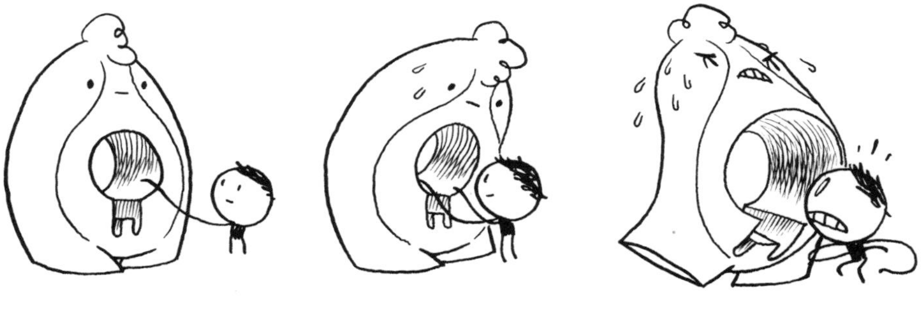

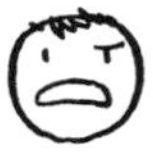

"Hey! Heeeeeyyy...!"

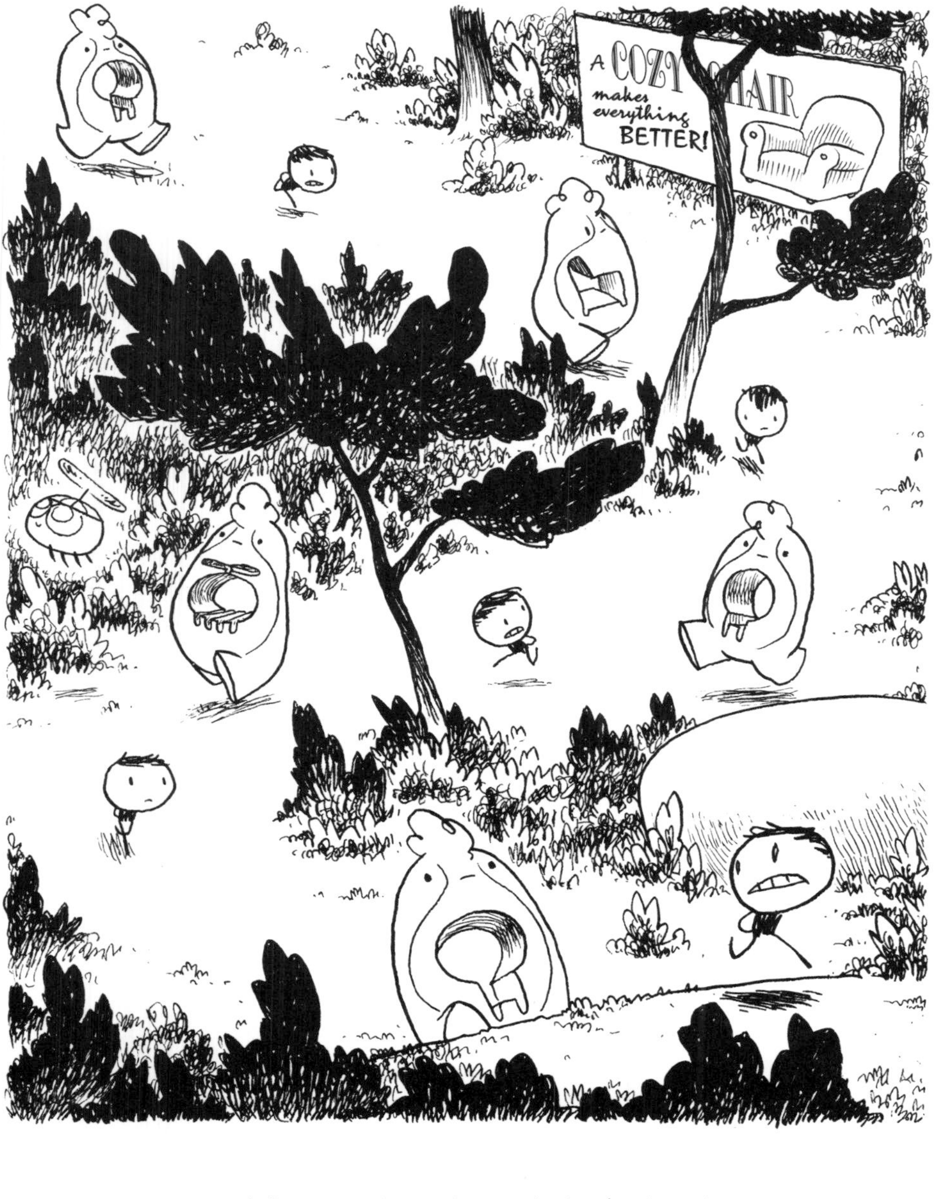
A COZY CHAIR
makes everything BETTER!

Alphonse thought Hole looked sad.

But he also looked kinda creepy.

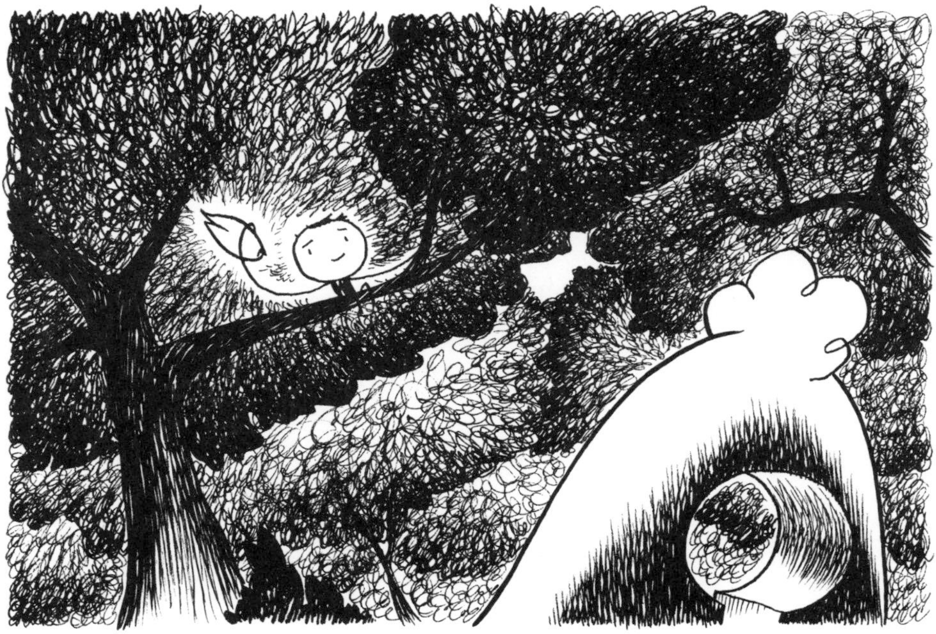

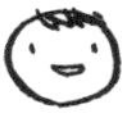

"I'm tired of playing chase. I'm gonna eat.
Do you want an endive?"

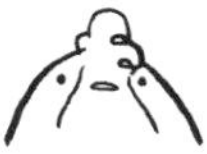

"Yes."

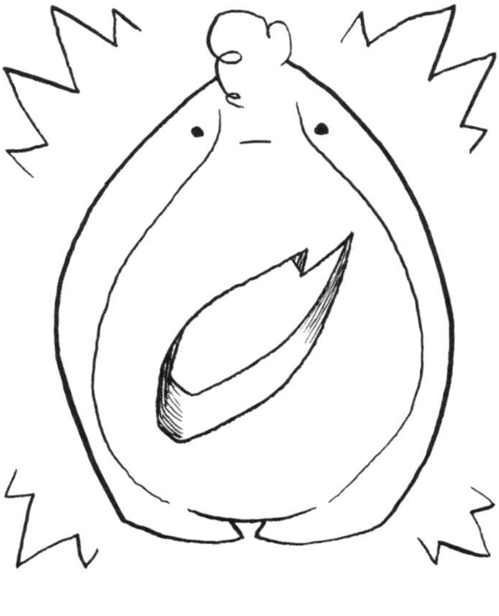

The hole in Hole took the shape of an endive.

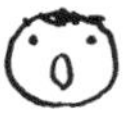

"Ha! How funny!
Don't move.
I wanna try
something..."

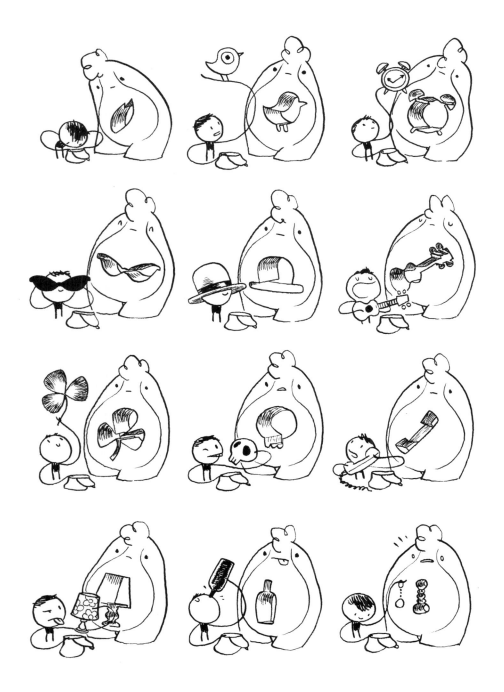

And just then...

SHLUUURP!

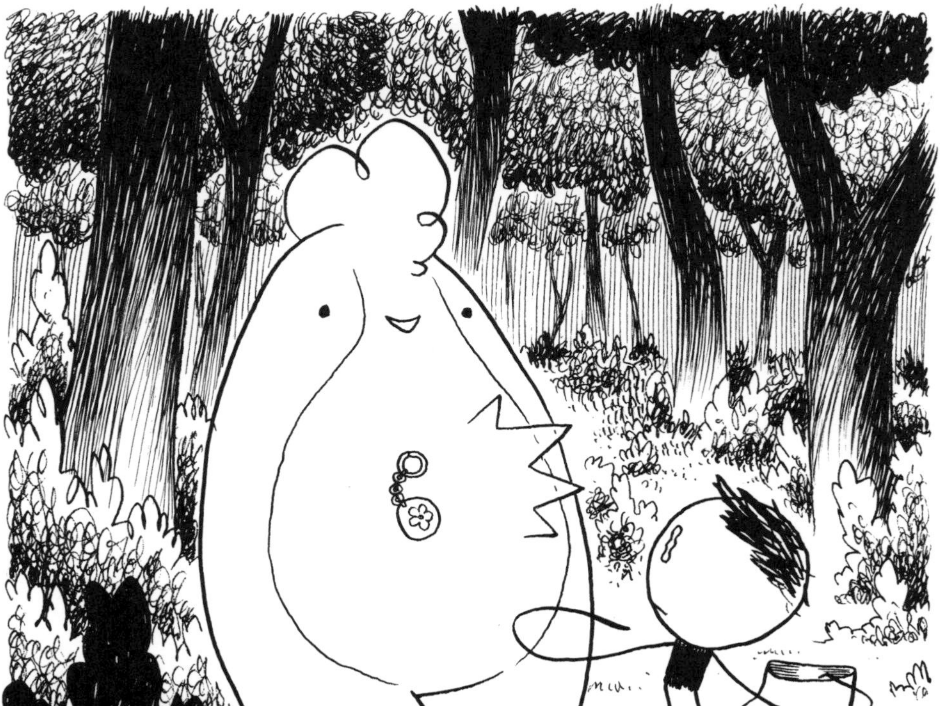

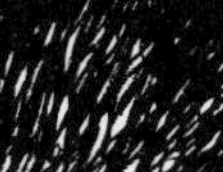
"HEY! Give it back! That's mine!"

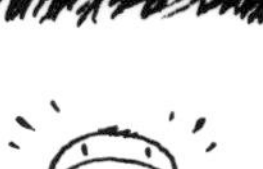
"I don't know how!"

But for the first time, Hole was smiling.

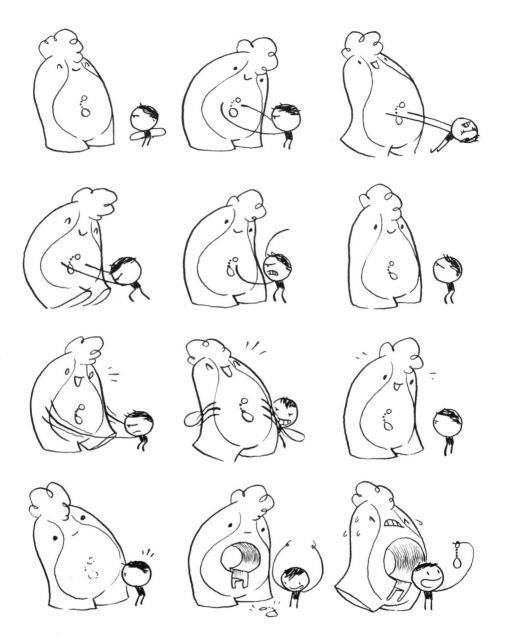

Alphonse felt oddly relieved.

 "Whew! Thanks!"

SHLUUURP!

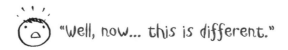 "well, now... this is different."

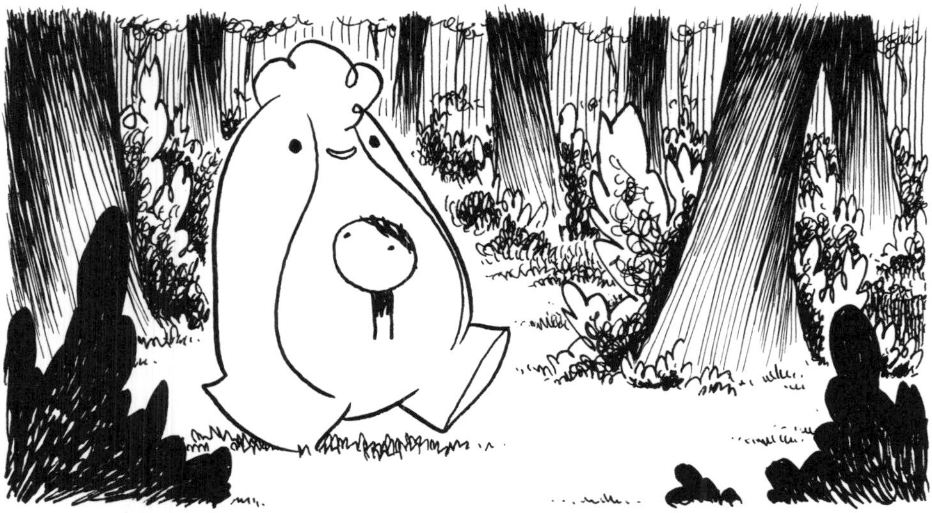

"This is good. I feel good. You're gonna feel good, too, you'll see! I'll take you on trips and we'll go for walks... come on! There's some cool stuff this way..."

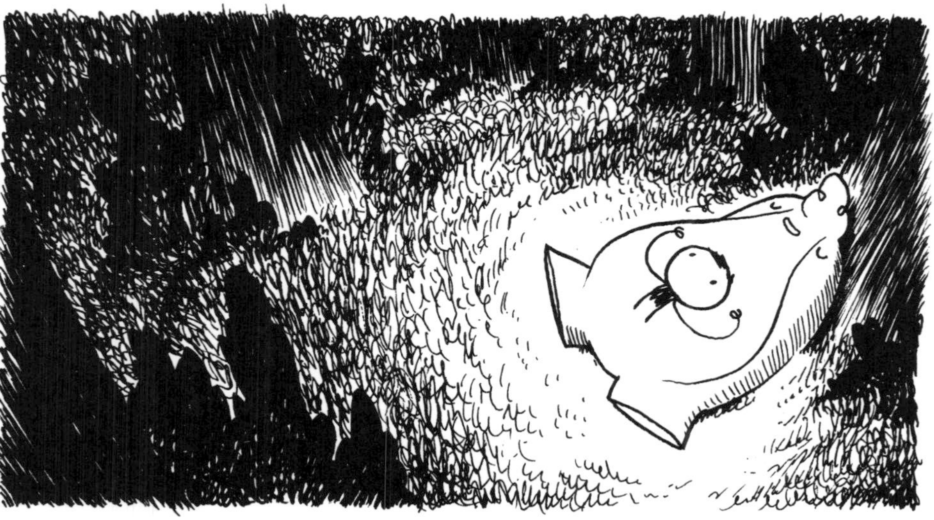

Hole fell asleep with a big smile on his face.

"Hey! Hey, HOLE! HEY!"

But Hole was fast asleep.

He slept for several days and nights.

Alphonse tried to wiggle free,
but it was no use.

 "Hey, come on! I'm getting bored in here!"

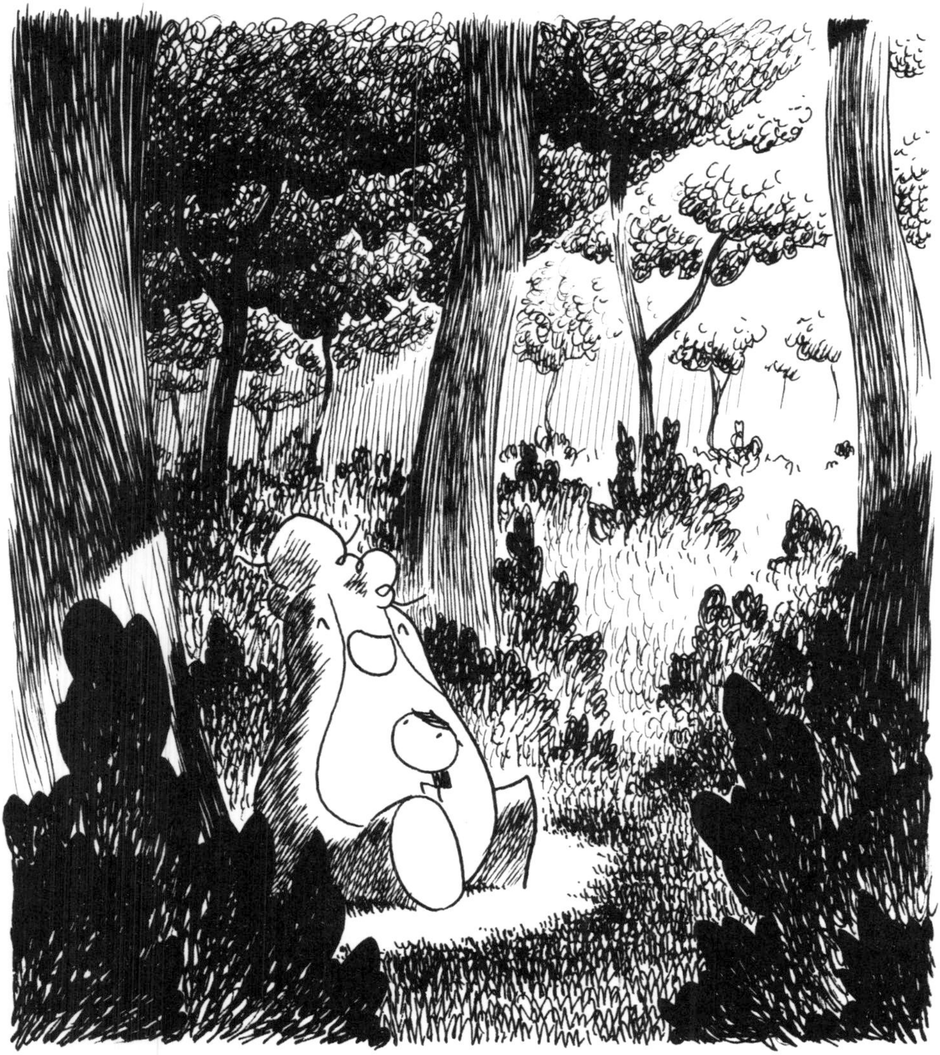

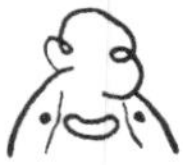

"Okay, let's go!"

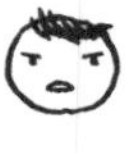

"I'd like to go on my own.
I don't want to be a burden."

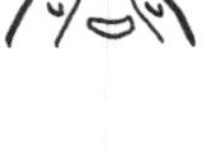

"You're not a burden at all!
See how good this feels?"

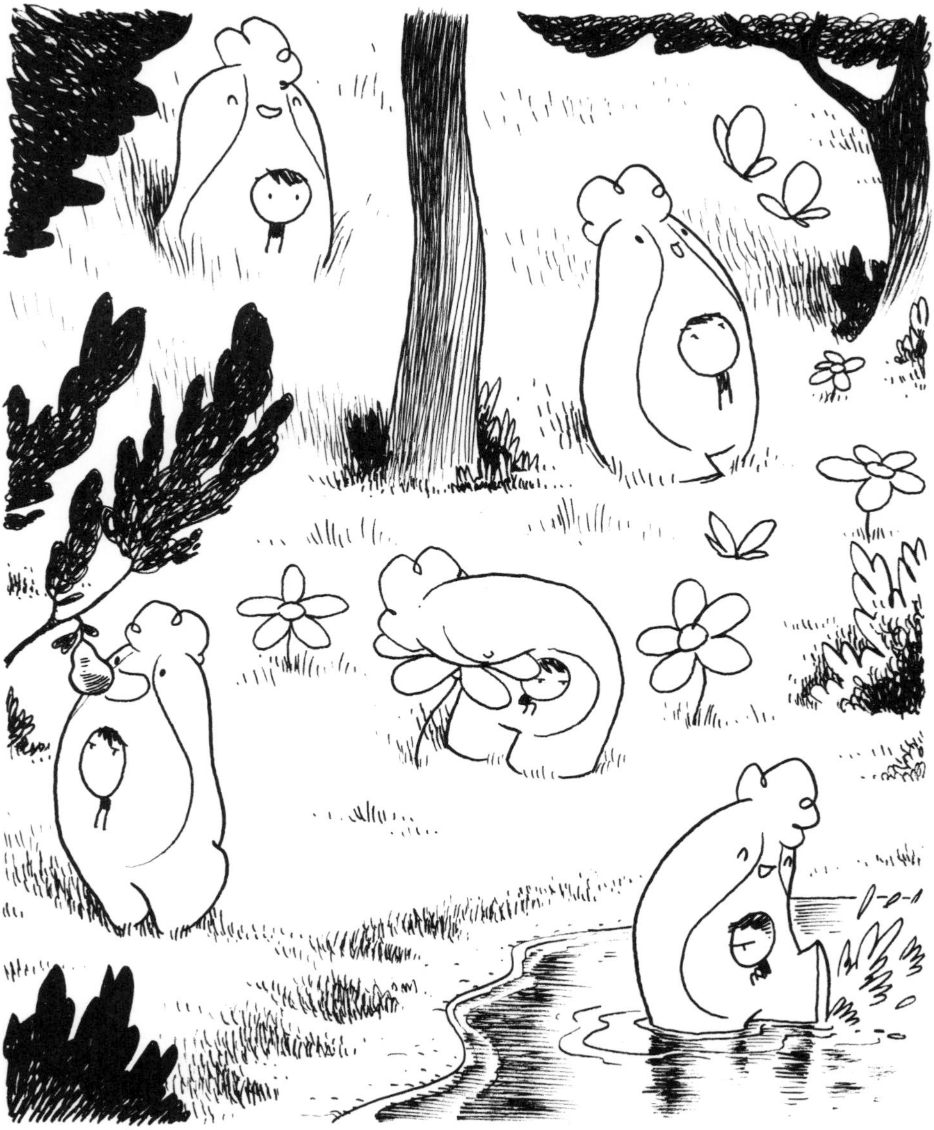

Hole sniffed flowers, splashed in ponds, and did
a whole bunch of other fun things.

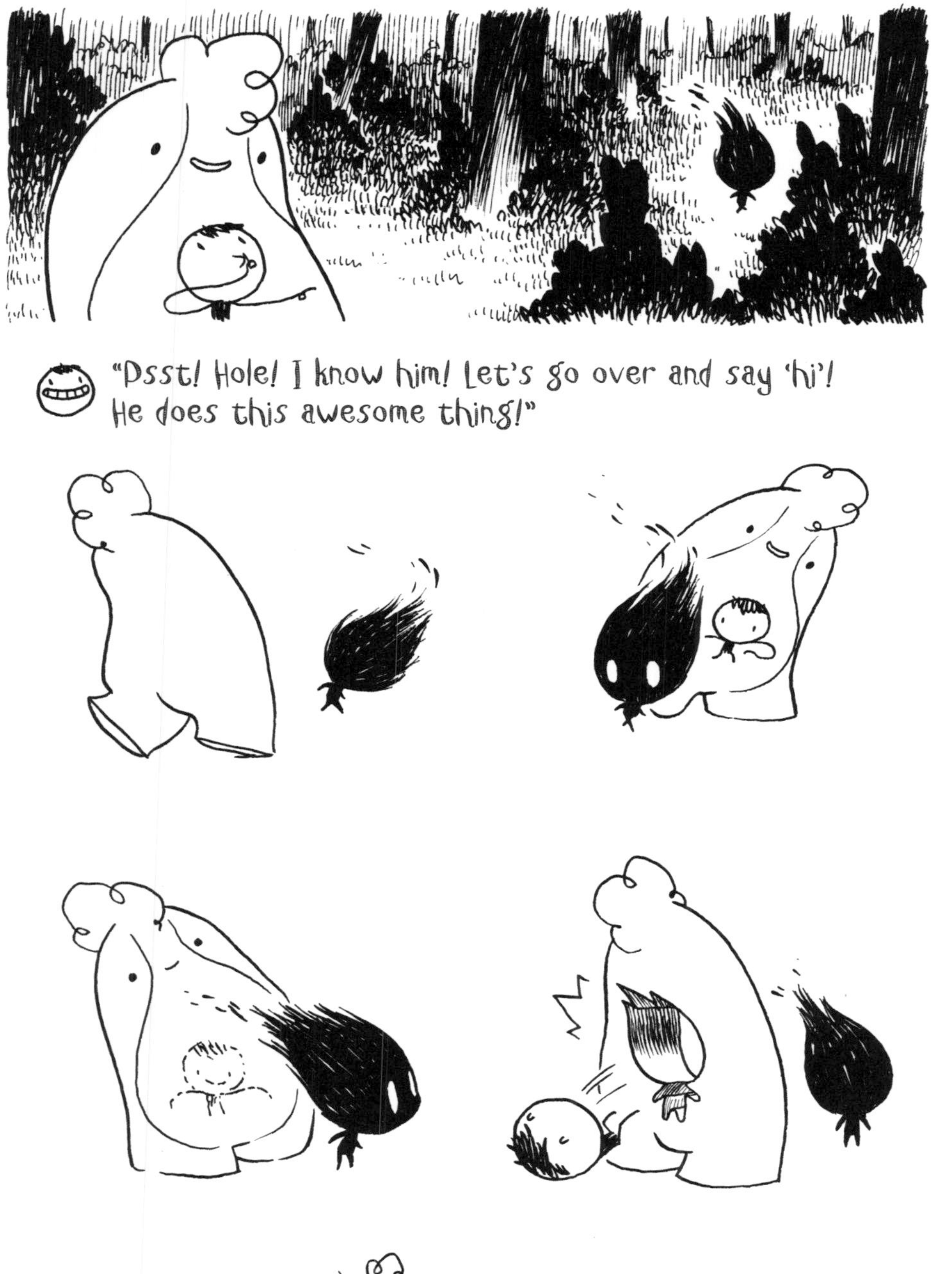
"Psst! Hole! I know him! Let's go over and say 'hi'! He does this awesome thing!"
"Whoa!"

While Hole stared at the smoking pile of ashes,
Alphonse ran away.

Hole's hole wasn't shaped like anything anymore.

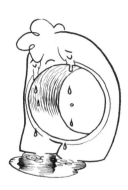

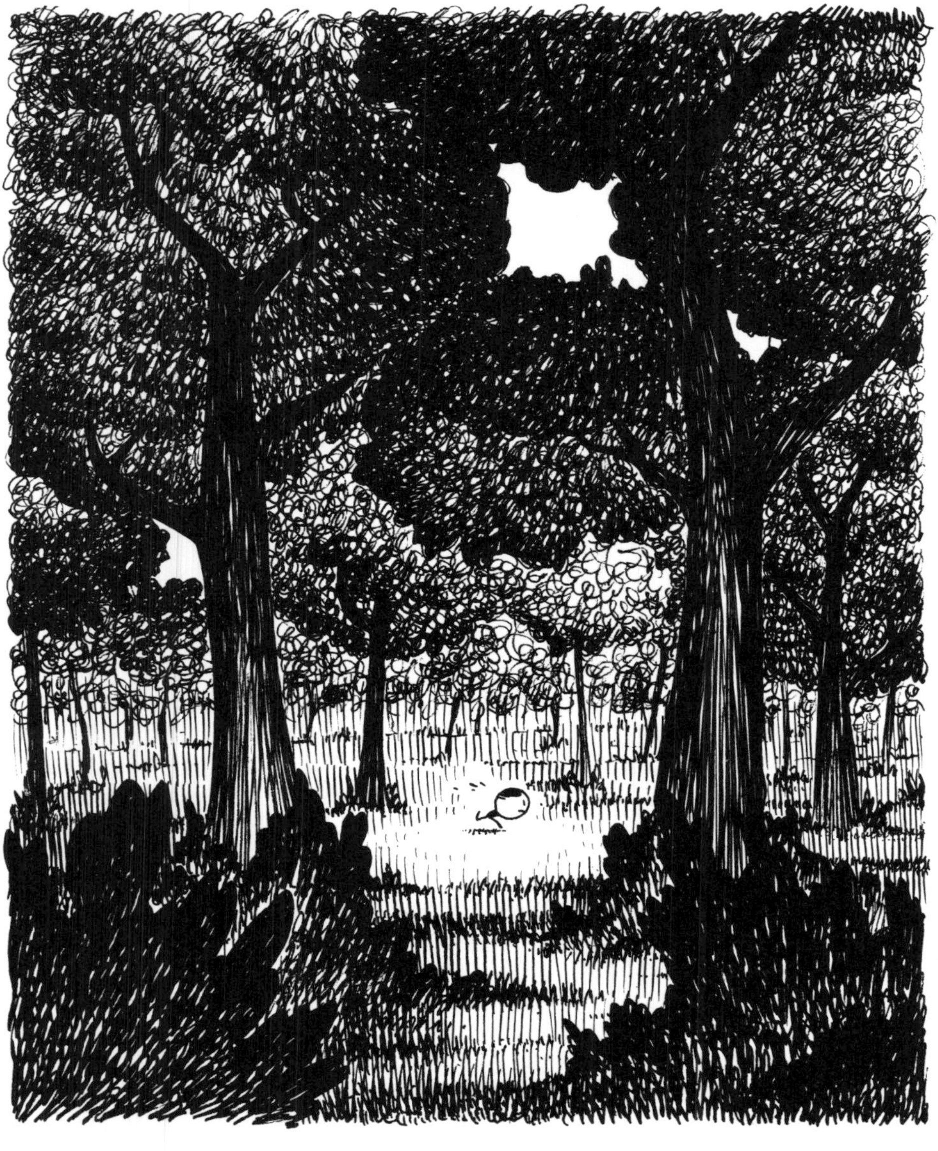

Alphonse kept running, to get as far away as he could.

And then, behind a soft, little hill, he saw...

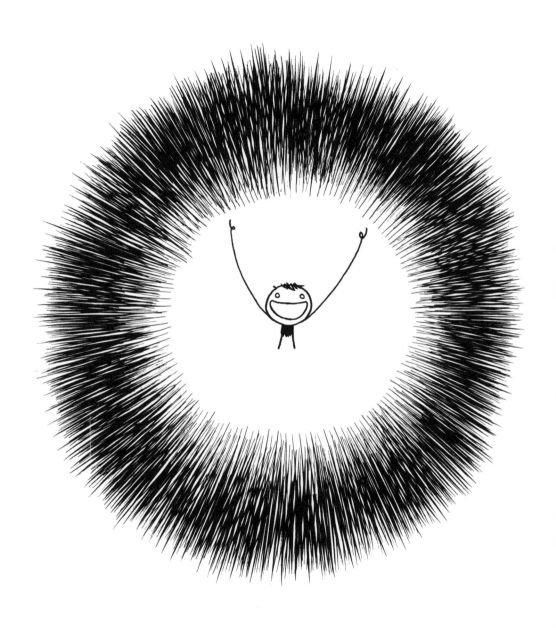

"Big Man! There you are!"

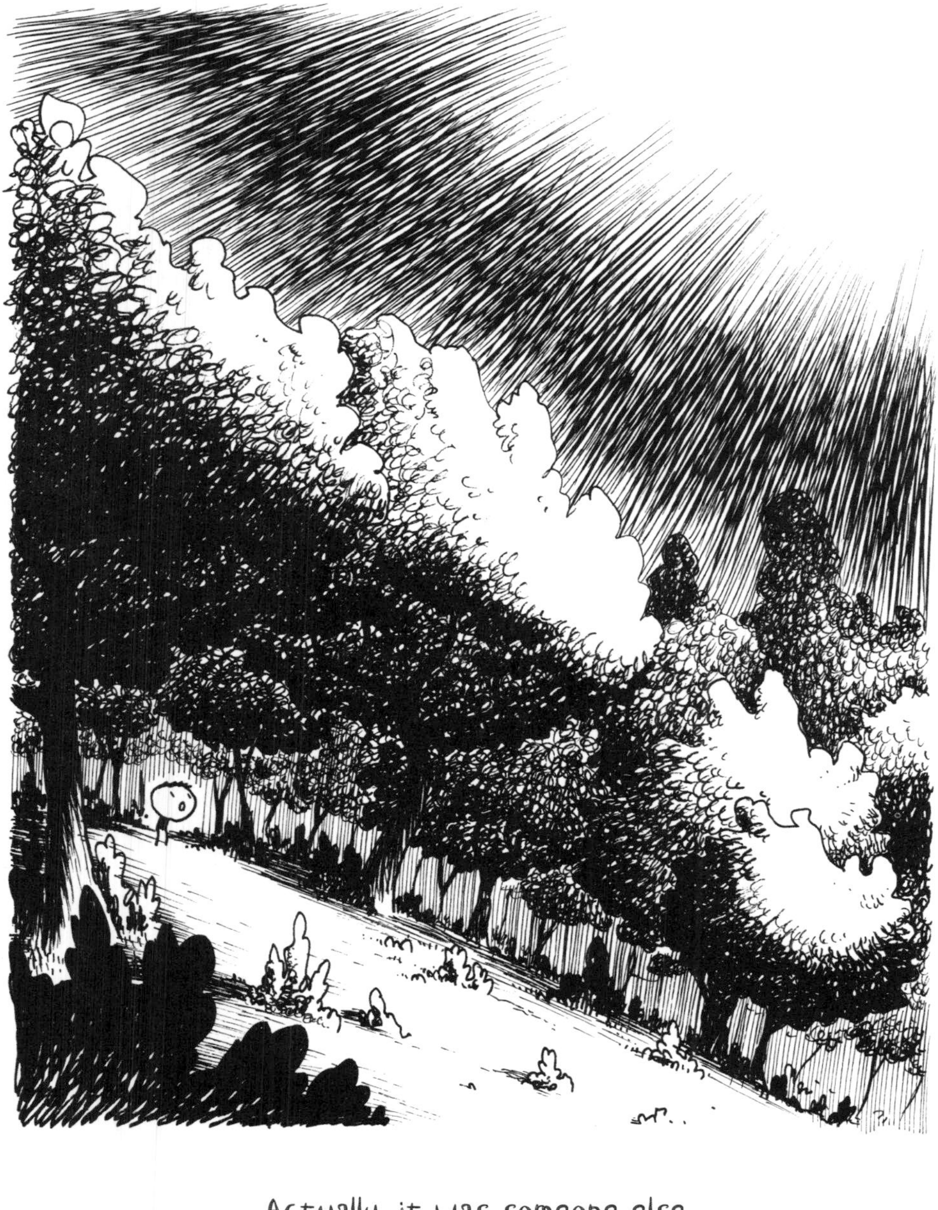

Actually, it was someone else.

Someone very, very beautiful.

He shone like all the hope in the universe.

Everyone was following him.

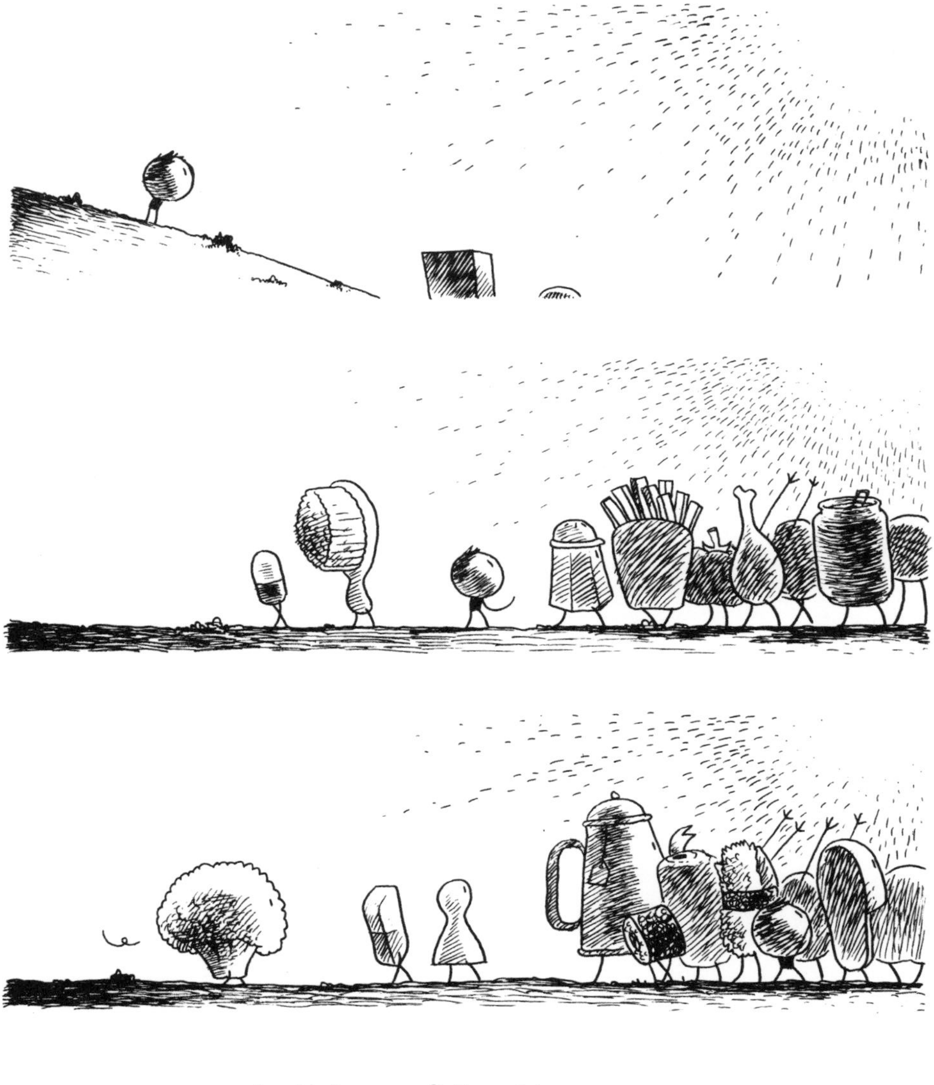

So Alphonse follwed him, too.

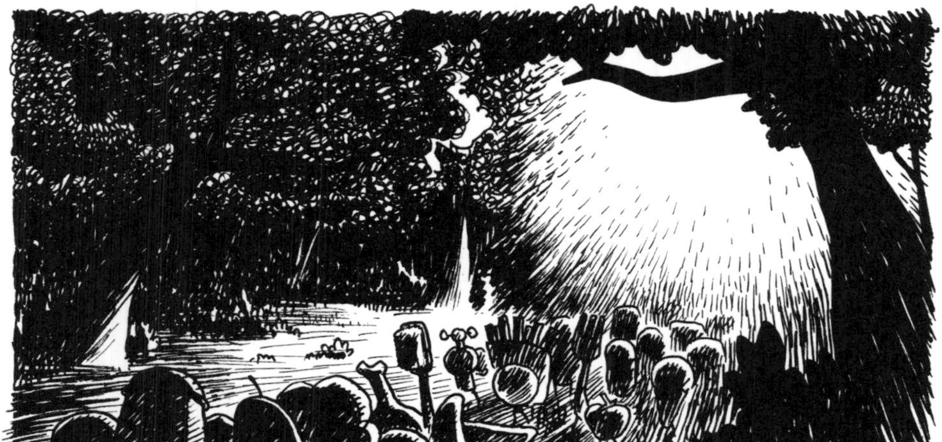
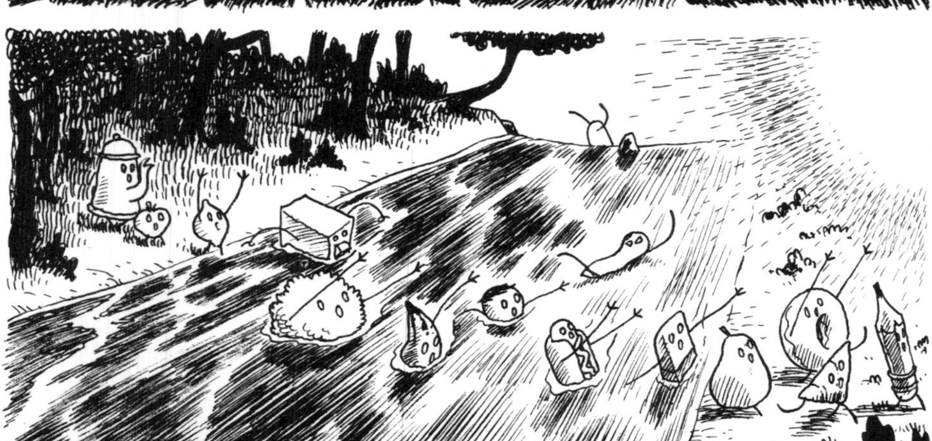
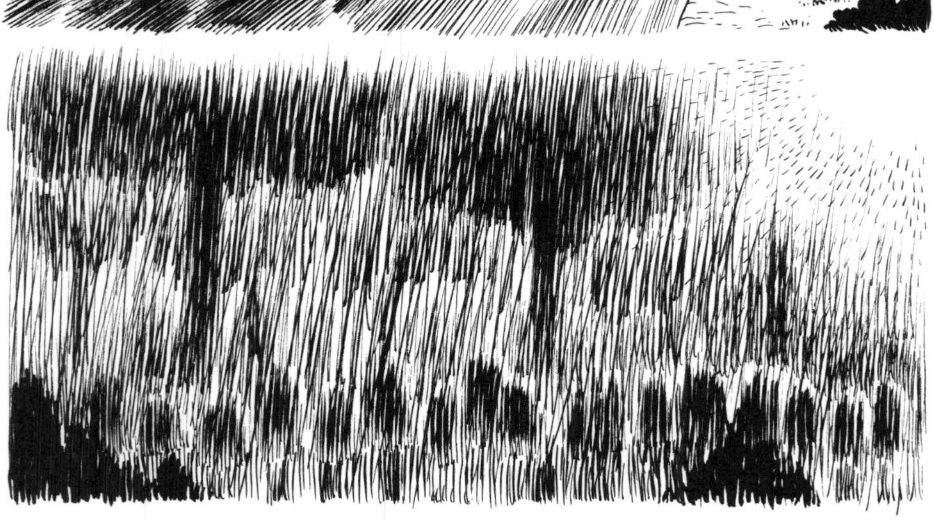

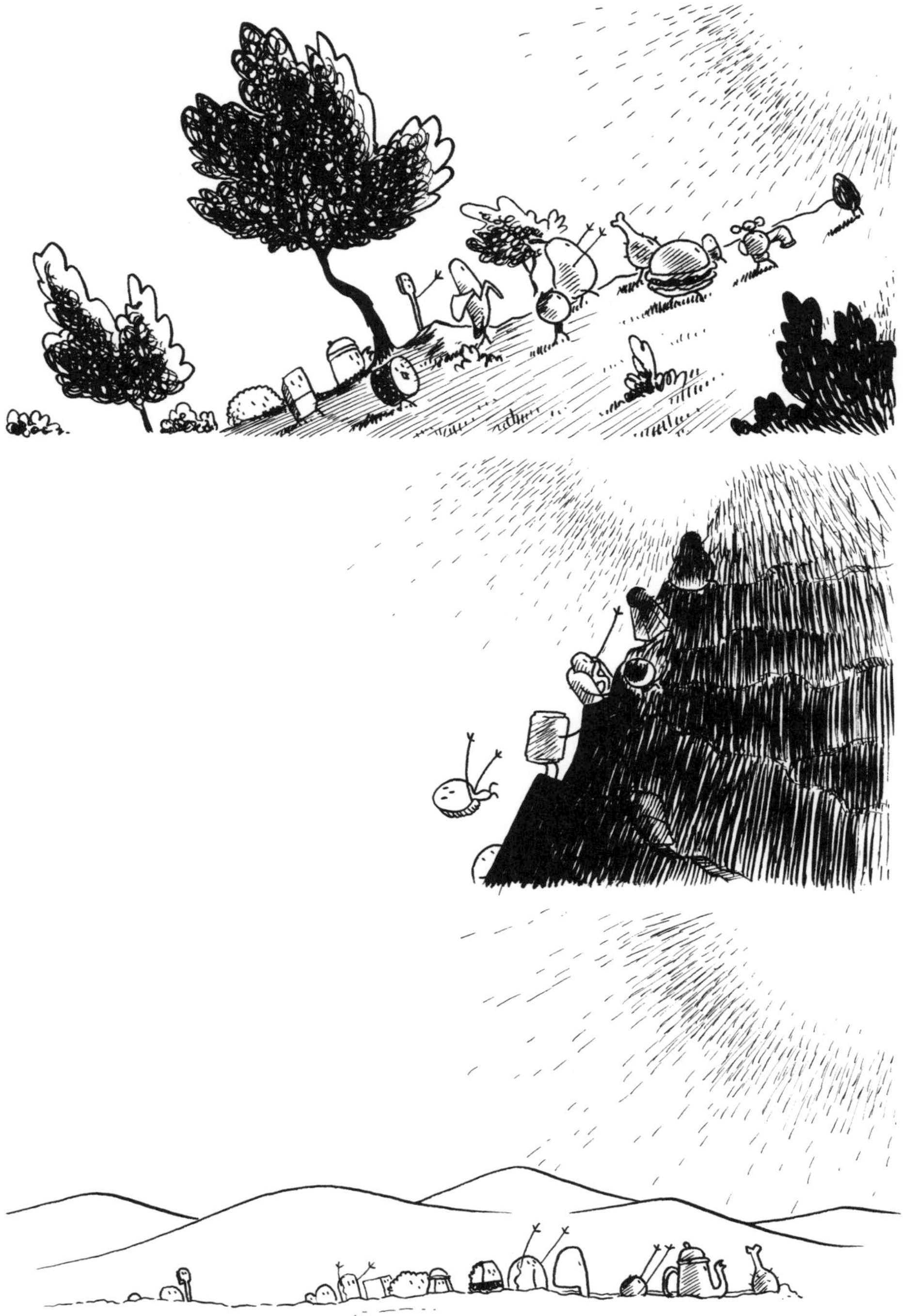

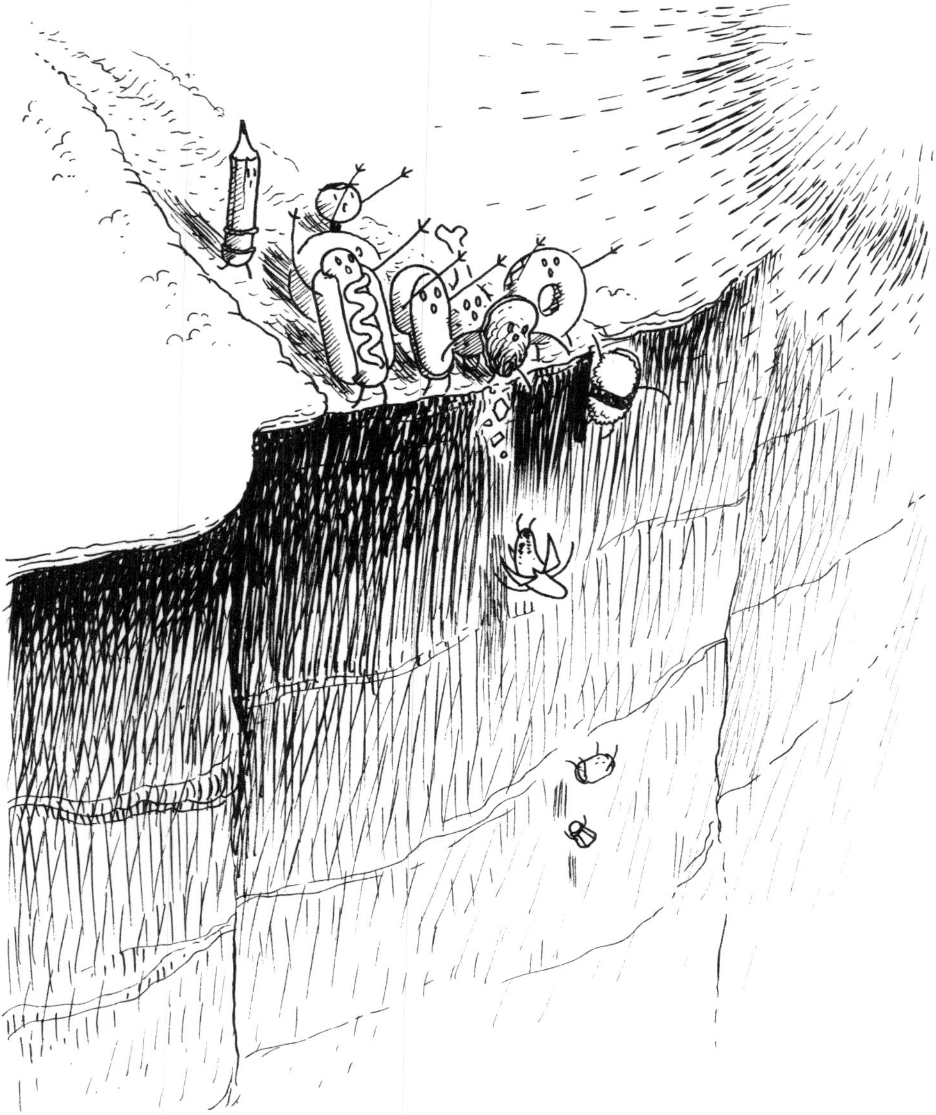

When they reached the end of the world, the Shining One
kept right on going without looking back.

Some followers fell. Others stopped.

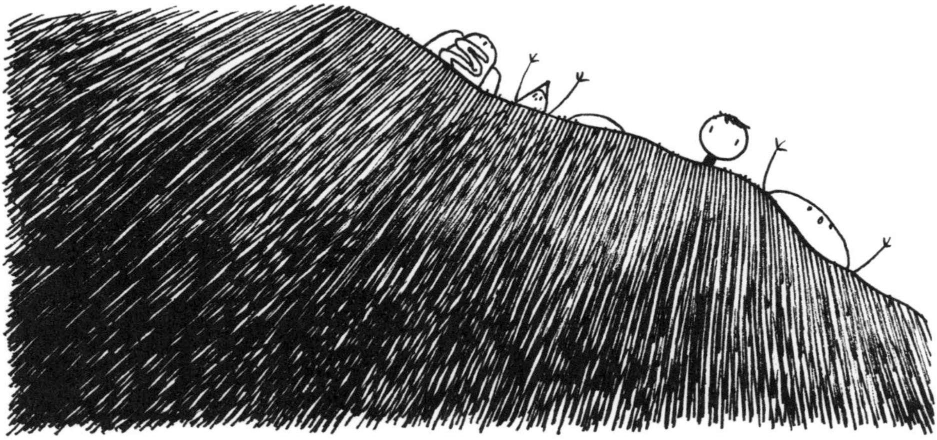

"whoa... uh..."

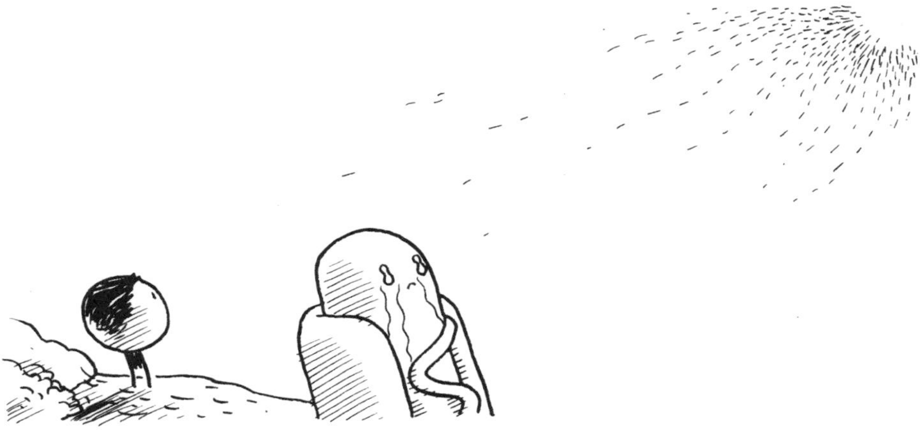

So he left.

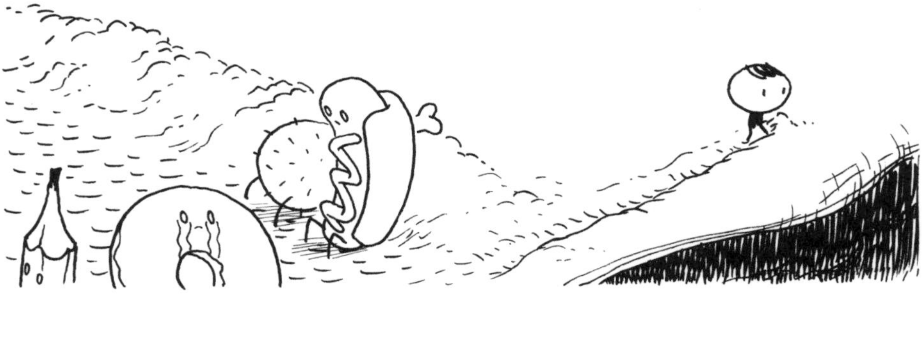

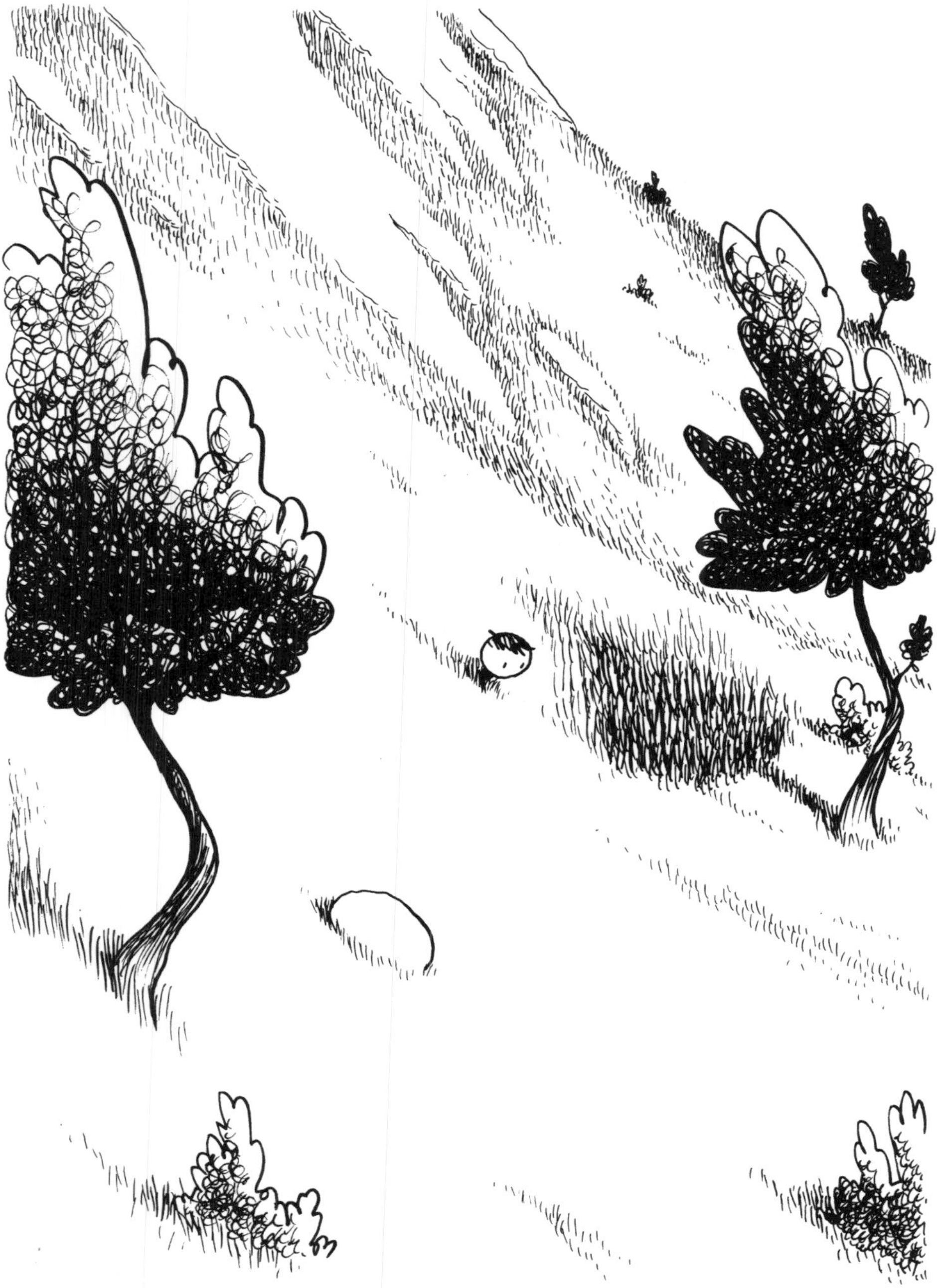

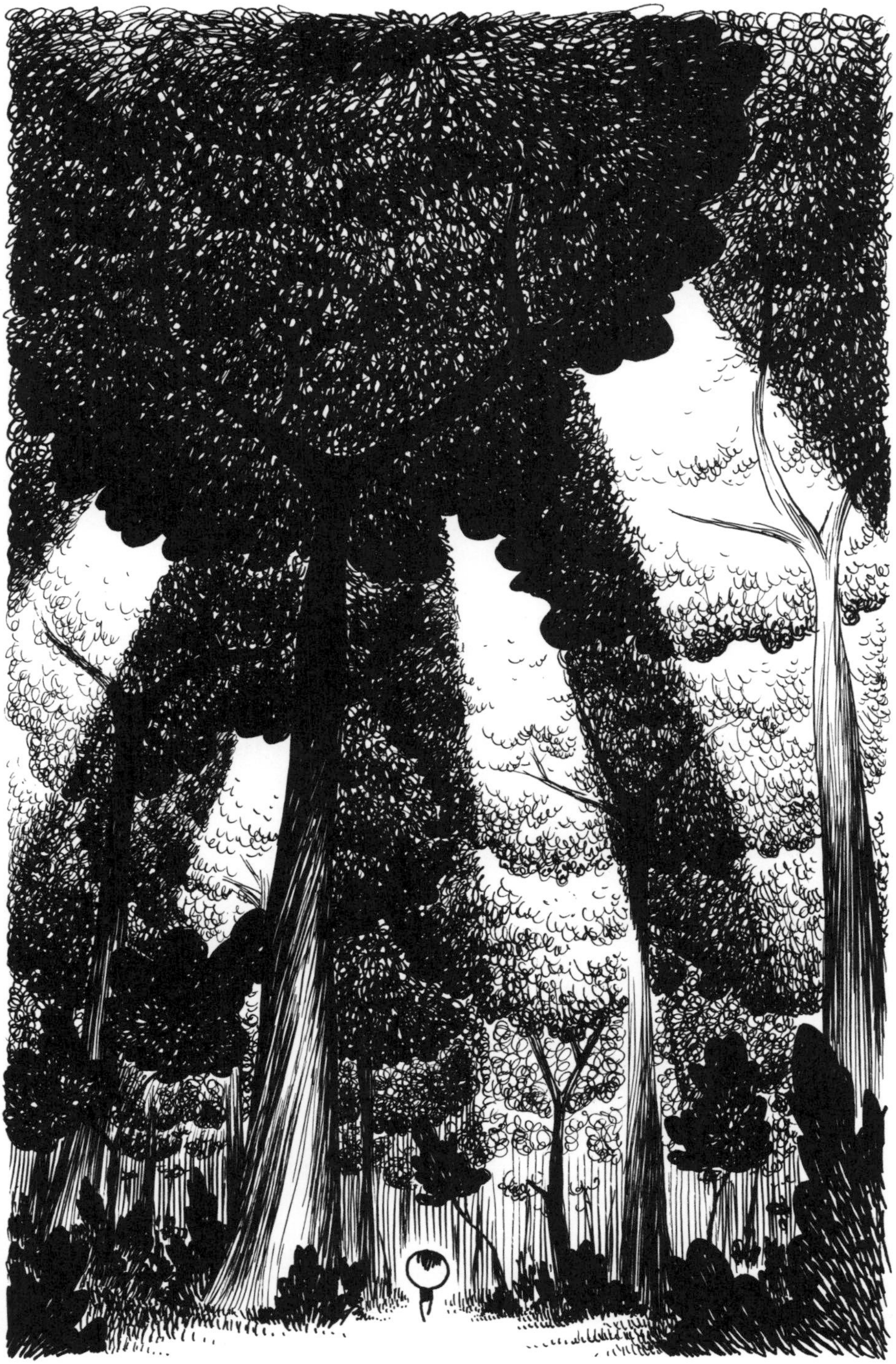

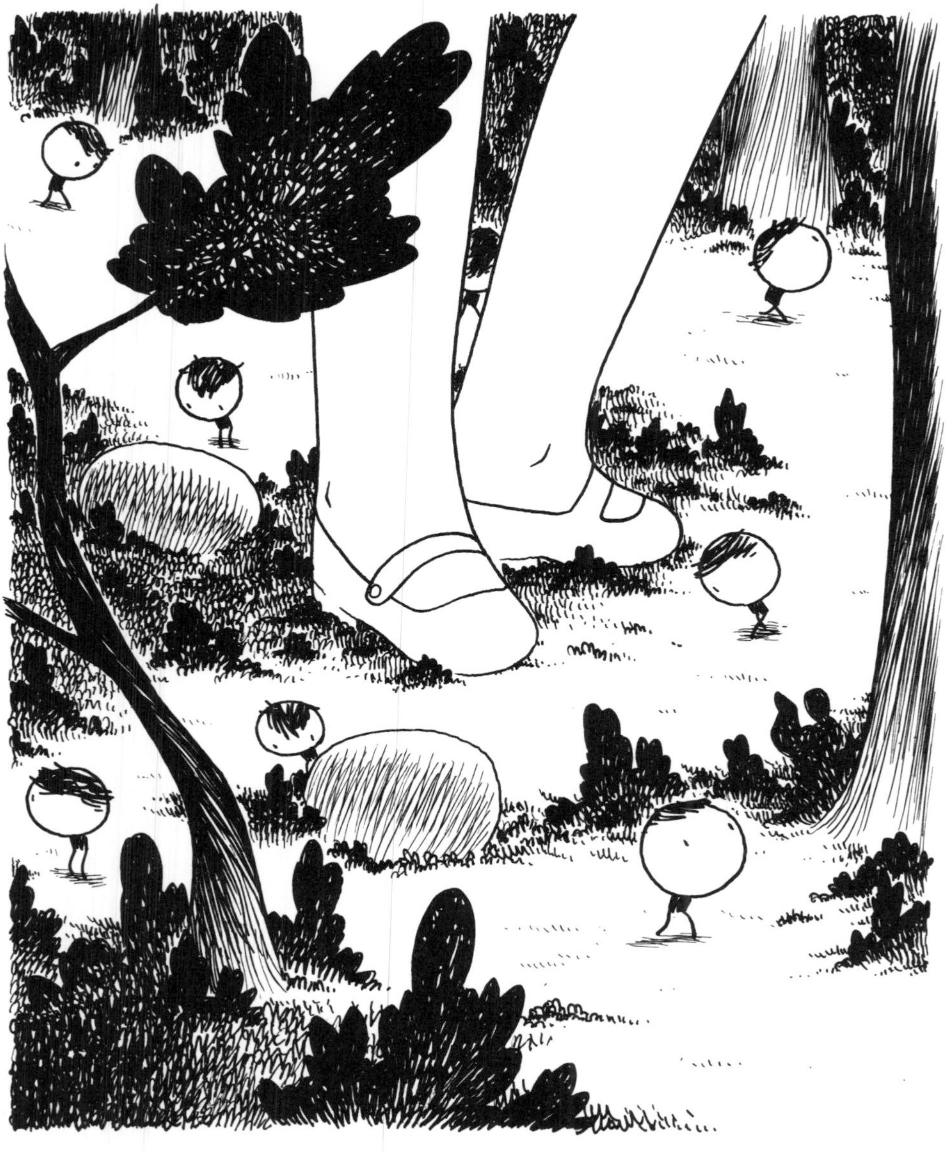

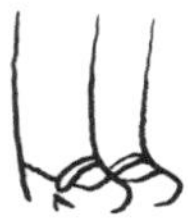

"Hey there, little guy! Whatcha doing?"

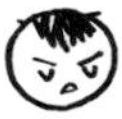
"Leave me alone. I'm looking for something."

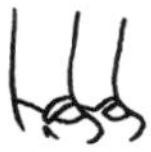
"Yeah, I can tell. I'm looking for something, too."

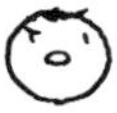
"Oh yeah? What are you looking for?"

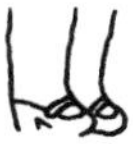
"Someone like you.
We can be alone together.
What's your name?"

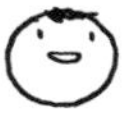
"Alphonse Tabouret!"

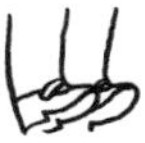
"Ha ha ha! That's a funny name!
My names Penelope Achoo."

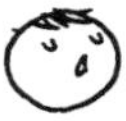
"That's not much better, if you ask me."

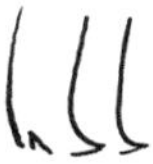
"I didn't ask you.
Besides, I make the rules out here."

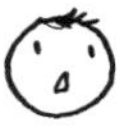
"Say what?"

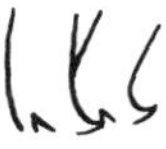
"Come on, let's go play that game where
we race and I win."

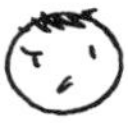
"But what if I win?"

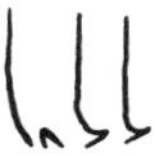
"Then you'll obviously be cheating."

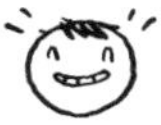
"Okay, let's do it!"

All day long...

...Alphonse lost to Penelope.

And she was happy.

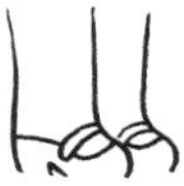

"You can sleep with me tonight. My feet get cold."

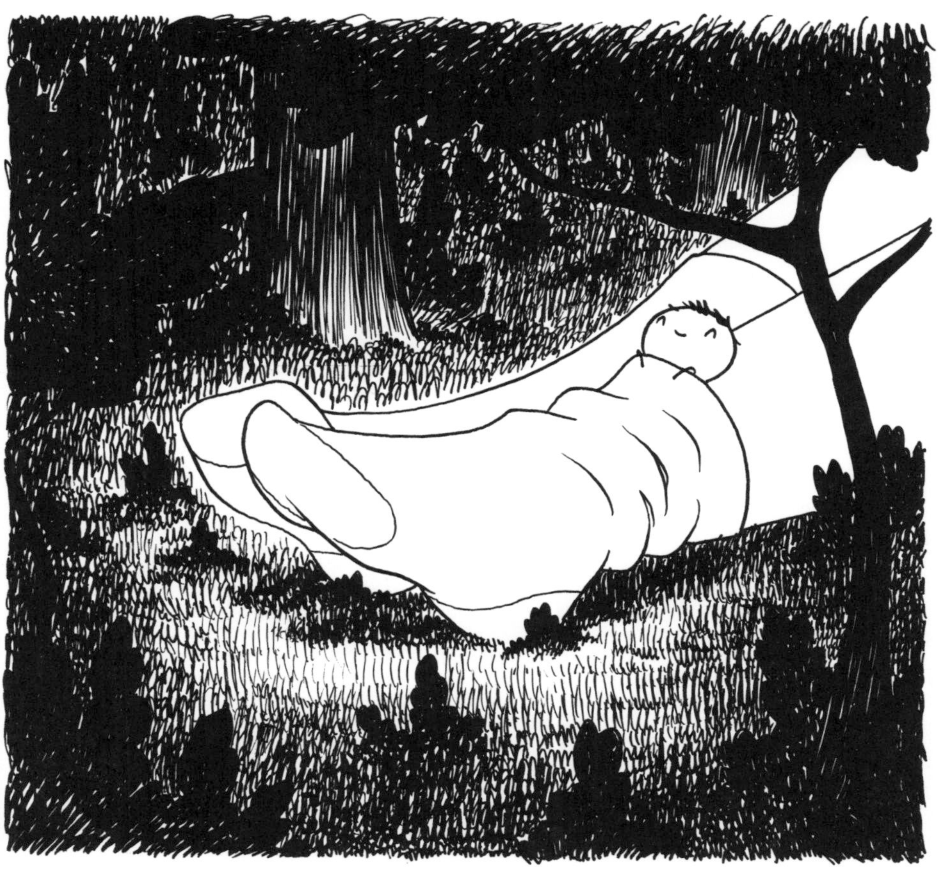

They laid down together,
with Alphonse tucked into her sock.

And when she was finally quiet,
he thought she was terrific.

In the morning, she awoke in a very bad mood.

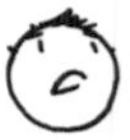
"To say the least..."

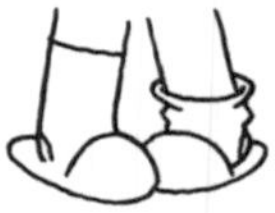
"I slept terribly. My back hurts, my legs hurt, my whole--"

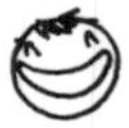
"Your hole hurts?"

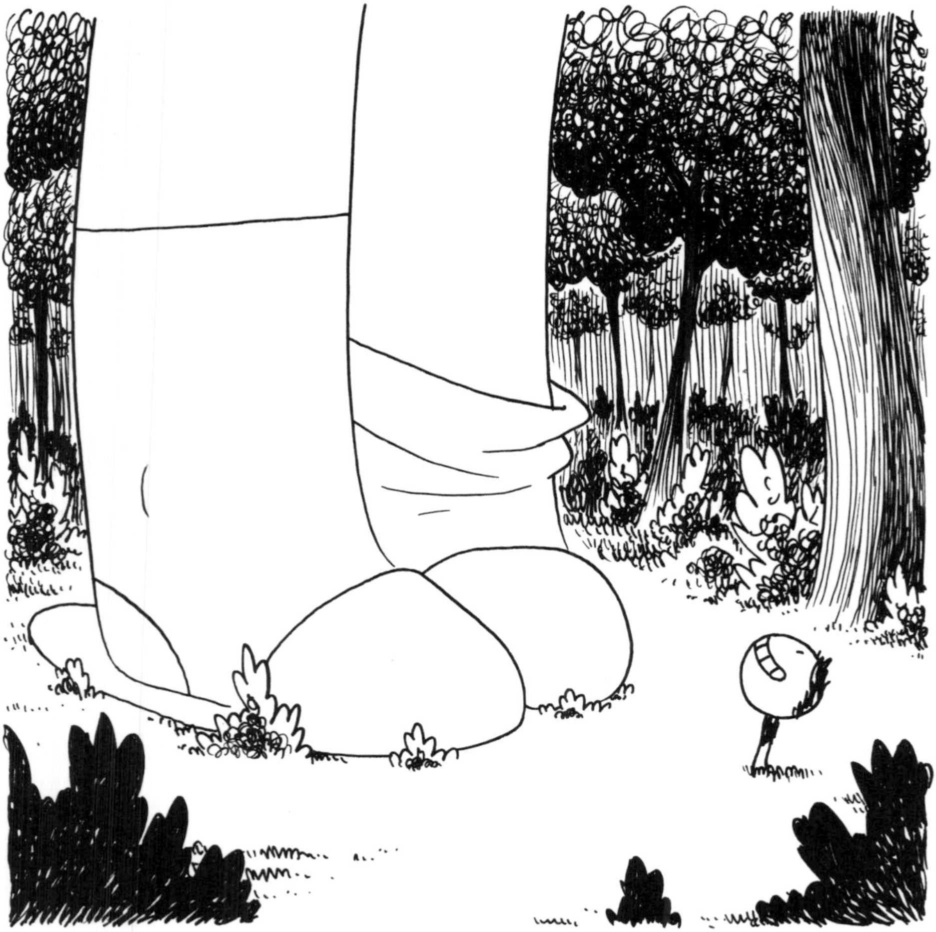

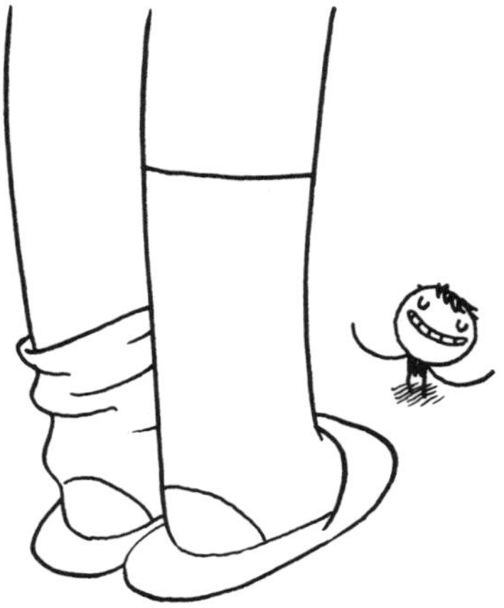

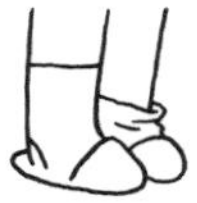

"What a stupid thing to say.
I don't have any holes!"

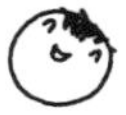

"It was just a joke. A pun.
I wanted to make you laugh."

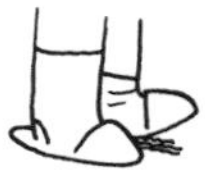

"I hate puns. You're not funny.
Why don't you go build us a
cabin or something."

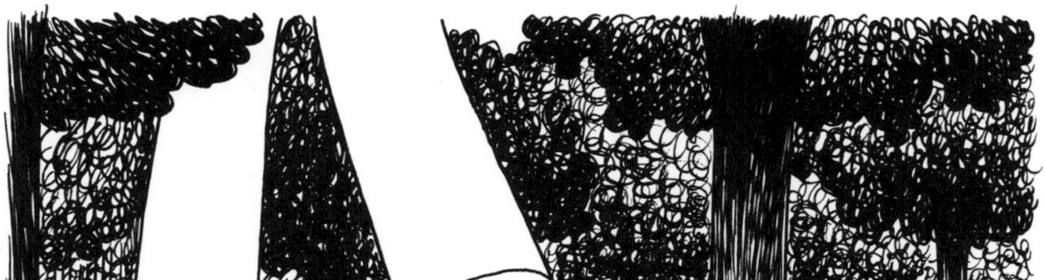

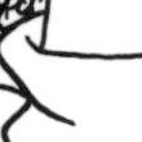

"Yeah, why not? A house of our own could
be nice! I bet Penelope misses having a
door to slam!"

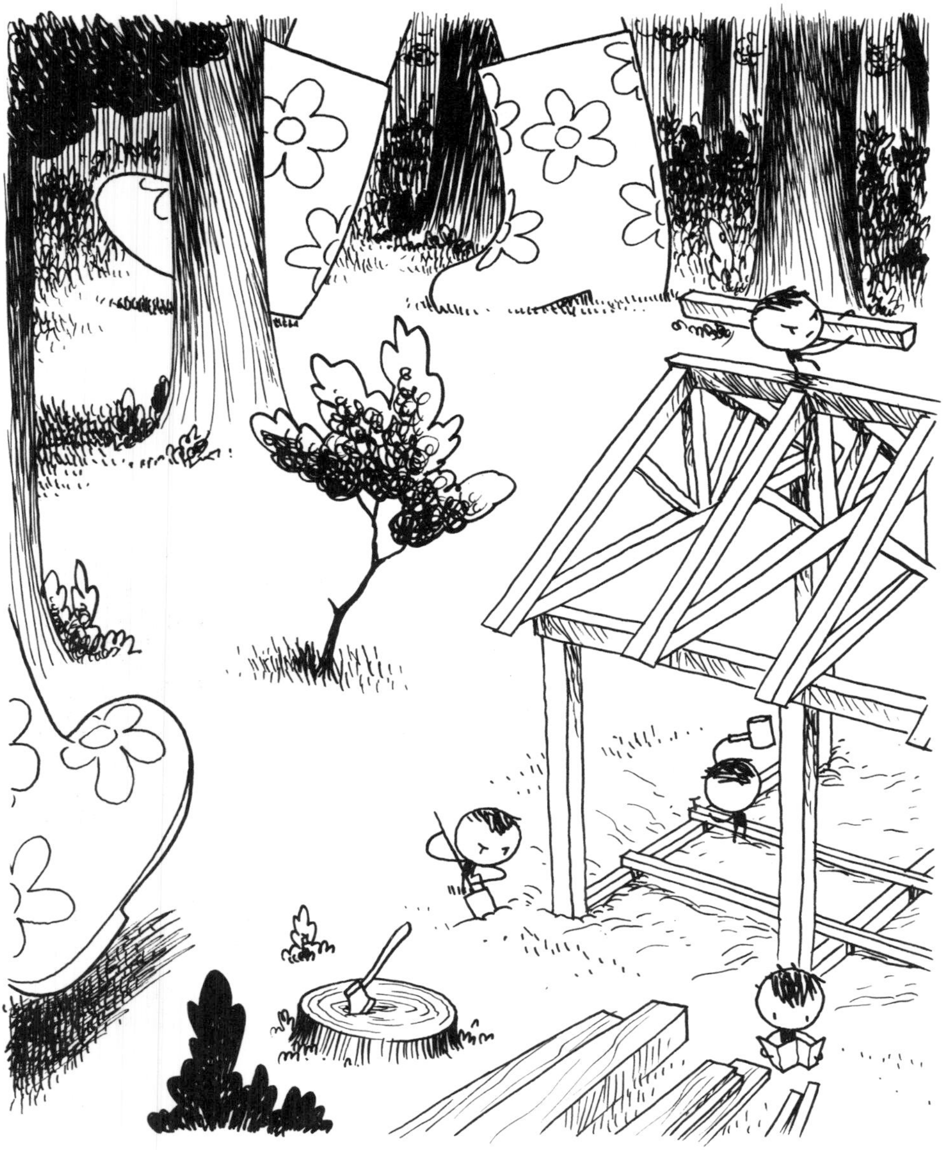

While Alphonse worked, Penelope went for a stroll, picking flowers to put in her hair.

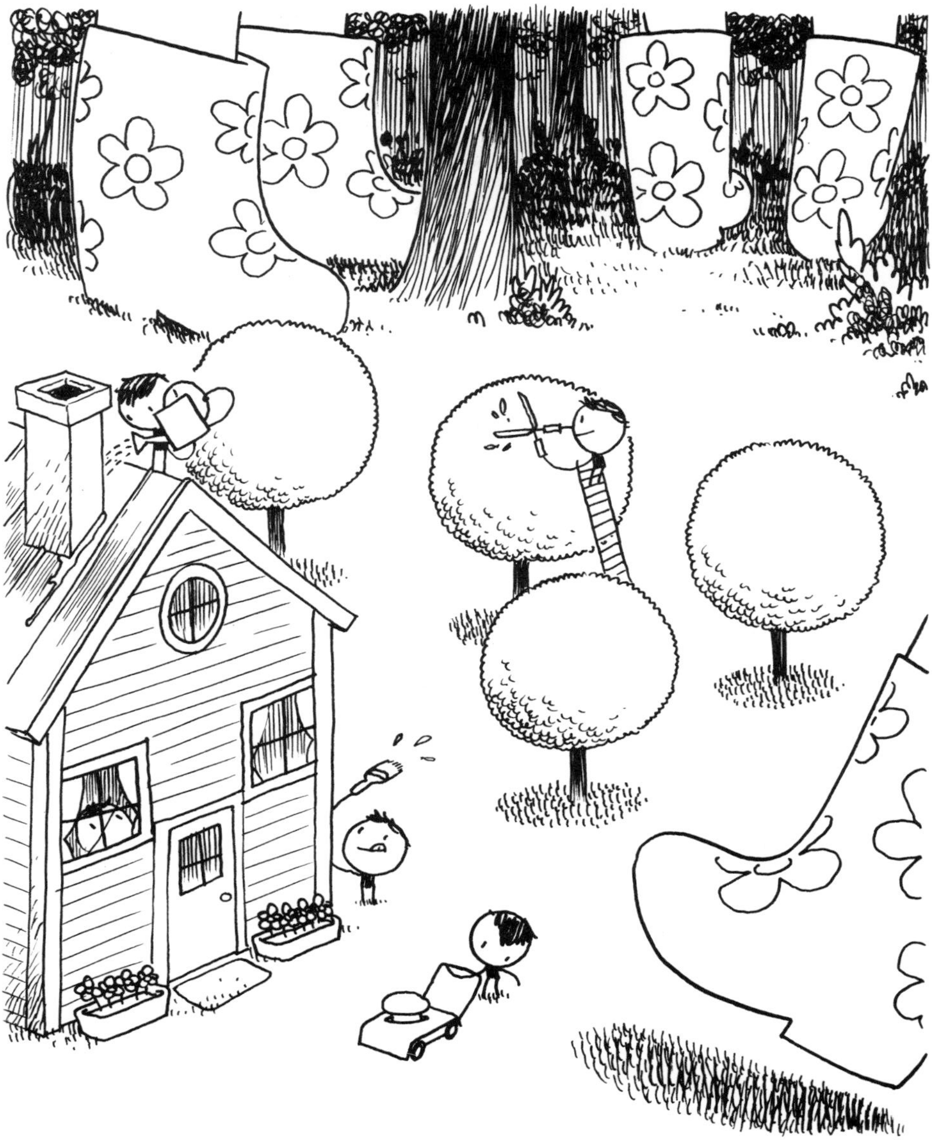

She returned just as Alphonse finished putting up the chimney.

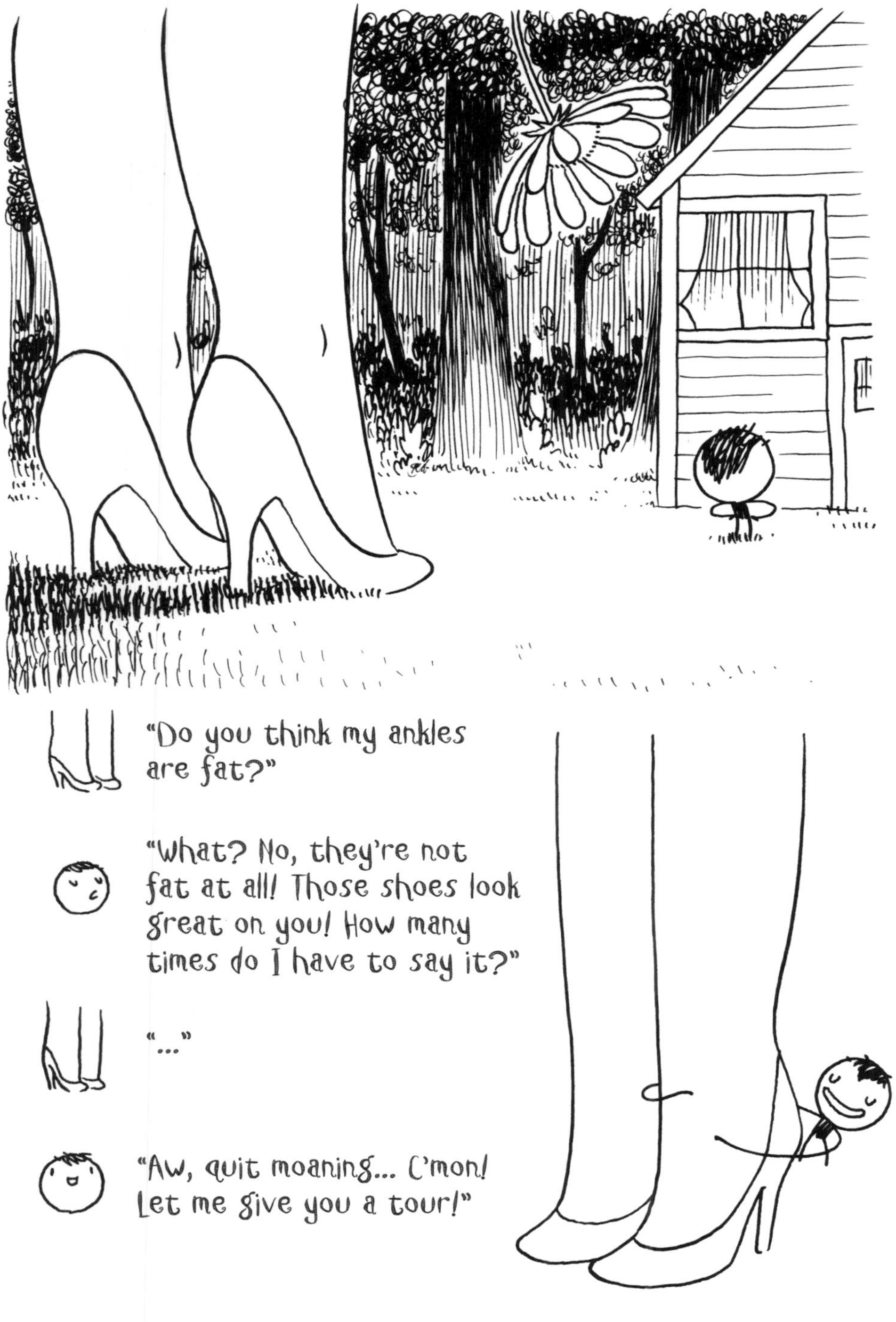
"Do you think my ankles are fat?"
"What? No, they're not fat at all! Those shoes look great on you! How many times do I have to say it?"
"..."
"Aw, quit moaning... C'mon! Let me give you a tour!"

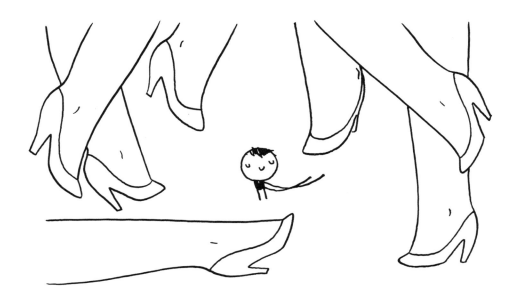

first he showed her around the property,
then he gave her a tour of the house.

"What a mess! You just
stuck stuff anywhere!"

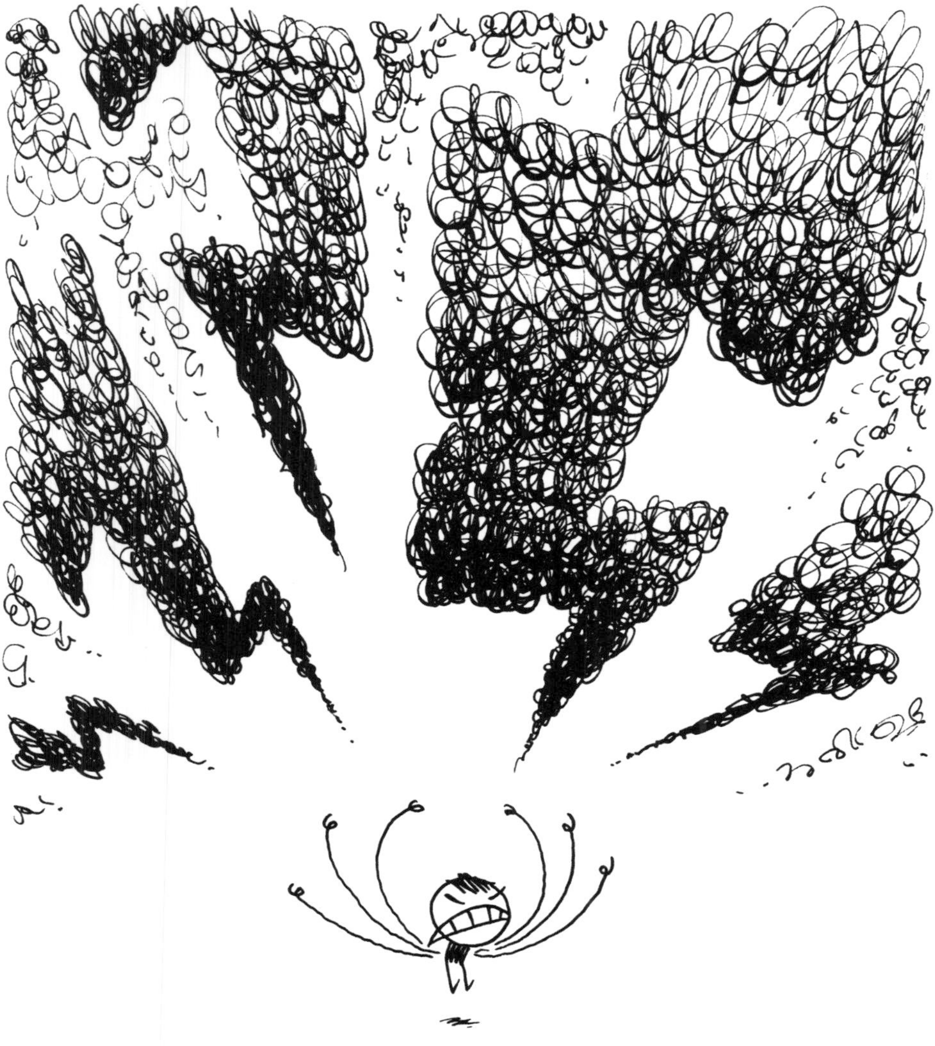

Alphonse was tired, but proud of the house he'd built, so he started screaming.

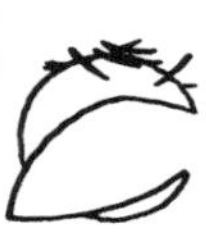

"What's your problem?! Nothing I do is ever enough! I worked all day long, and here you are complaining! Whine, whine, whine!"

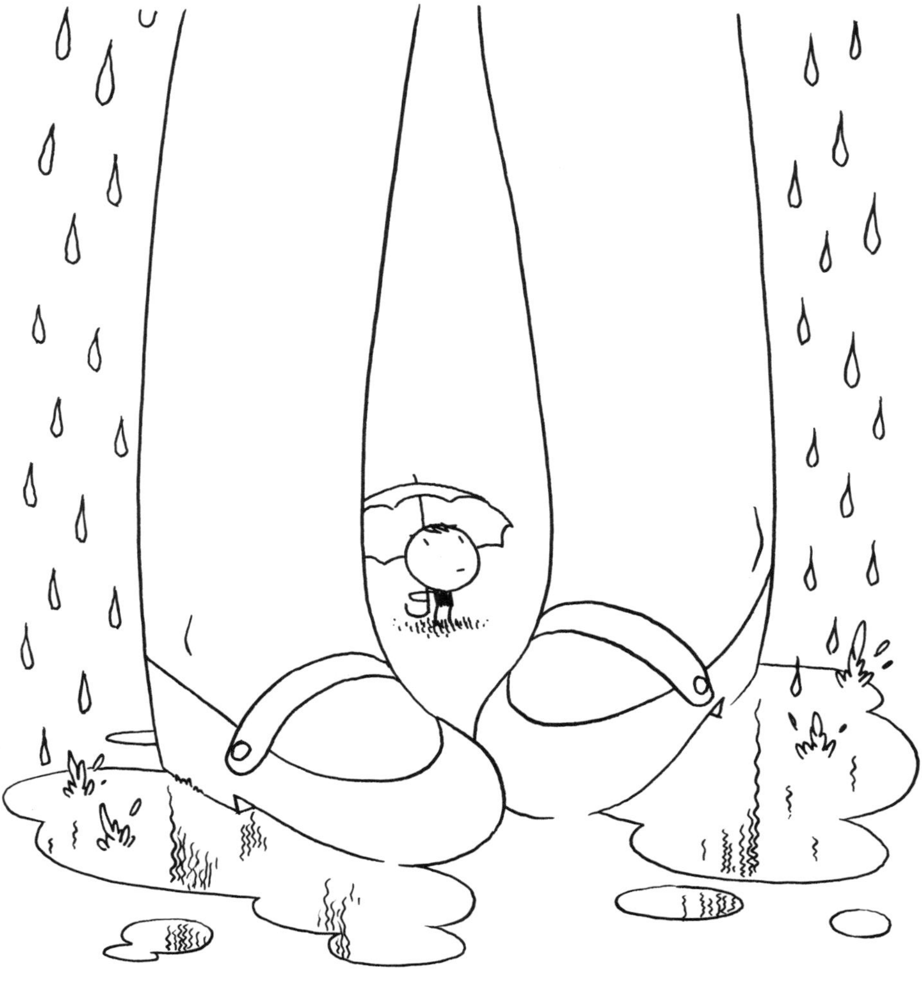

Suddenly, tears sprang from her eyes,
making puddles everywhere.

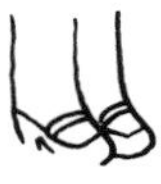

"Boohoohoo! Can you even hear how mean you're being? Boohoohoo! I'm so unhappy!"

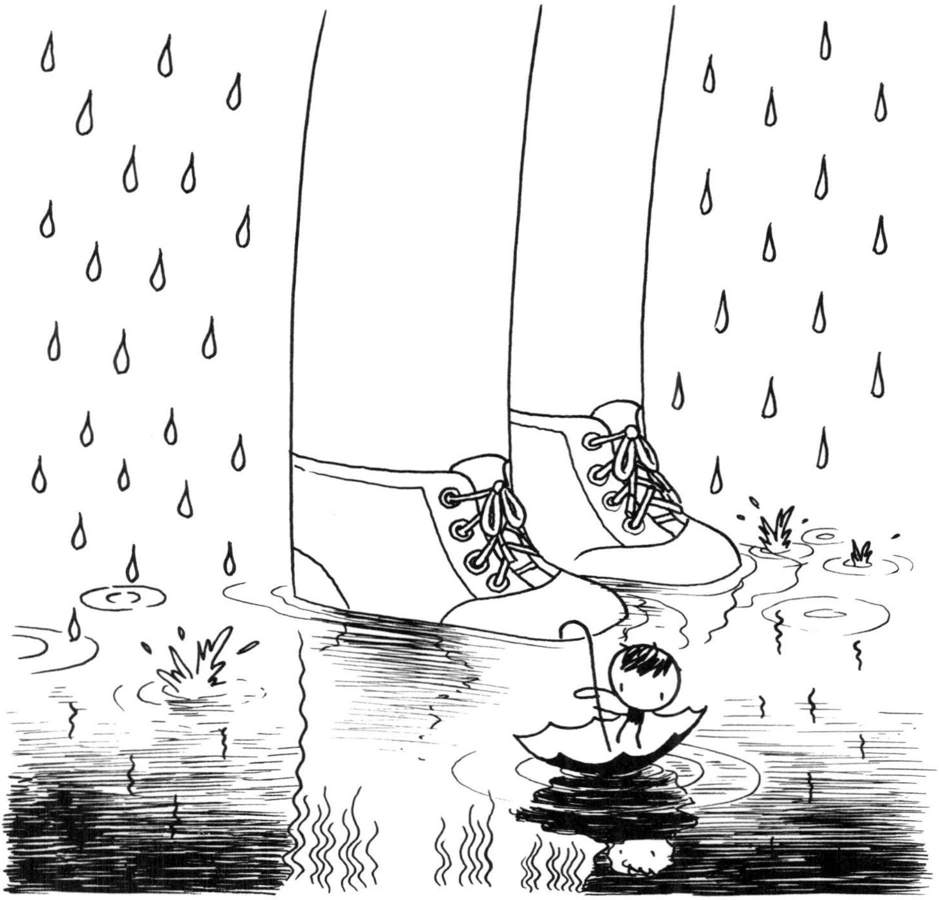

Alphonse felt very sorry and embarrassed.

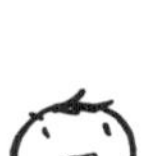

"Hey, hey... you're like a crocodile: you have a nasty bite, but you're always crying, too. C'mere, let me cheer you up. Tell me how you want everything, and I'll do exactly what you say."

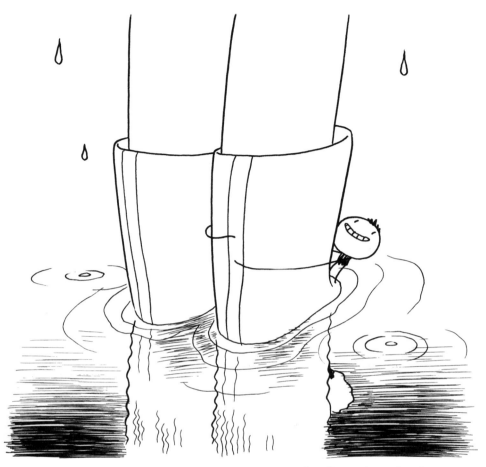

 "(sniffle) Well, things would be fine already if you'd listened to me in the first place before going off and doing your own thing..."

 "Sure, sure, you're absolutely right."

 "I know I am... (sniffle)"

Alphonse looked up at the sky far, far above until he could see stars he'd never seen before.

Then he listened to her every complaint.

And when it came to complaining...

  "I really want a necklace."

"What for?"

"To be pretty."

"Your neck is fine already."

"I know, but still..."

So Alphonse went back to the Knickknack Shop.

 "Meh, it's okay..."

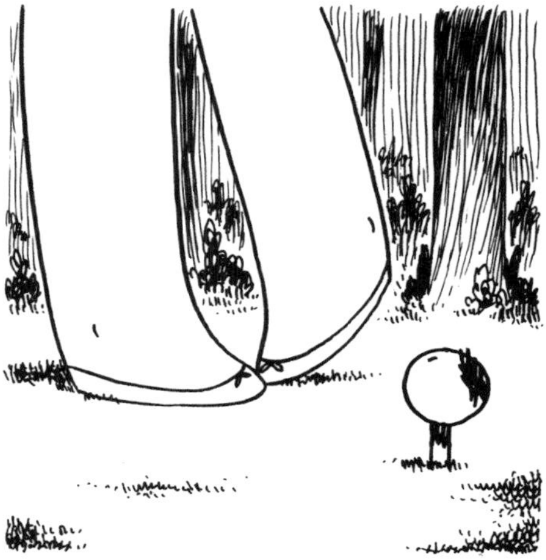

"You never give me flowers."

"Of course not. When you pick a flower, it dies."

"Yeah, I know. But still."

So Alphonse went out to pick flowers.

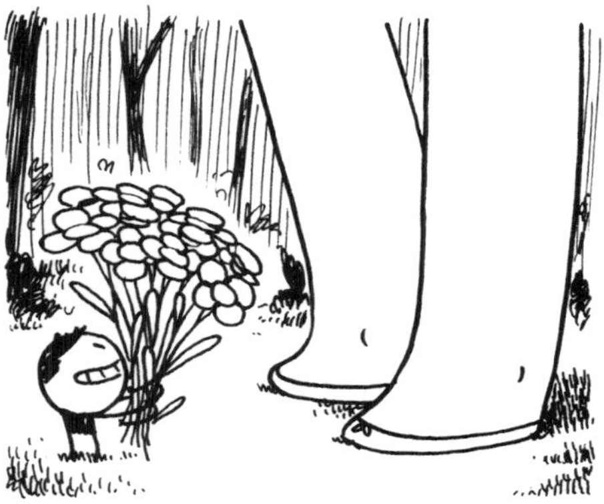

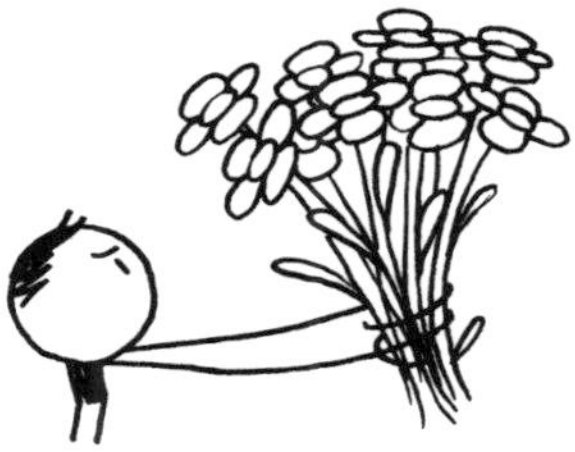

"But they're all white."

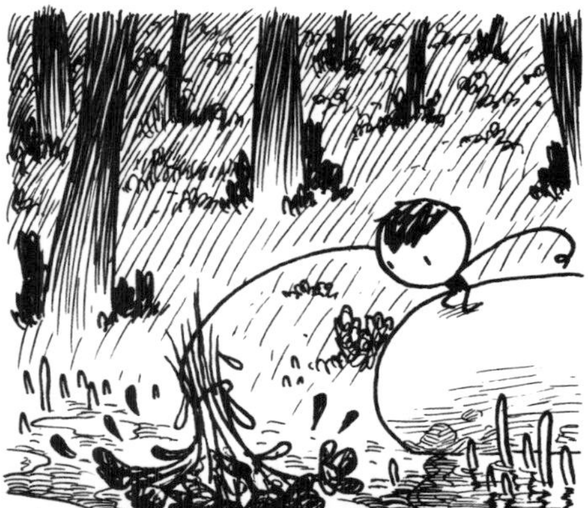

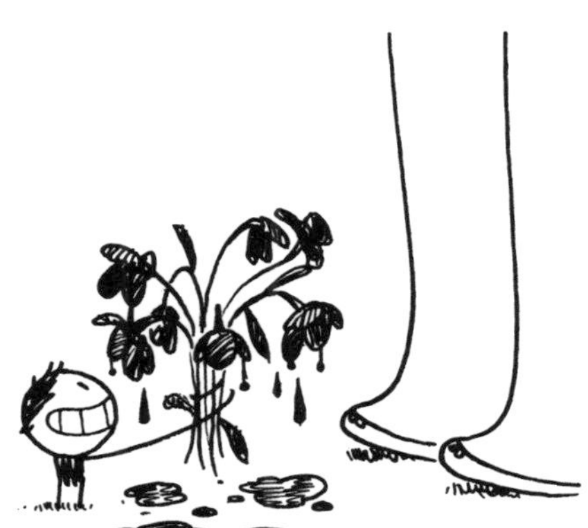

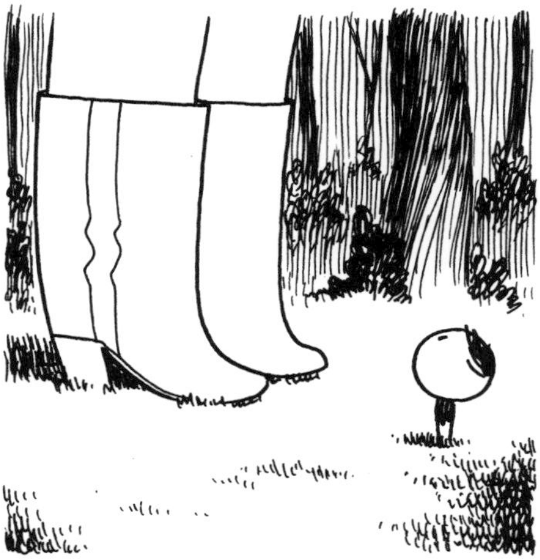

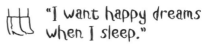

"I want happy dreams when I sleep."

"But you always smile in your sleep."

"Yeah, I know. But still."

So Alphonse took a nap.

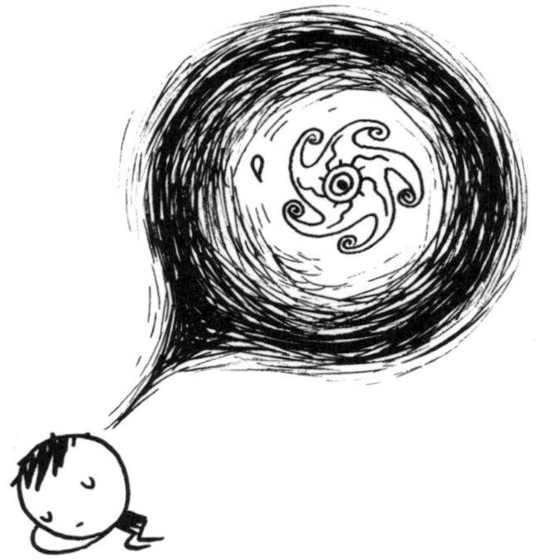

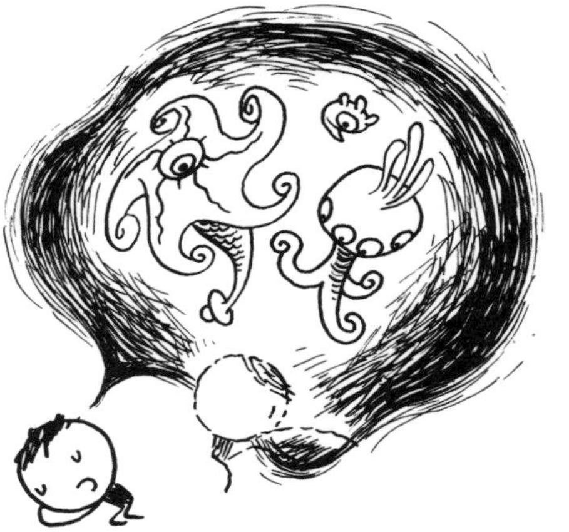

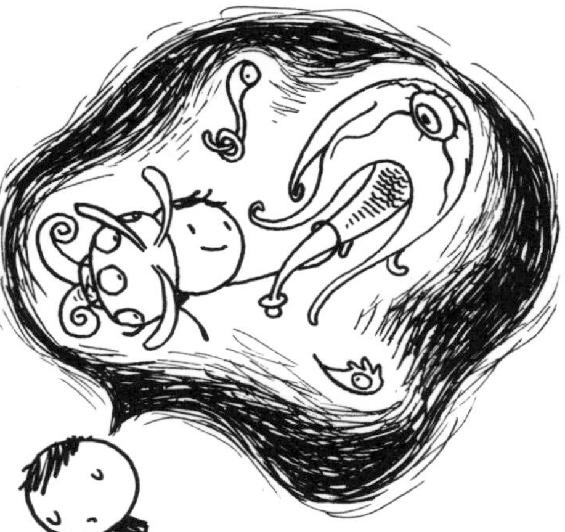

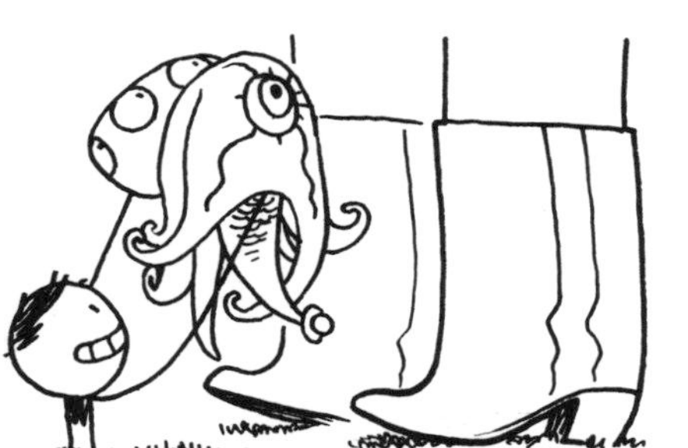

"That doesn't go with any of my outfits..."

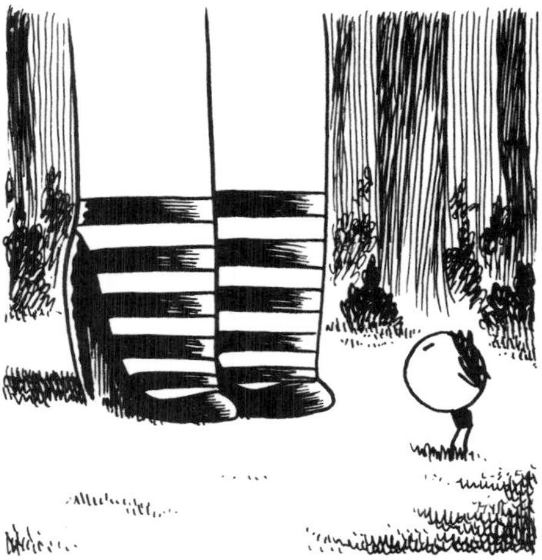

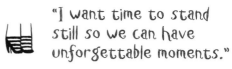

"I want time to stand still so we can have unforgettable moments."

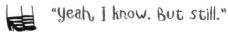

"Hmm, that's going to be a tough one."

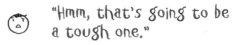

"Yeah, I know. But still."

So Alphonse did what he could.

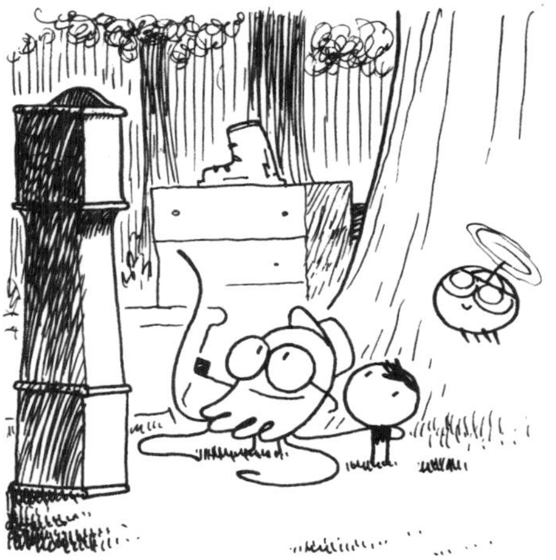

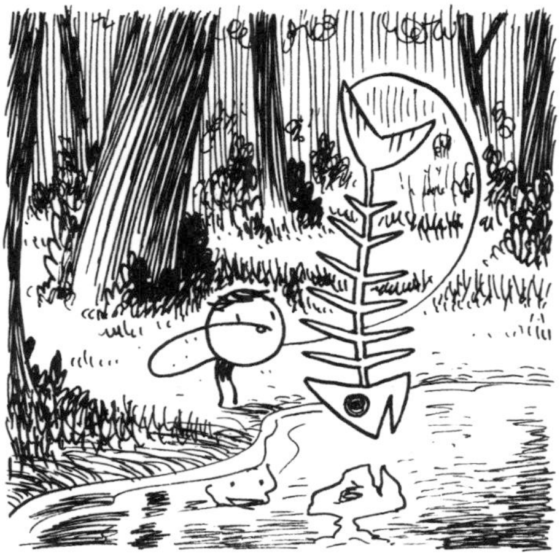

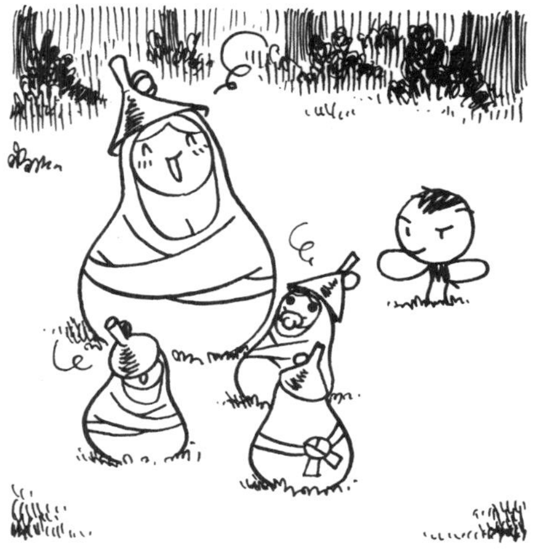

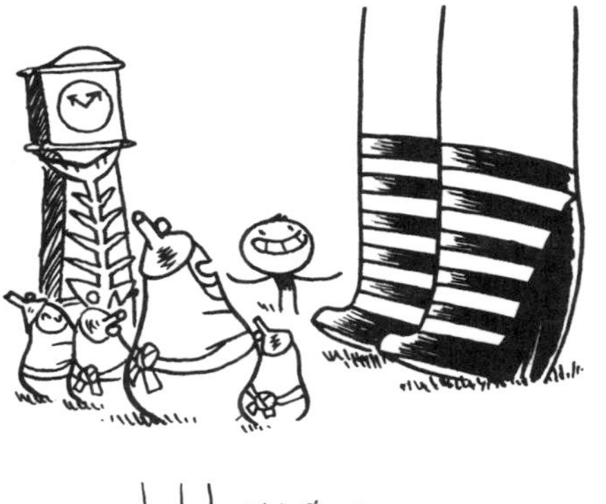

"Ugh."

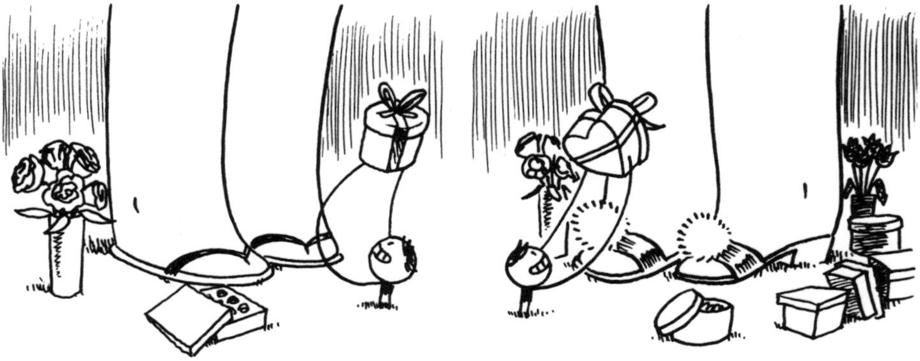

Penelope's wishes became more and more complicated.

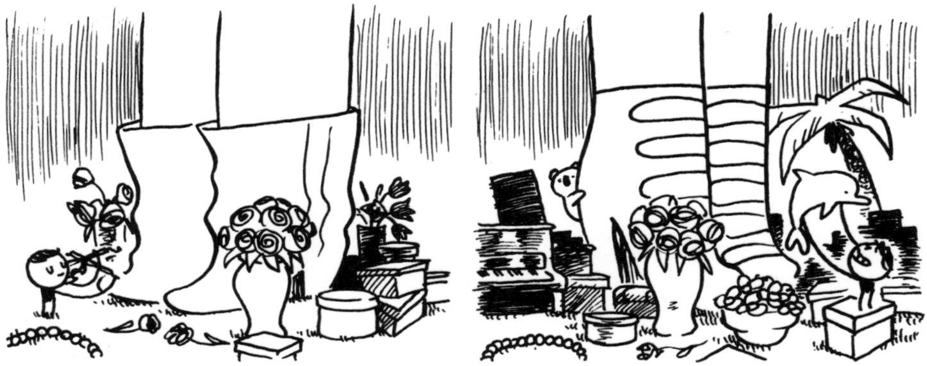

And numerous. And even more complicated.

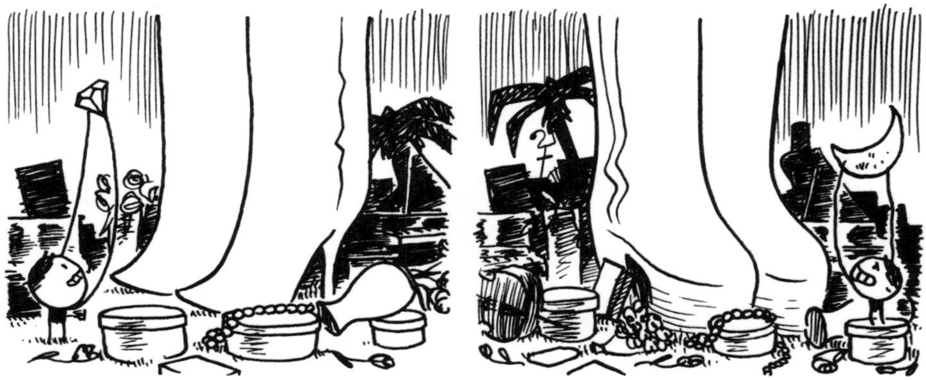

And Alphonse kept getting them wrong.

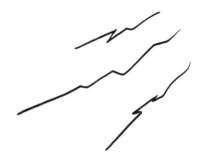

She'd overflow with anger...
then switch to satisfaction.

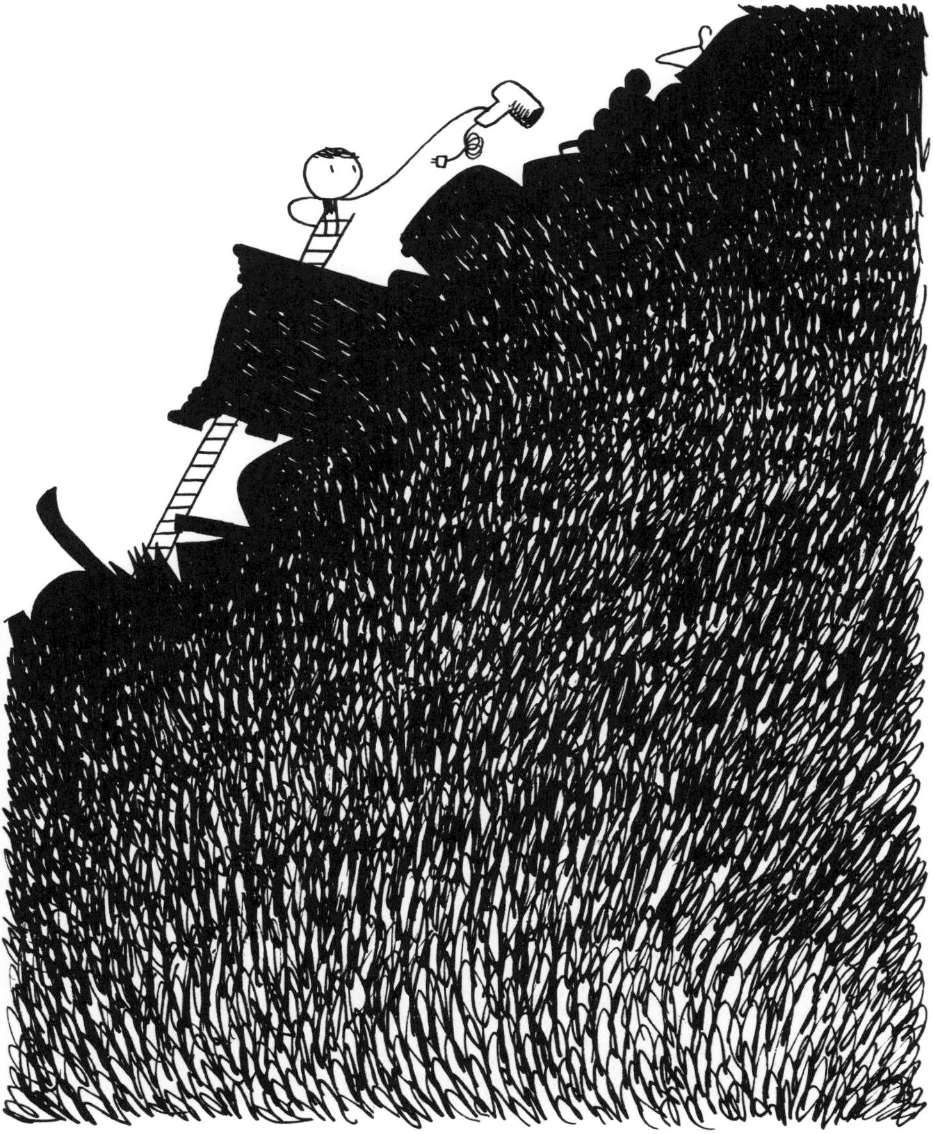

Alphonse would scale Penelope Mountain on a ladder and cover her in heaps of whatever she wanted.

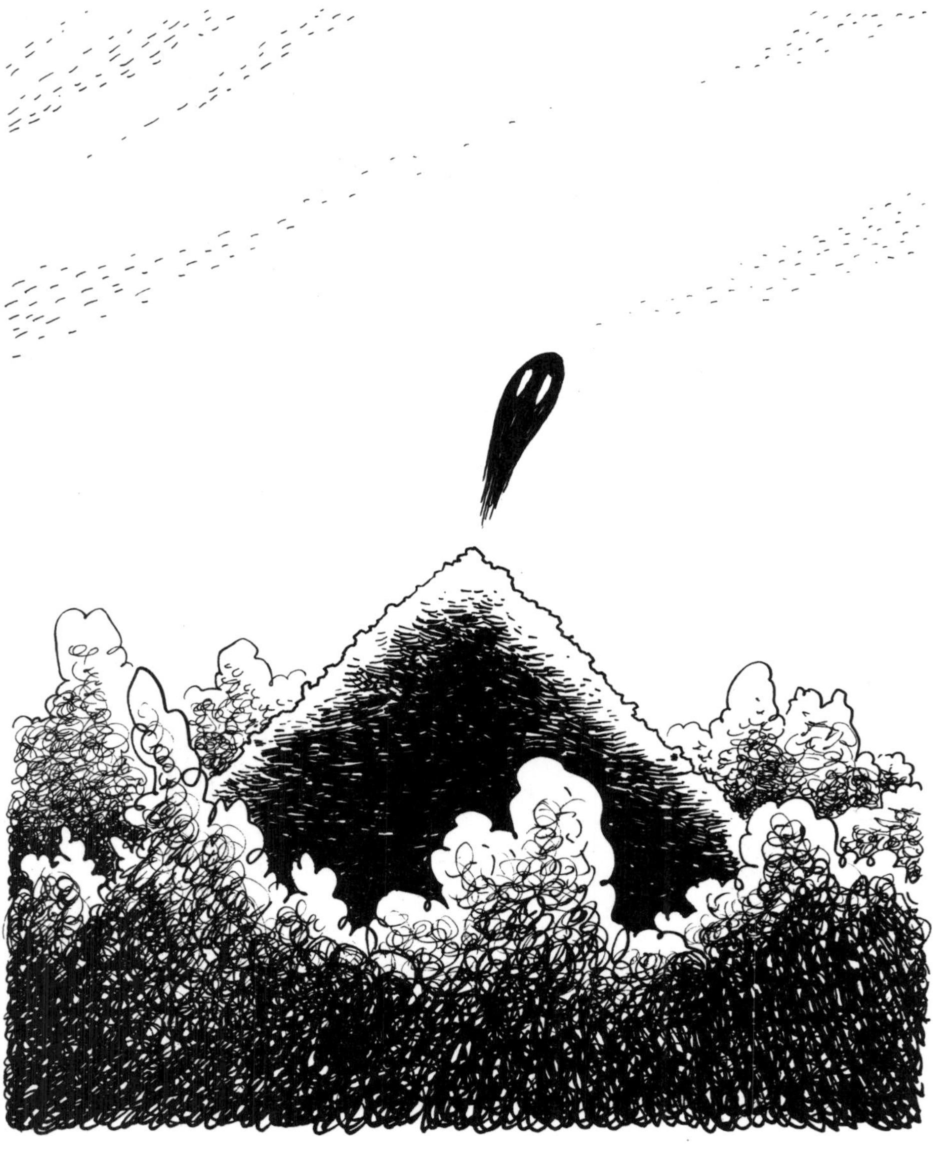

Then, one day, smothered by her satisfaction,
she gave up the ghost.

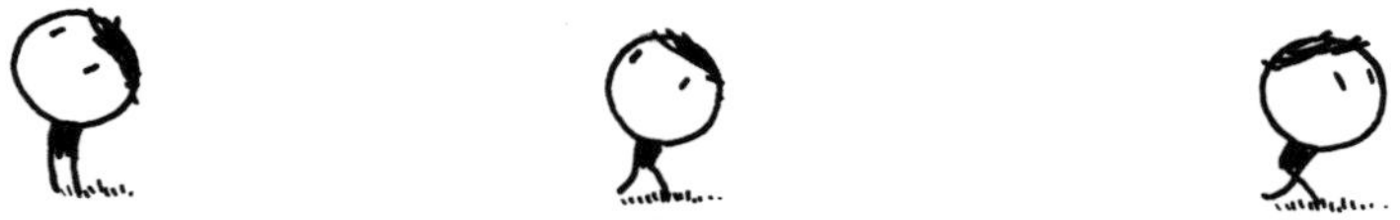

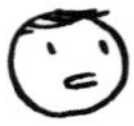

"Huh.
Well, huh.
Guess I should go back to
looking for the Big Man again."

 "Hey, it's you! You sure helped me out of a pickle last time!"

 "Really?"

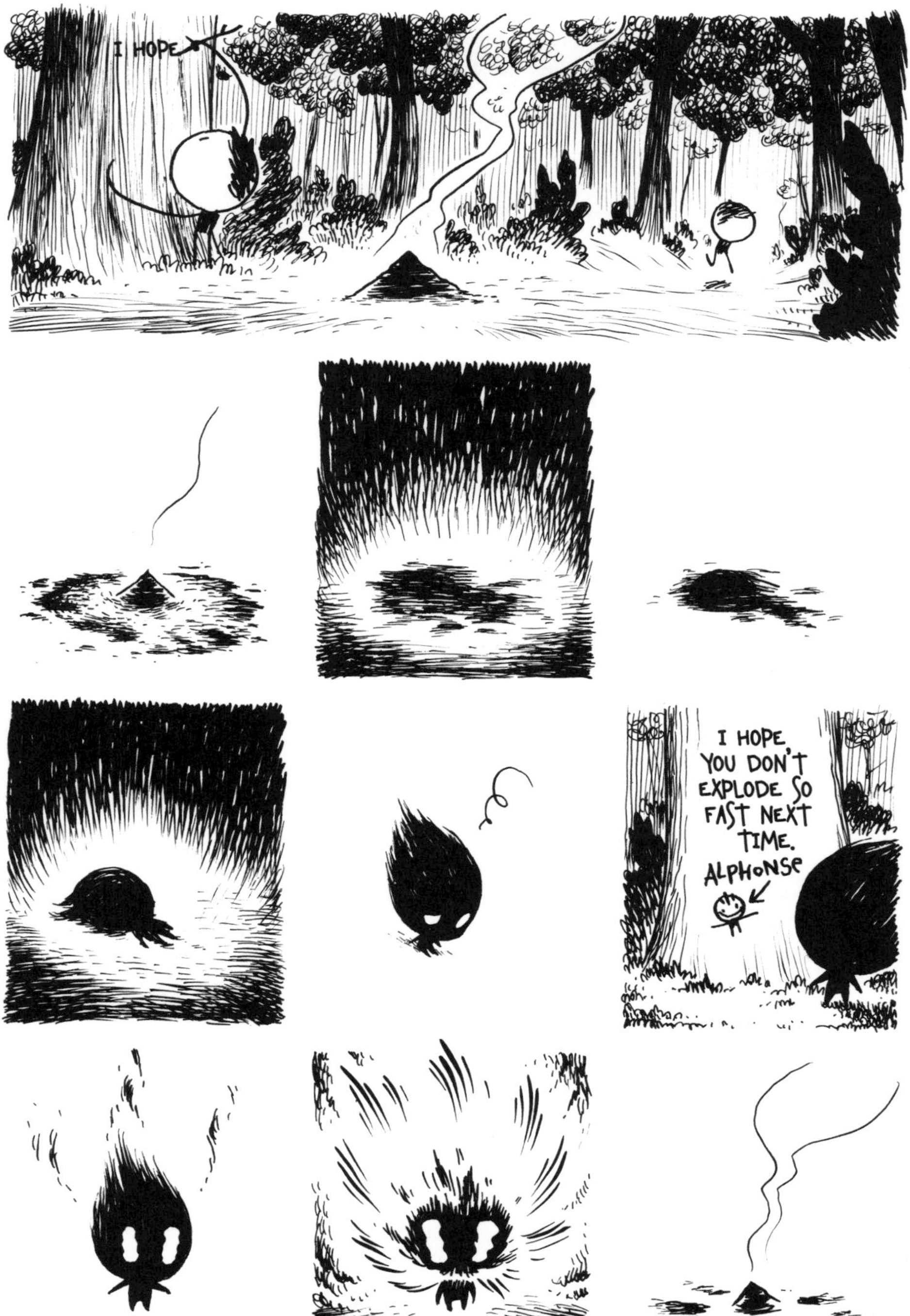
I HOPE
I HOPE YOU DON'T EXPLODE SO FAST NEXT TIME.
ALPHONSE

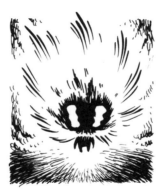

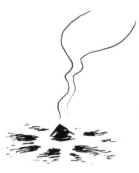

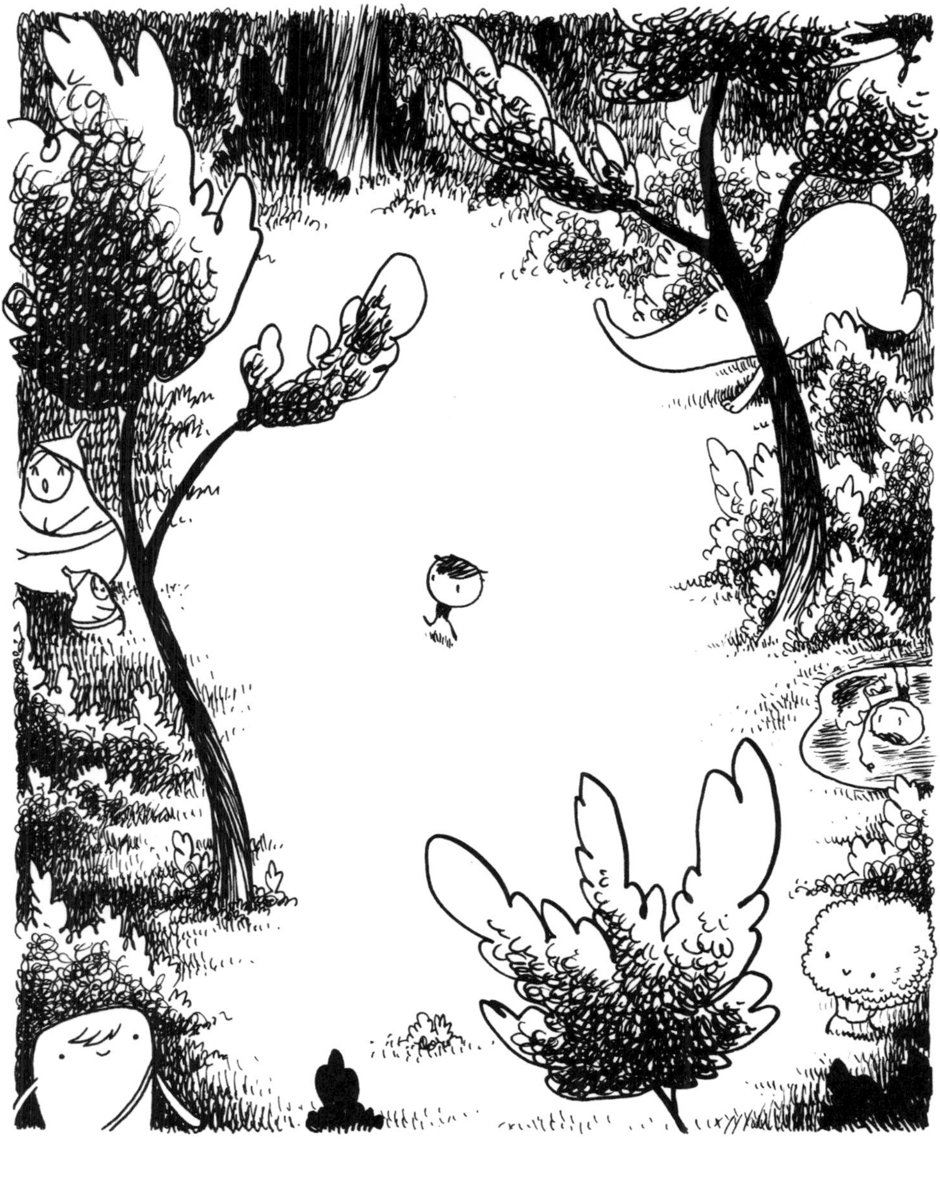

Alphonse didn't know if he wanted his life to be full or empty anymore.

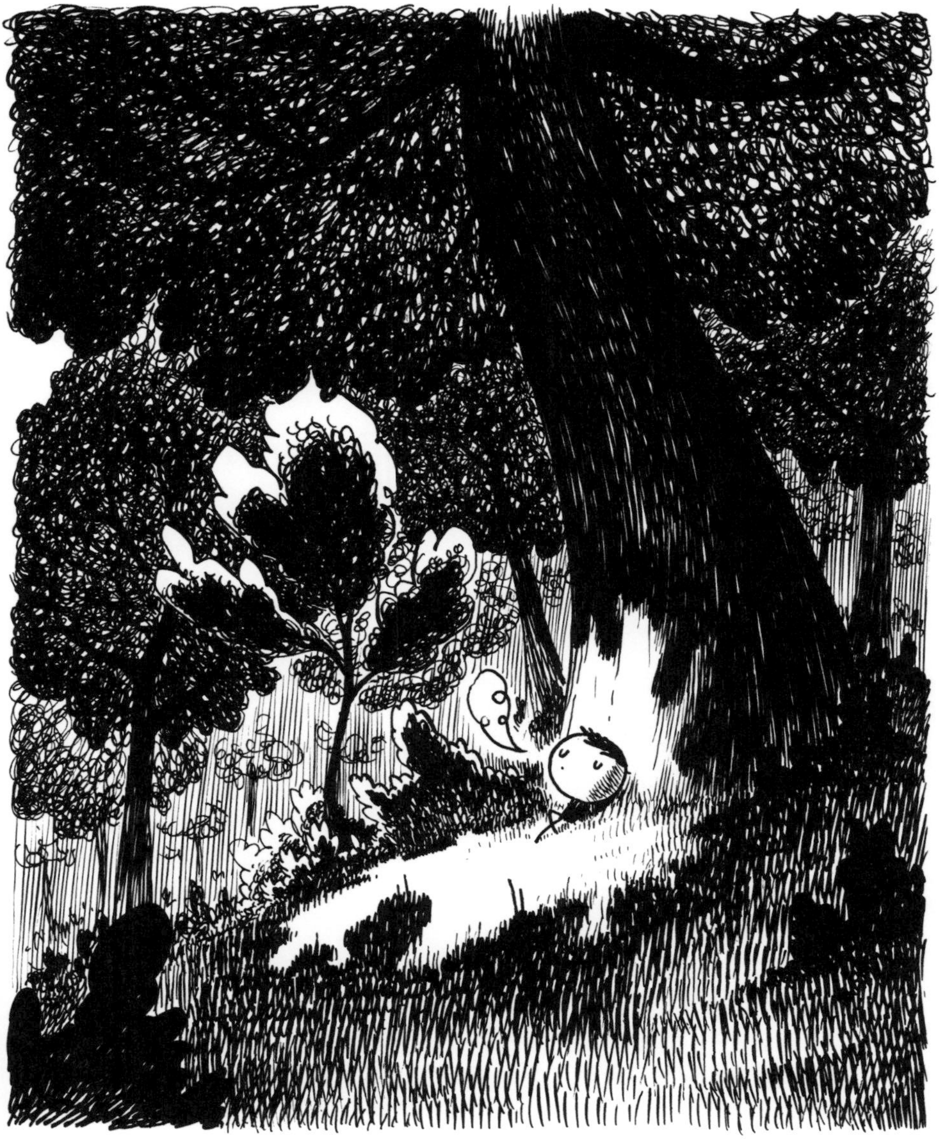

He was tired, so he decided to rest for a bit.

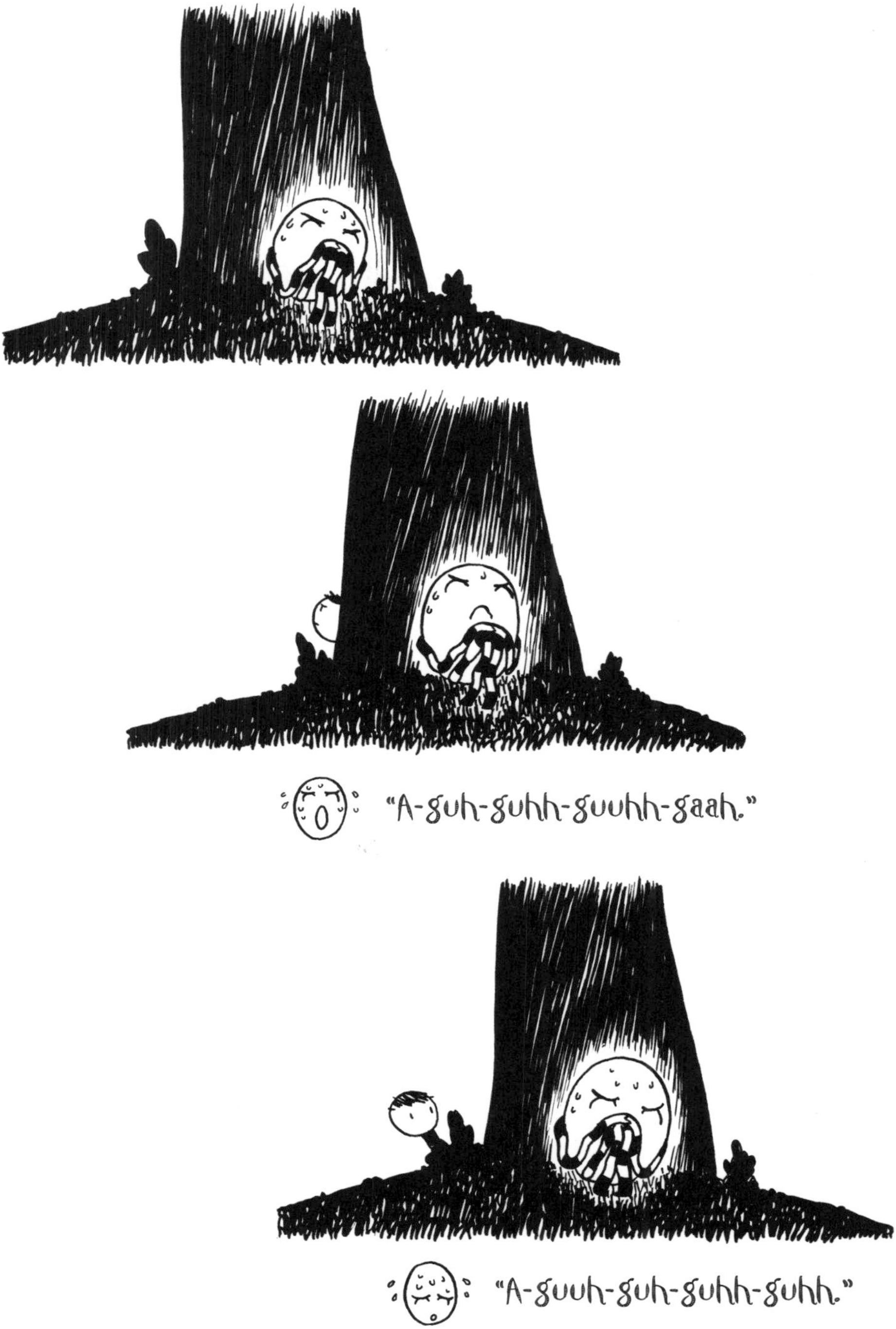
"A-guh-guhh-guuhh-gaah."
"A-guuh-guh-guhh-guhh."

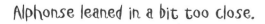

Alphonse leaned in a bit too close.

"Aaaaaaaaaaaaaaaaaaaaaaaaaaaaaaah!"

This frightened Alphonse, who also said,

 "Aaaaaaaaaaaaaaaaaaaaaaaaaaaaah!"

And so they ran around and around the tree,
chasing each other and screaming.

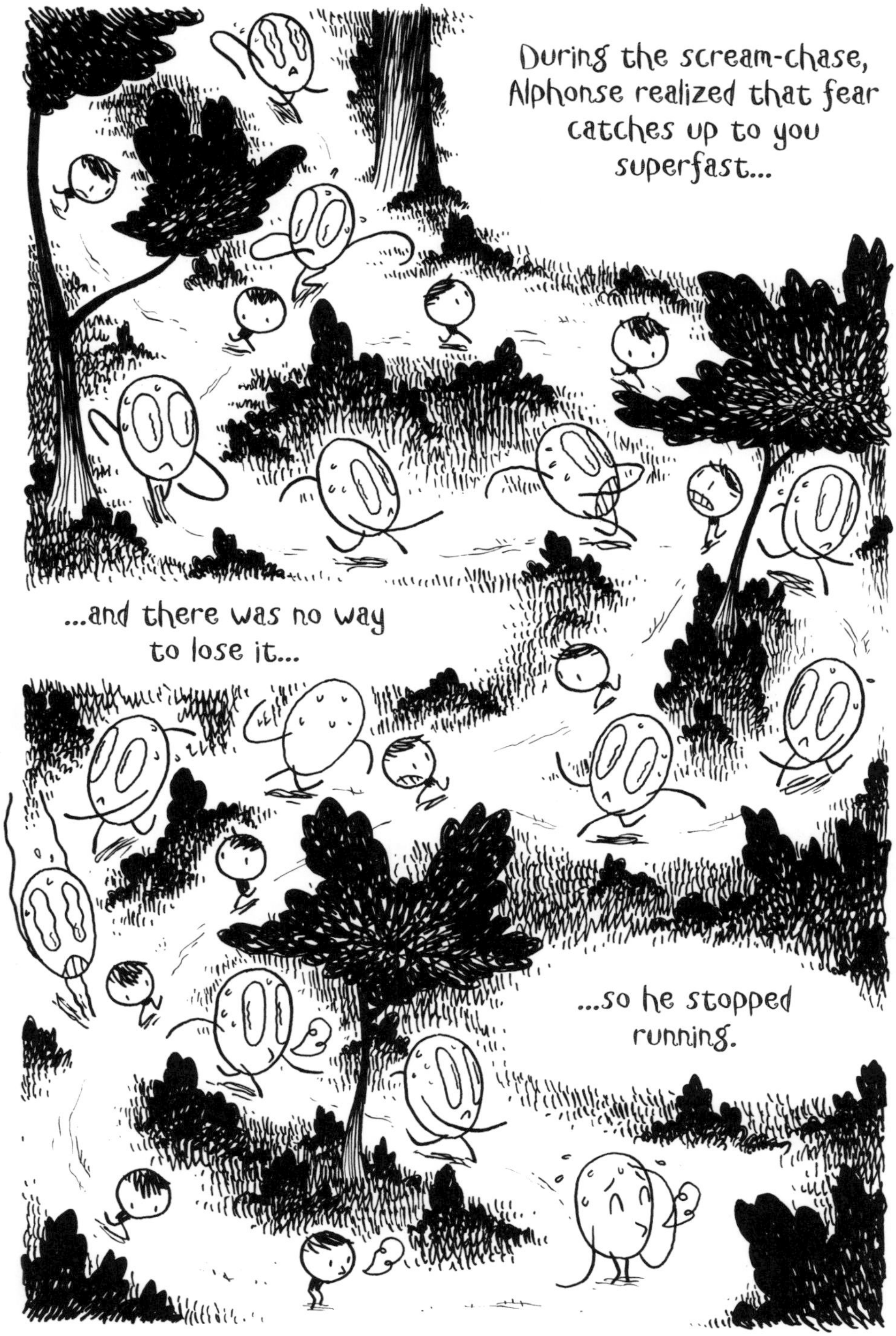
During the scream-chase, Alphonse realized that fear catches up to you superfast...
...and there was no way to lose it...
...so he stopped running.

They both looked pale and nervous. Especially Guish.

"Are you cold?"

"Huh? N-no... oh... no..."

"Sorry to wake you up."

"Oh, good thing it was just you.
I could've been eaten by something really scary!
Or rolled over and off the edge of the world!
Or gotten chewed on by a carrot-nibbler!
Or had a bee fly up my nose!
Then I really would have been in trouble!"

"Uh... right. Later."

But Guish fell in step behind Alphonse and they walked together for a while.

They met different people along the way, exchanging glances with them but never really stopping.

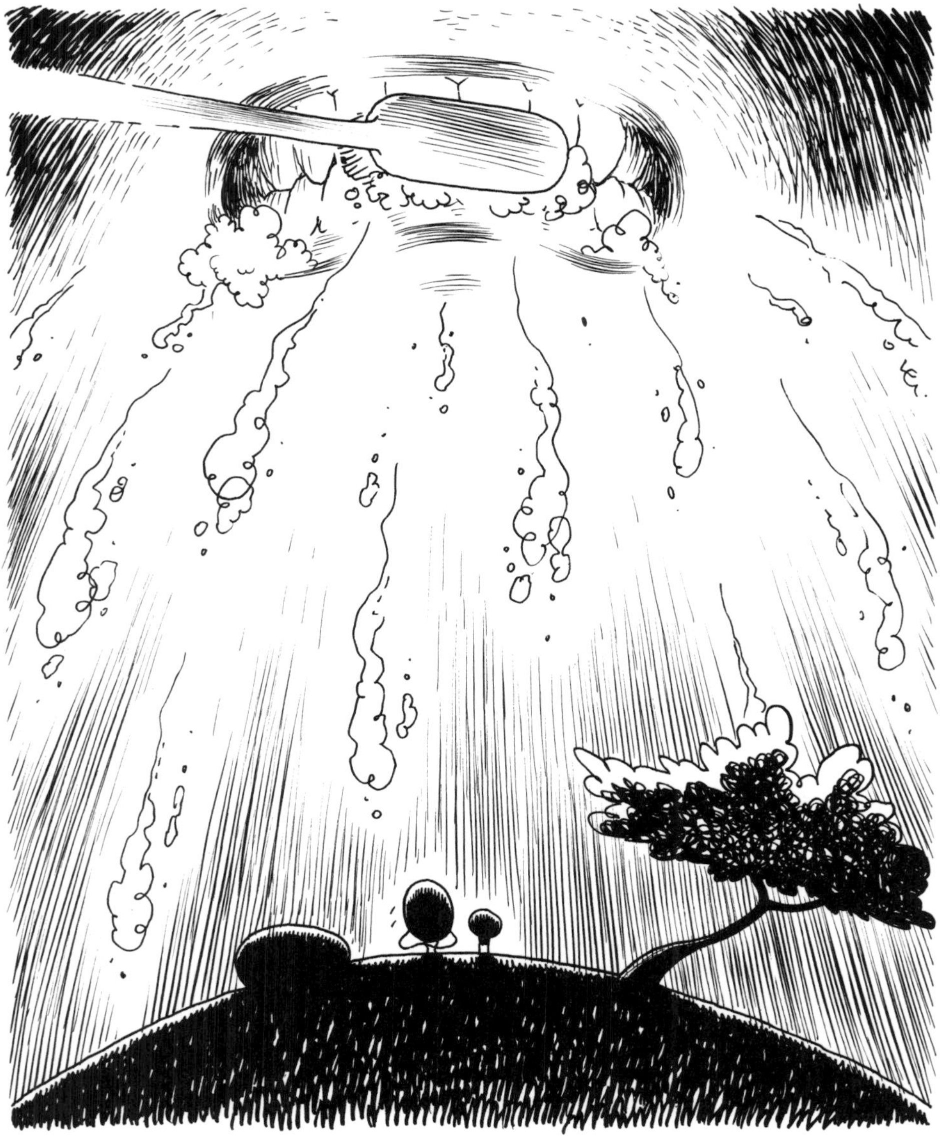

They kept walking until it began raining toothpaste.

There were two others sitting there, staring up at the sky.

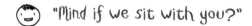 "Mind if we sit with you?"

"Only if you pay the toll."

"That's not exactly what I meant... (sigh)"

"Can I sit down anyway?"

"Whatever. (sob)"

"I'm Anxtie. This is Hole."

 "Oh, hey! Where'd you go? While you were gone, Anxtie and I got together and formed a club..."

 "The CLUB OF THE LEAGUE OF OOLA OOLA Z!"

 "Good call doubling up on 'club' and 'league'... sounds classy!"

 "I know, right?"

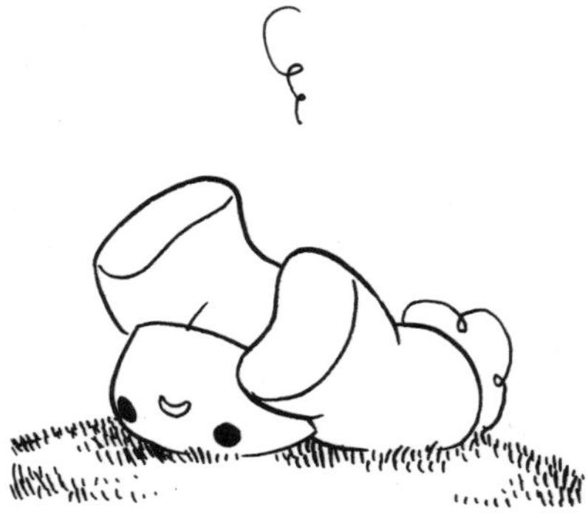

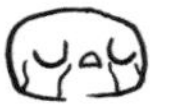

"But we kinda suck. You should just keep walking. (sob)"

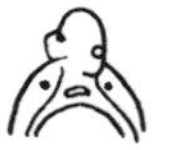

"Eh, Alphonse always leaves anyway."

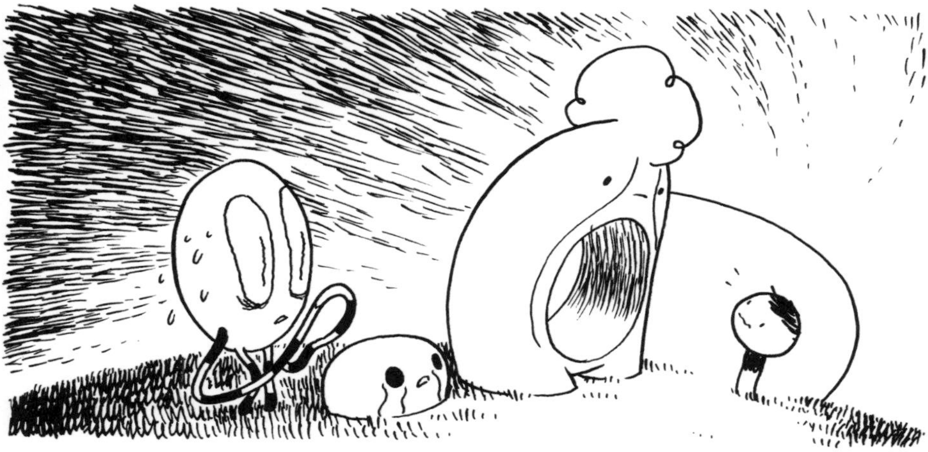

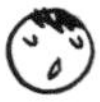

"That's so not true! We're staying! Right, Quish?"

"You're not gonna leave, are you?"

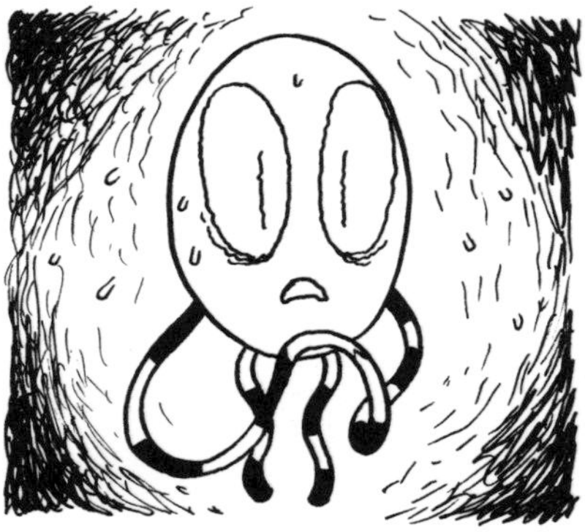

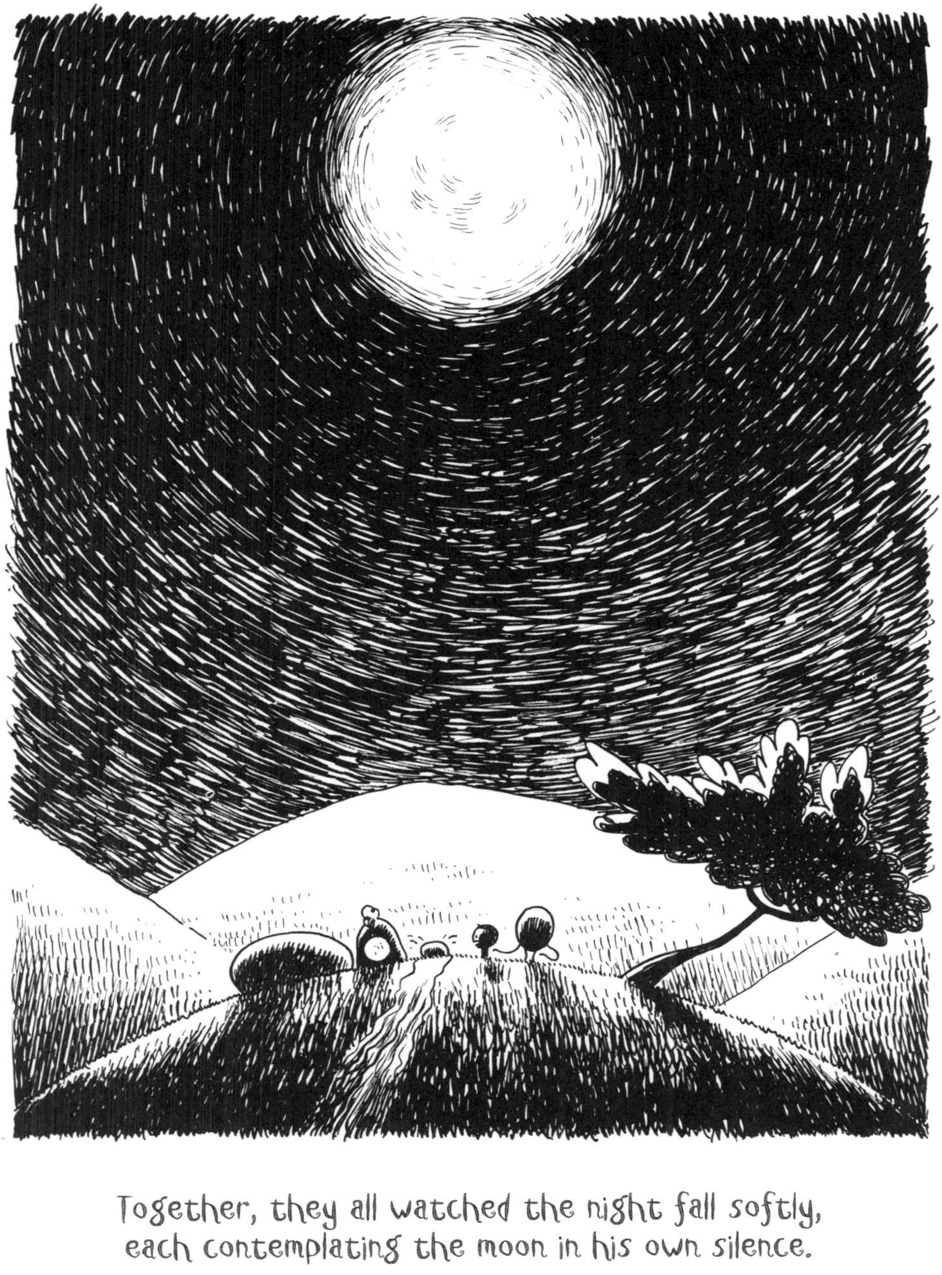

Together, they all watched the night fall softly, each contemplating the moon in his own silence.

"Your eyes sure leak a lot, Anxtie..."

When they woke up the next day, they saw that instead of being at the top of a hill, they were on a small island in the middle of a huge lake.

"Criminy flibbertigibbet! What the...?!"

"Oh no, oh no, oh no, oh no..."

"Sorry... I had some super-sad dreams."

"You cried a lake!"

"Yeah. Usually it's just a river."

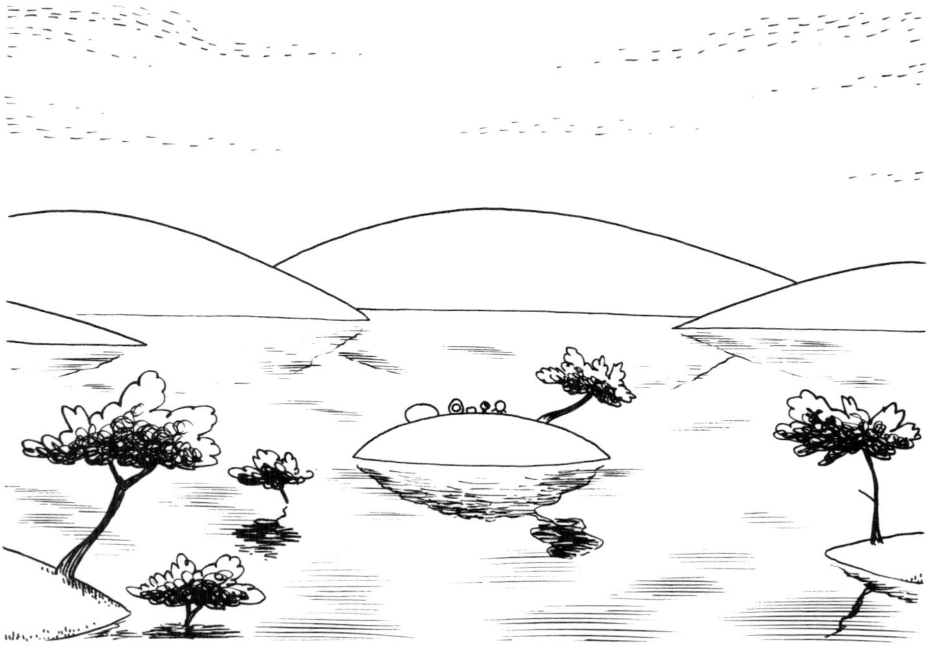

"It is kind of a pretty lake. I've never seen one like it."

"We'll call it LAKE UNA."

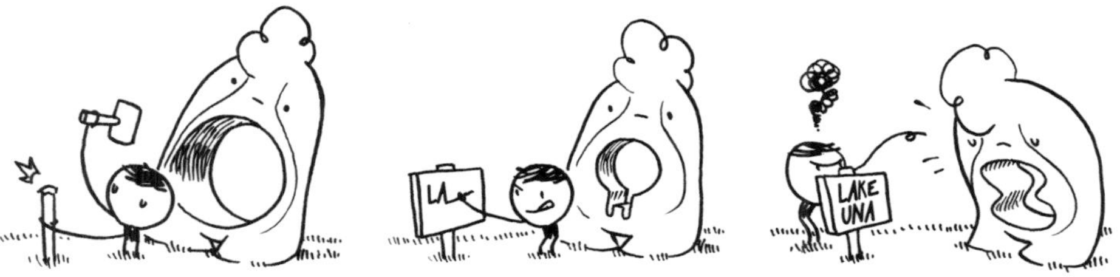
LA
LAKE UNA

"Oh no! Don't start that again!
Go bother Anxtie instead!"

"He's too wet and slippery."

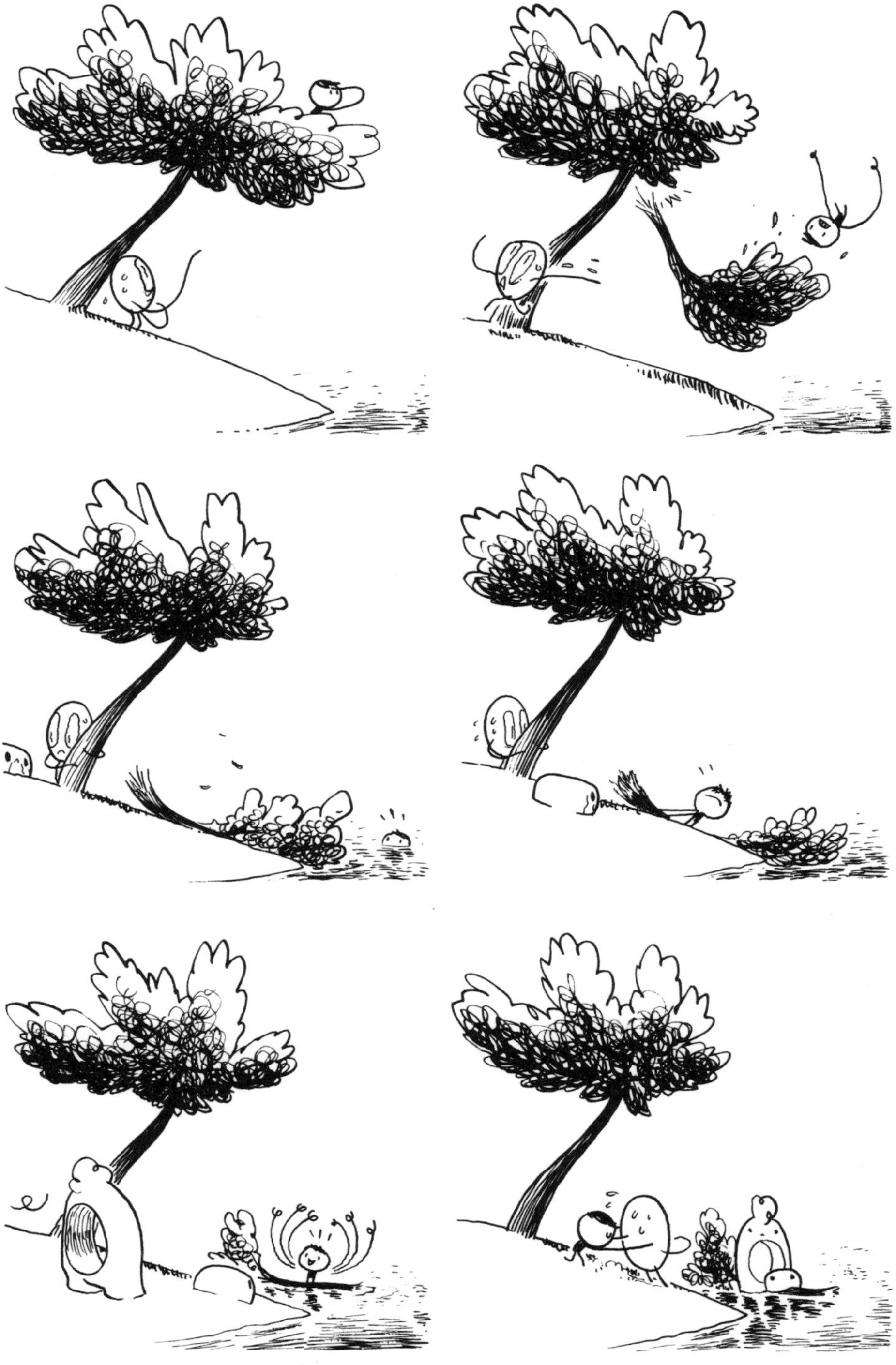

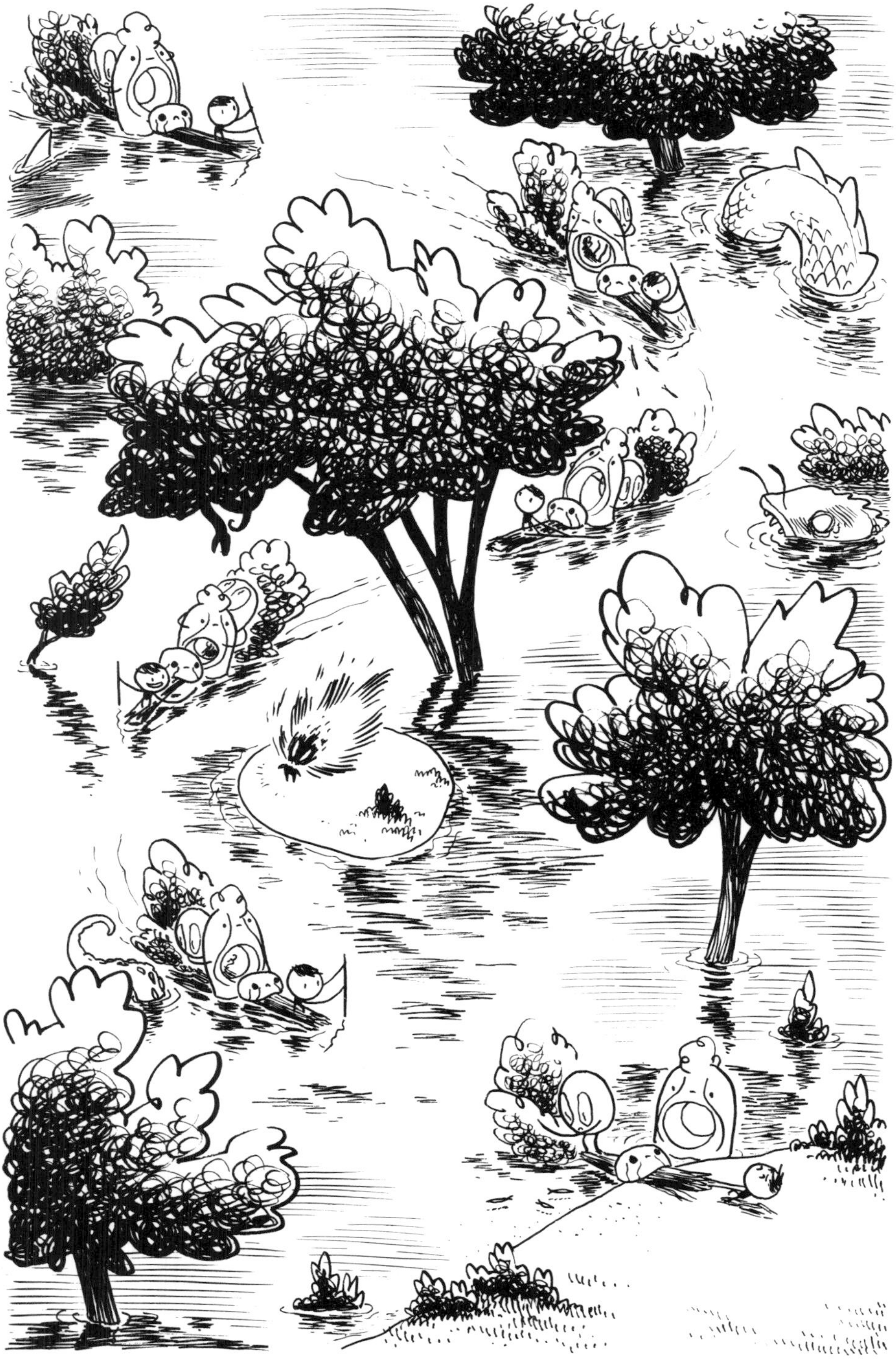

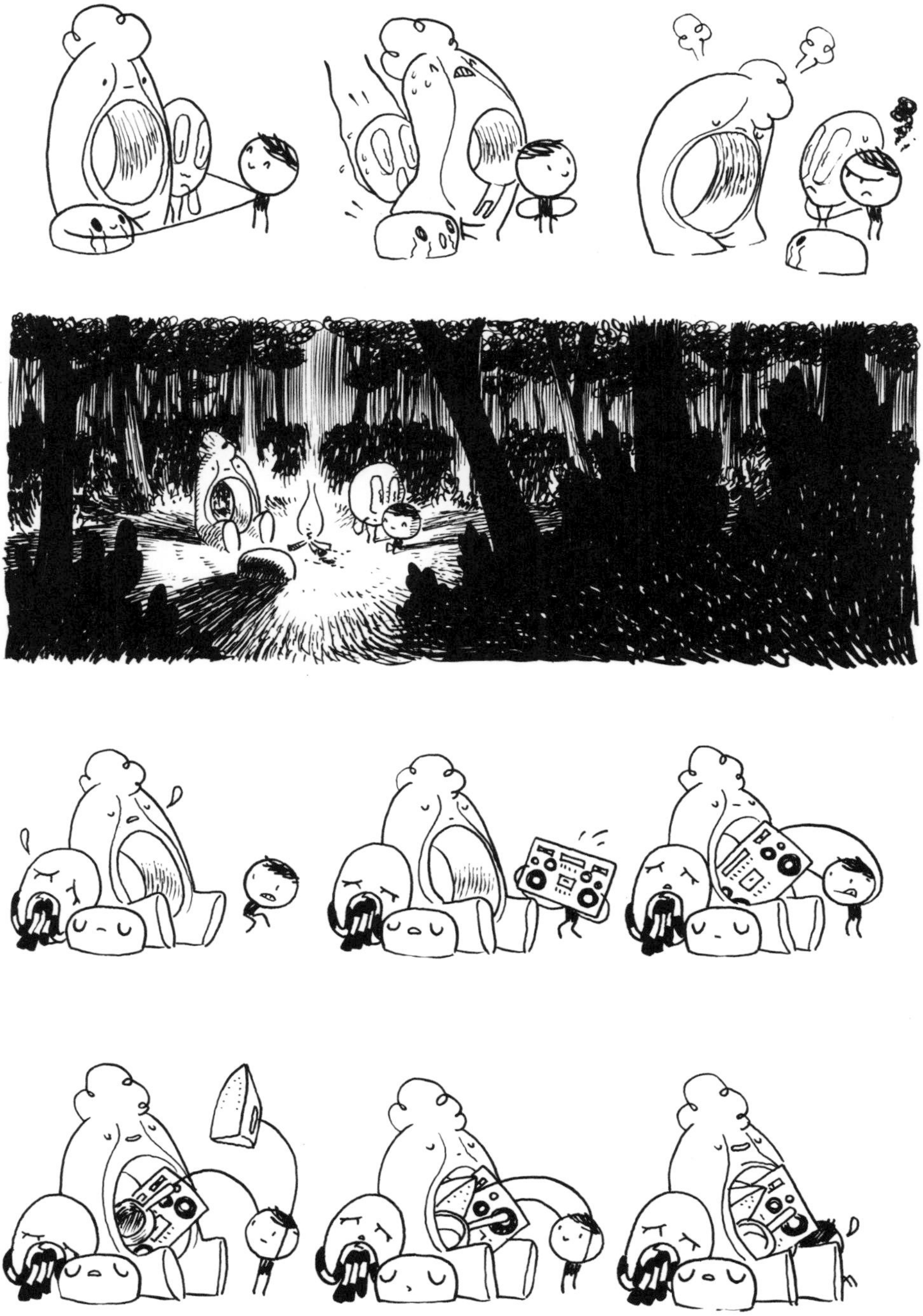

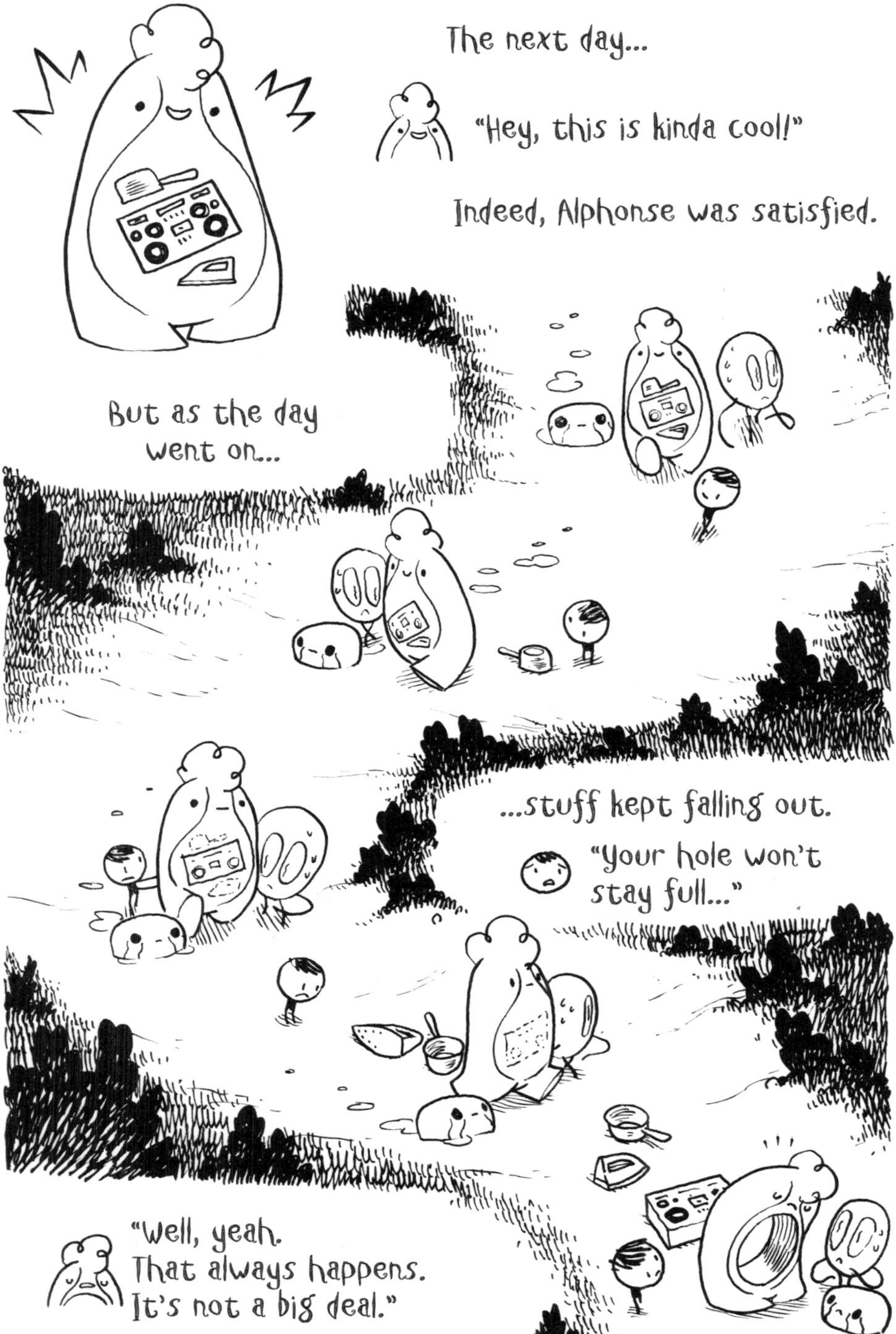

The next day...
"Hey, this is kinda cool!"
Indeed, Alphonse was satisfied.
But as the day went on...
...stuff kept falling out.
"Your hole won't stay full..."
"Well, yeah. That always happens. It's not a big deal."

"Hey, the sun's running away!"

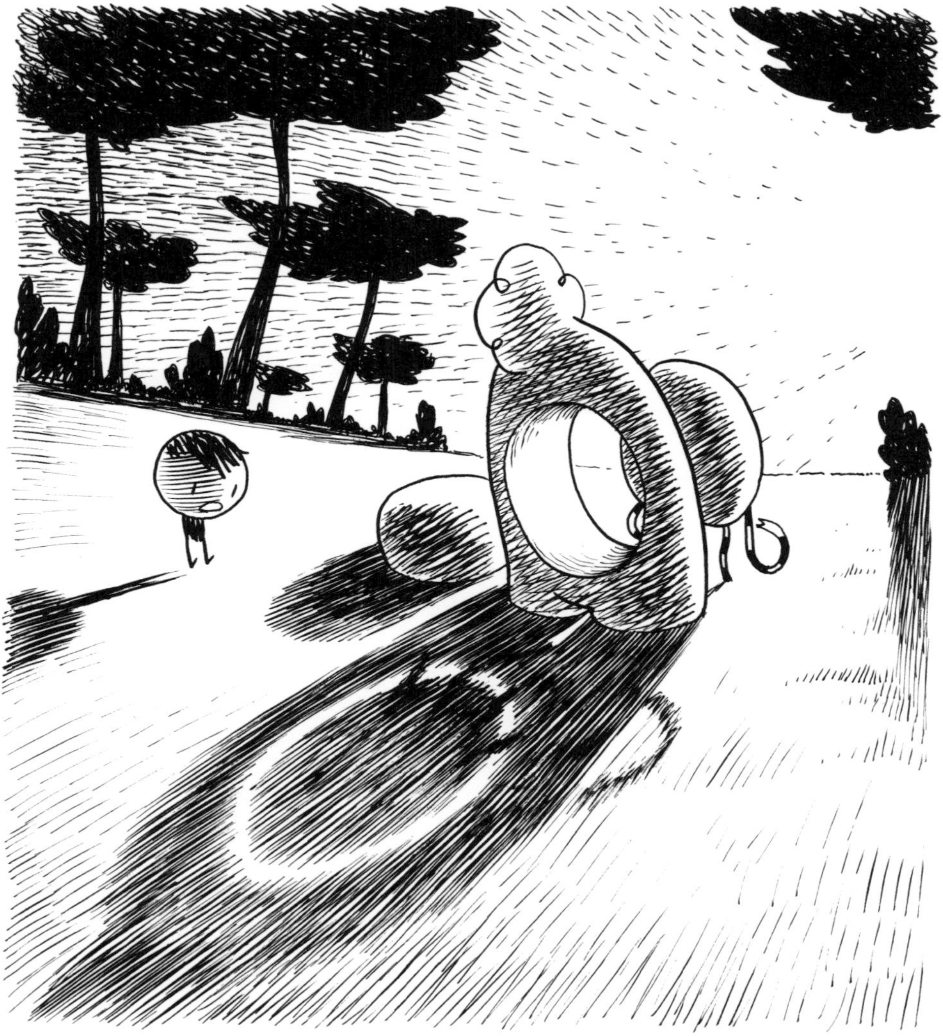

"Whoa! I'll be darned..."

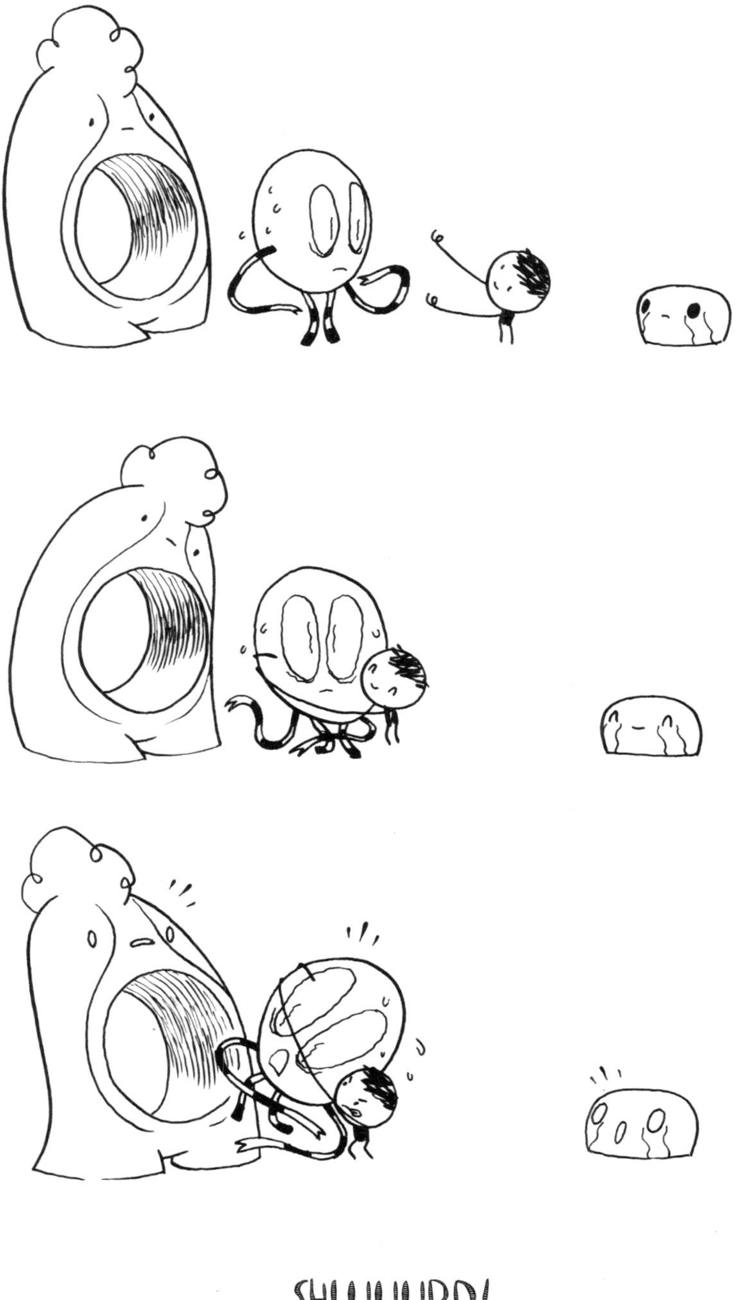
SHLUUURP!

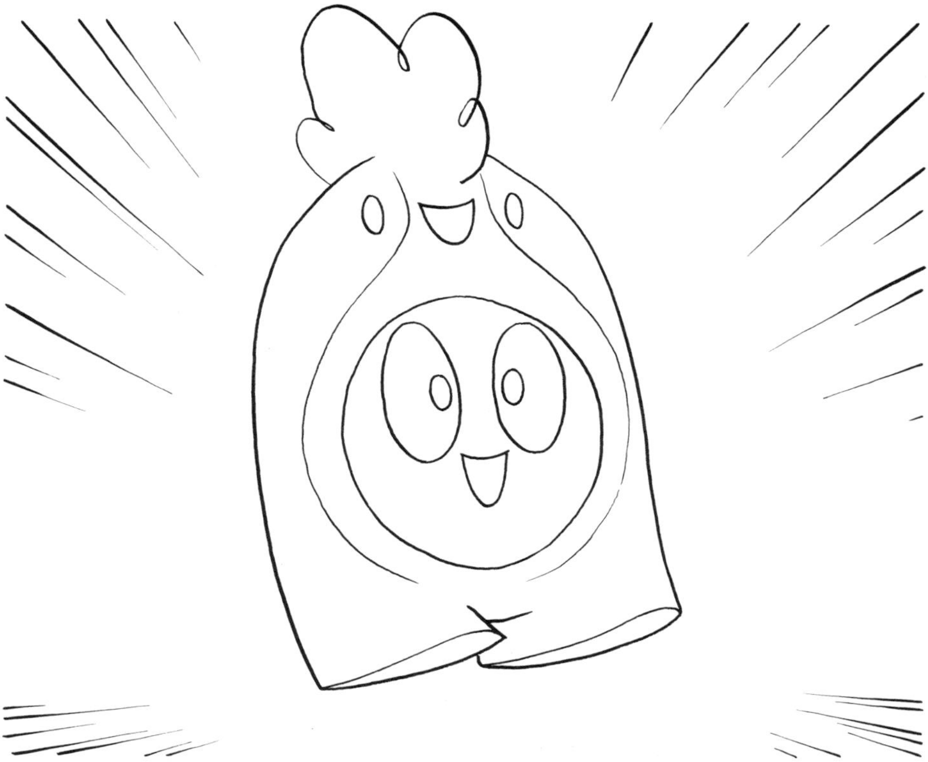

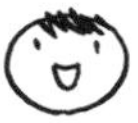 "Ta-daa! I fixed you!"

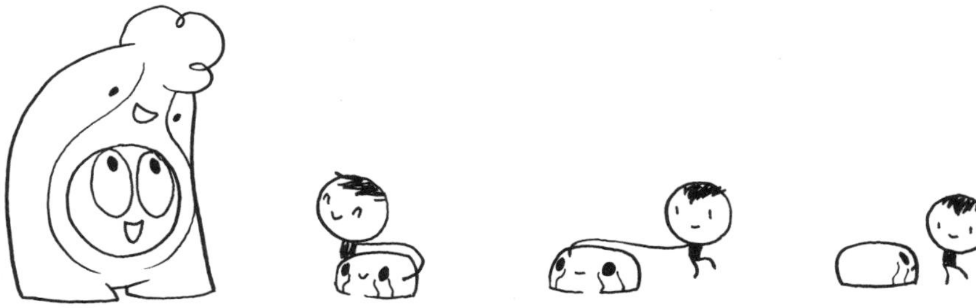

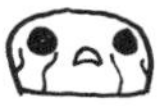 "But... now we'll never see them again! (sob)"

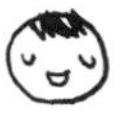 "Sure we will. But look... they're finally complete. They don't need anything else!"

"I'm sure they could've figured that out on their own eventually. C'mon, Anxtie. I'll carry you!"

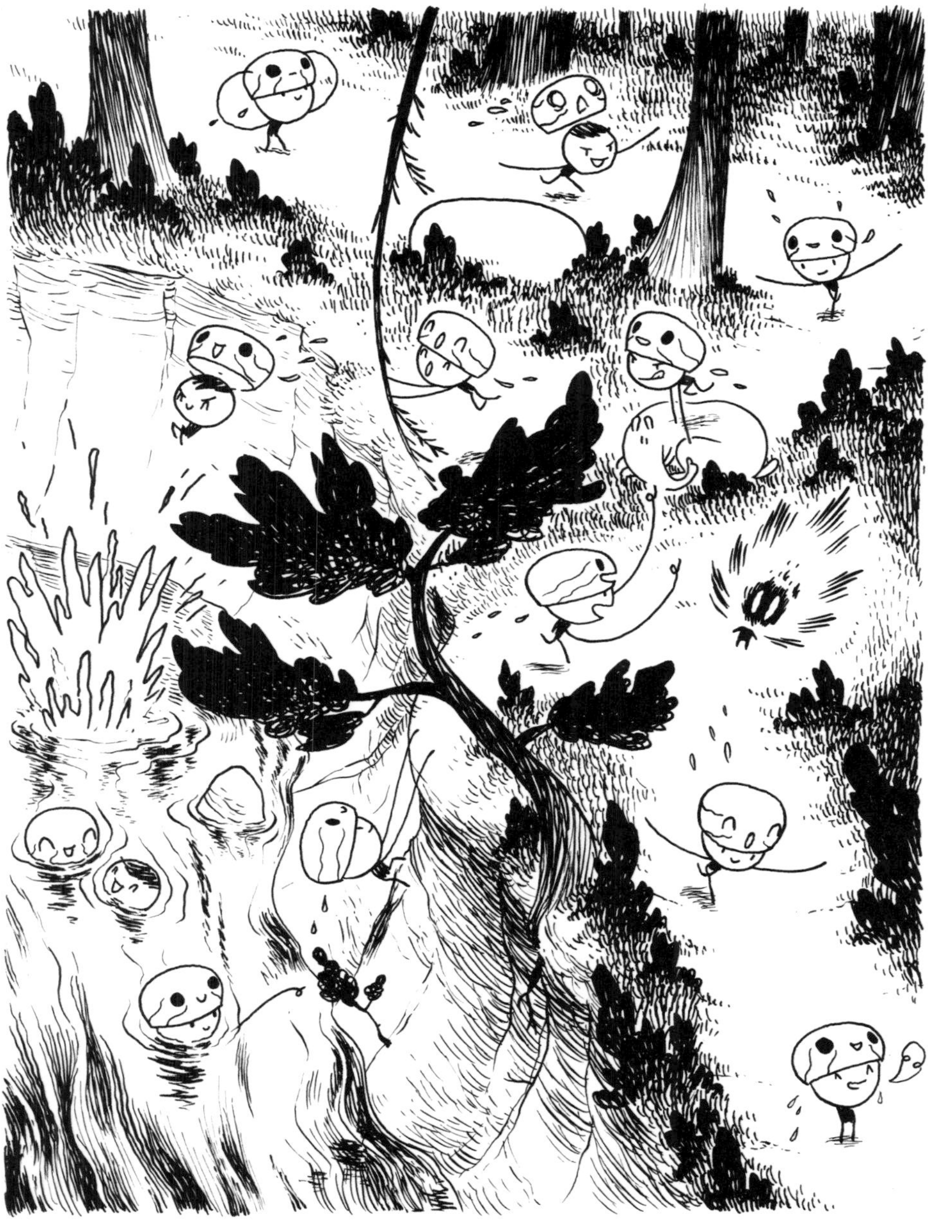

 "So what do we do now?"

 "I... I don't know anymore."

With both of their sadnesses combined,
Alphonse didn't see the Big Man pass nearby.

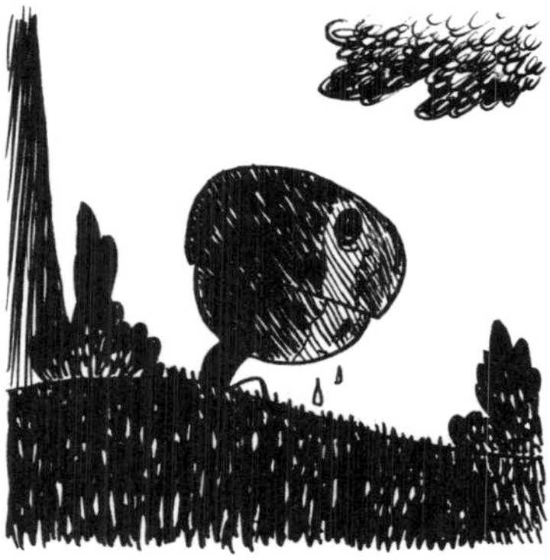

But Anxtie did.

"(sob) Wow, that guy's BIG..."

"What guy?"

"That guy, over there. See?"

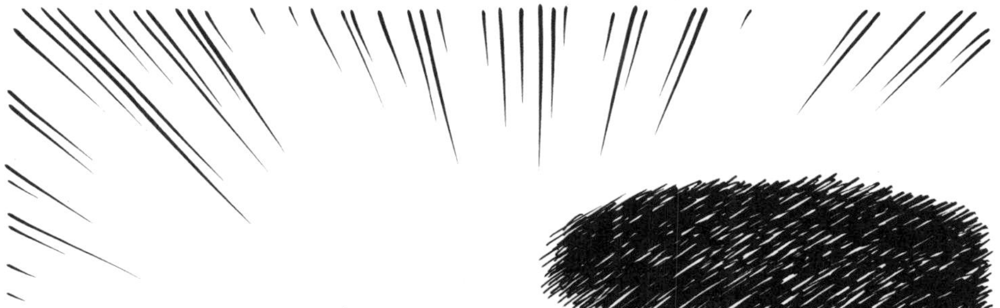

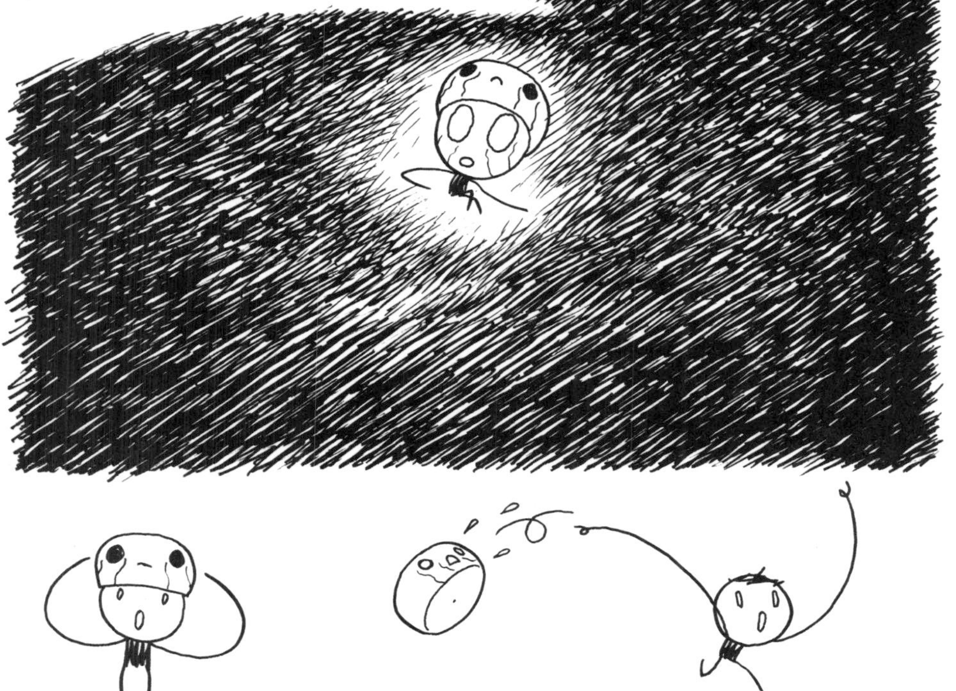

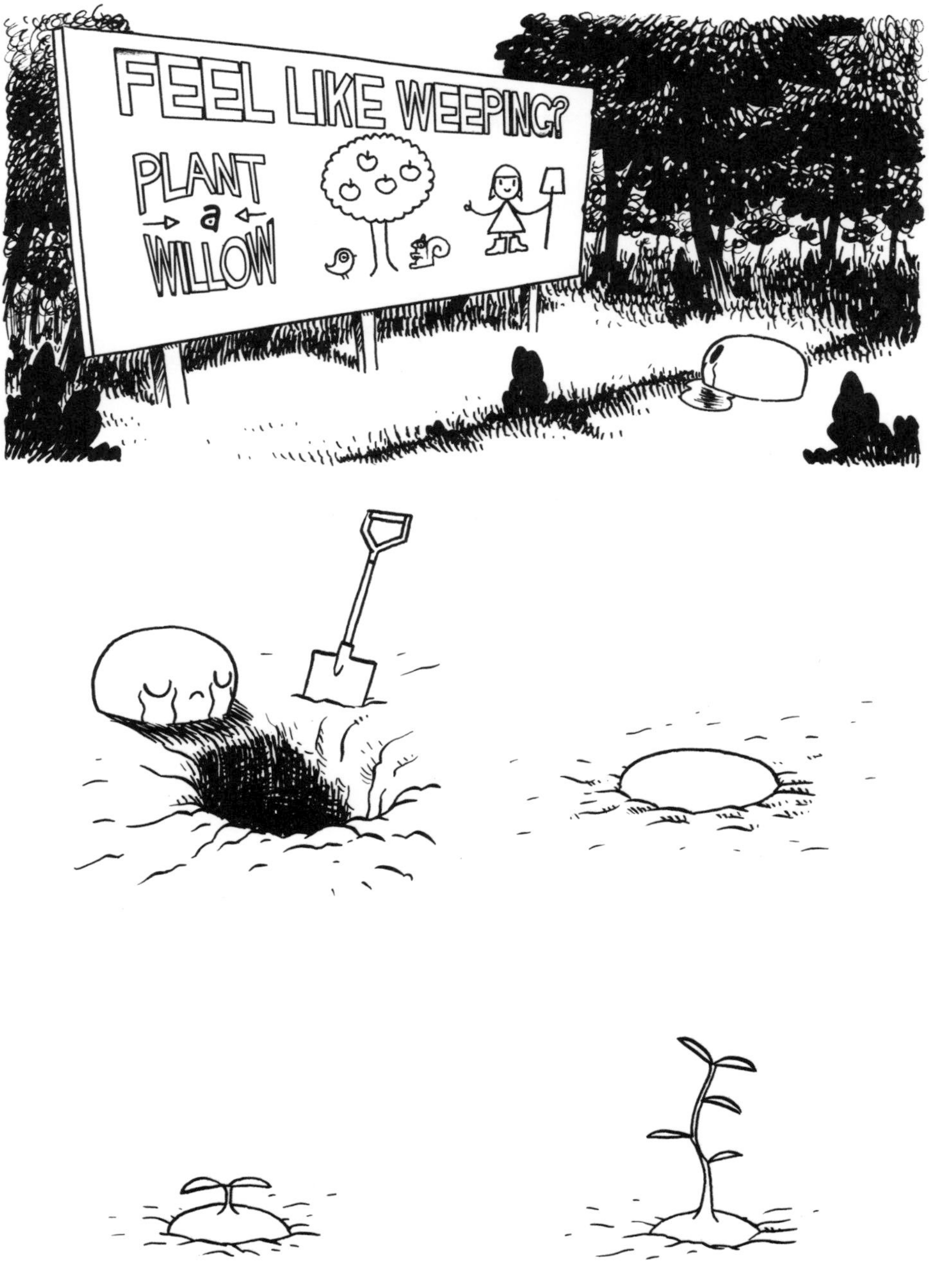
FEEL LIKE WEEPING?
PLANT
a
WILLOW

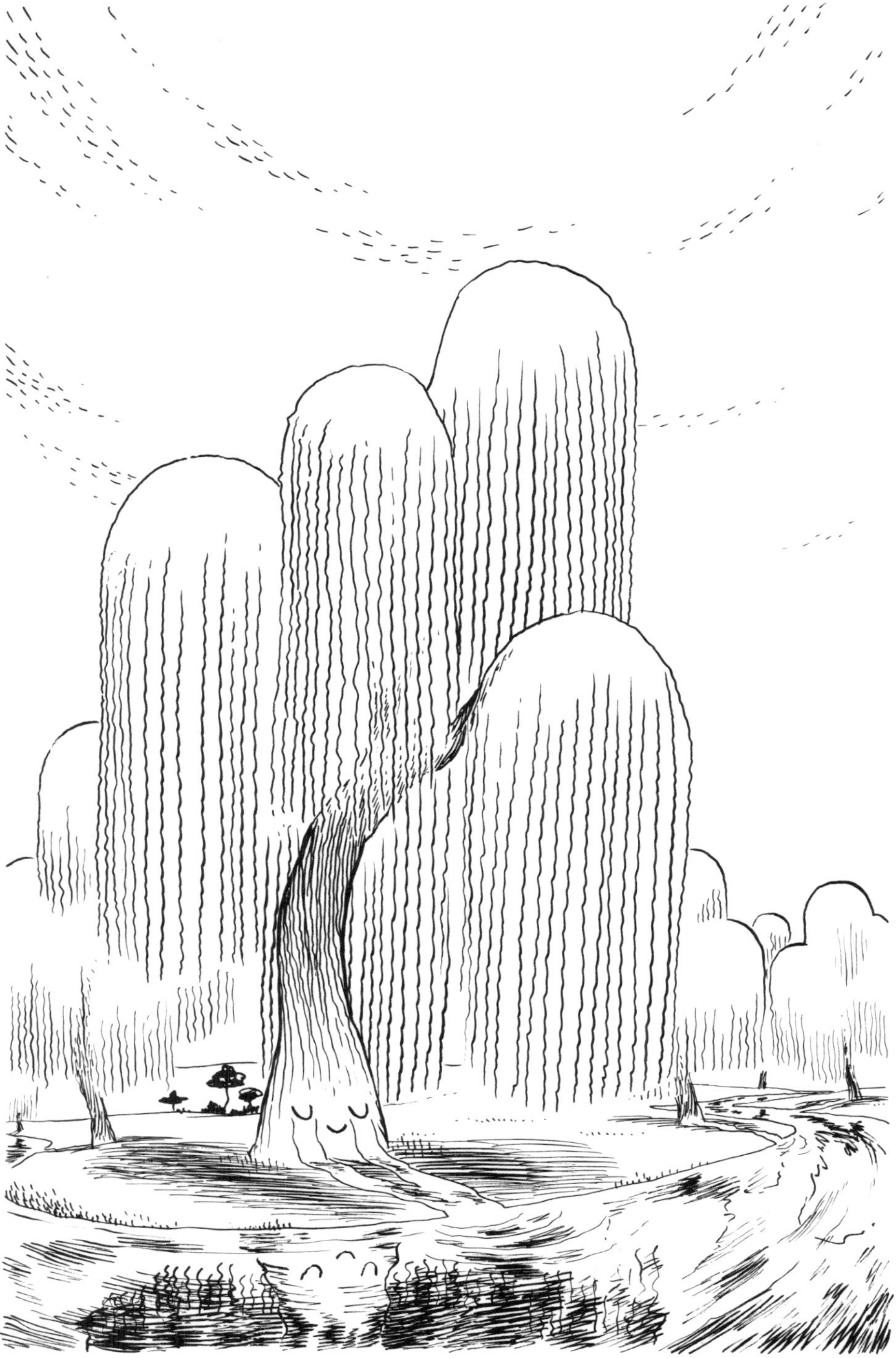

 "Woohoo! Big Man! Wait for me!
Where have you been? I've been looking
all over for you! You sure are a hard
man to find!"

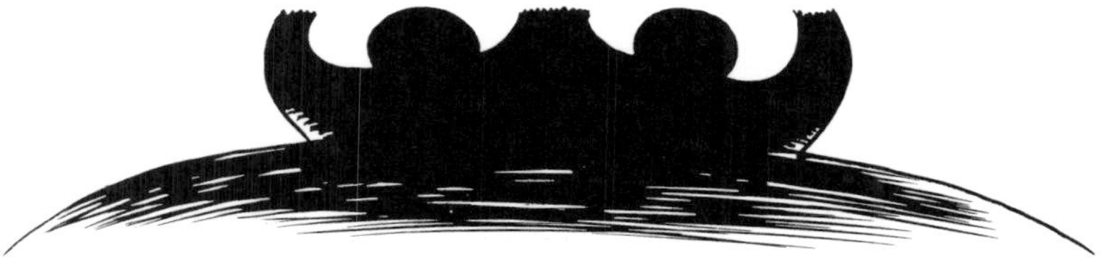

"I mean, I wasn't worried about you, of course. You can do anything! But me? Yeah, I was kind of worried about me. I got lost, and then I found a friend, and then someone drank him up, but it turned out he was just me. He was thirsty. The someone else, I mean, not my friend. And then there was Penelope, man oh man, if you only knew... she was pretty, for sure, but kind of high maintenance. And then I was alone again, and it was hard, you know, a real grind, and your heart gets all worn down when you're sad... I don't think I like being sad. But you know how it is, sometimes you don't have a choice, right? Oh man, if I knew you were here, I'd have brought you a gift... hey! Maybe we can go over to the Knickknack Shop together! Although they're probably closed at this hour... what should I do? I'm sure you know why everything's grinding me down all the time, but do you know how to make it stop? Well, I mean, of course you do, you know everything, but OH MAN, have I missed you! I mean, Hole and Guish and Anxtie were nice, but HEY! Speaking of which, where'd Anxtie go...? Anyway, they're all nice, but kinda lost and aimless, if you ask me. Well, I mean, they're better now, at least Hole and Guish are. Just goes to show, it doesn't take much, right, Big Man? So where are we going now that we're together again? I'm so happy! I've got tons of stuff to tell you!"

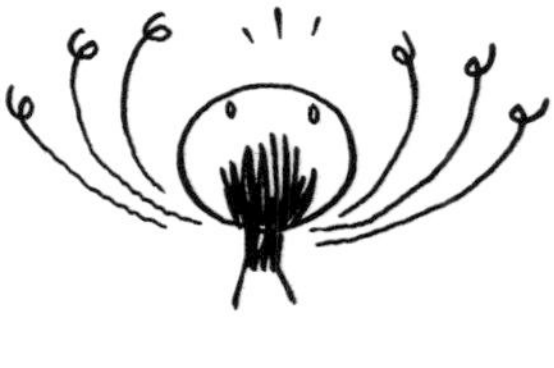

 "Oh yeah? And who are you, little motormouth?"

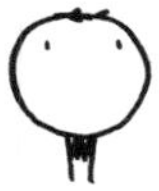

At that moment, something broke.

The being who'd meant the most to him in all the world since forever had forgotten who he was.

"I'm... I'm Alphonse Tabouret."

"Oh yeah?"

"You're... you're the one who started all this."

"Oh yeah?"

"Will you stop with the 'oh yeahs'?!"

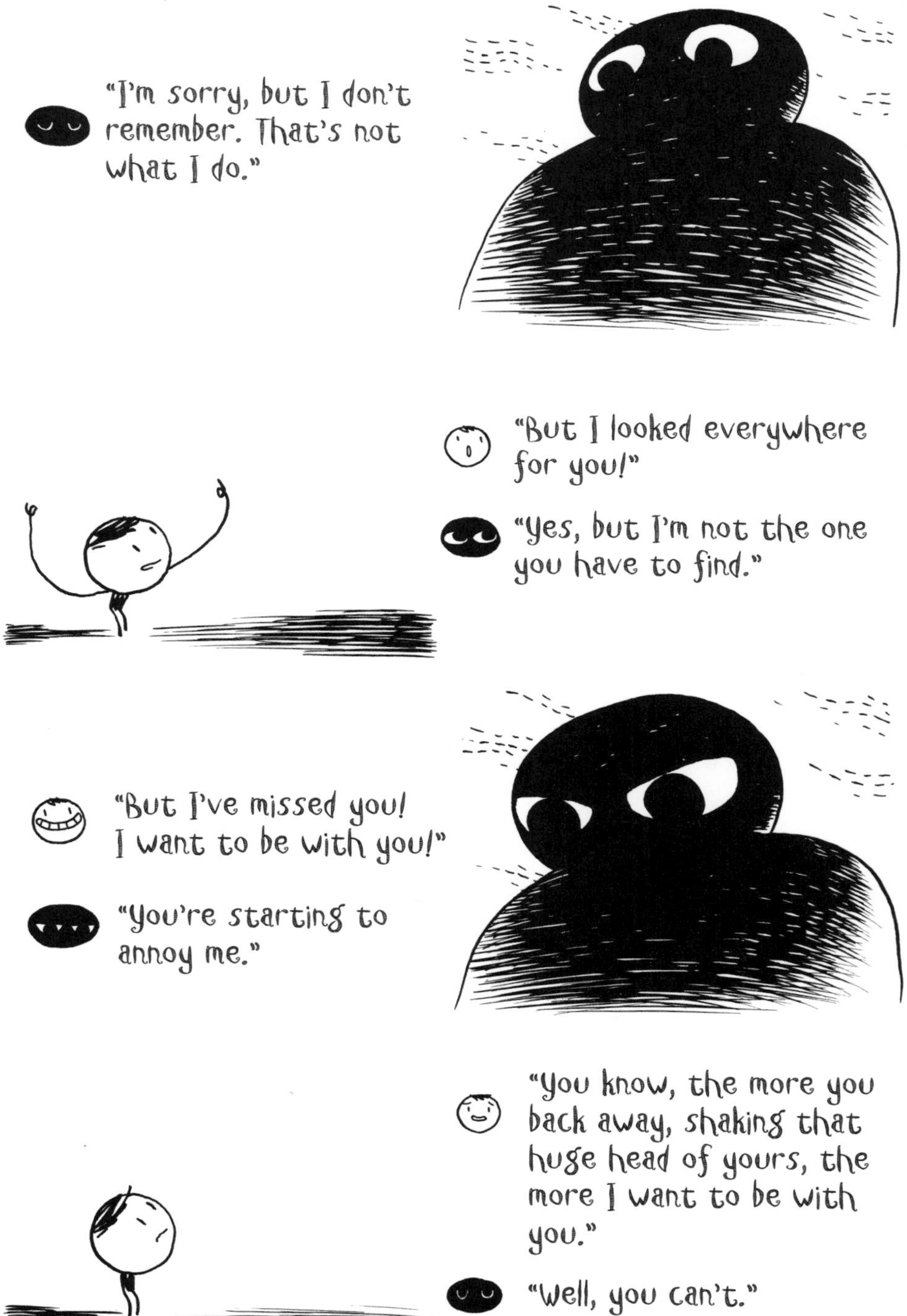
"I'm sorry, but I don't remember. That's not what I do."
"But I looked everywhere for you!"
"Yes, but I'm not the one you have to find."
"But I've missed you! I want to be with you!"
"You're starting to annoy me."
"You know, the more you back away, shaking that huge head of yours, the more I want to be with you."
"Well, you can't."

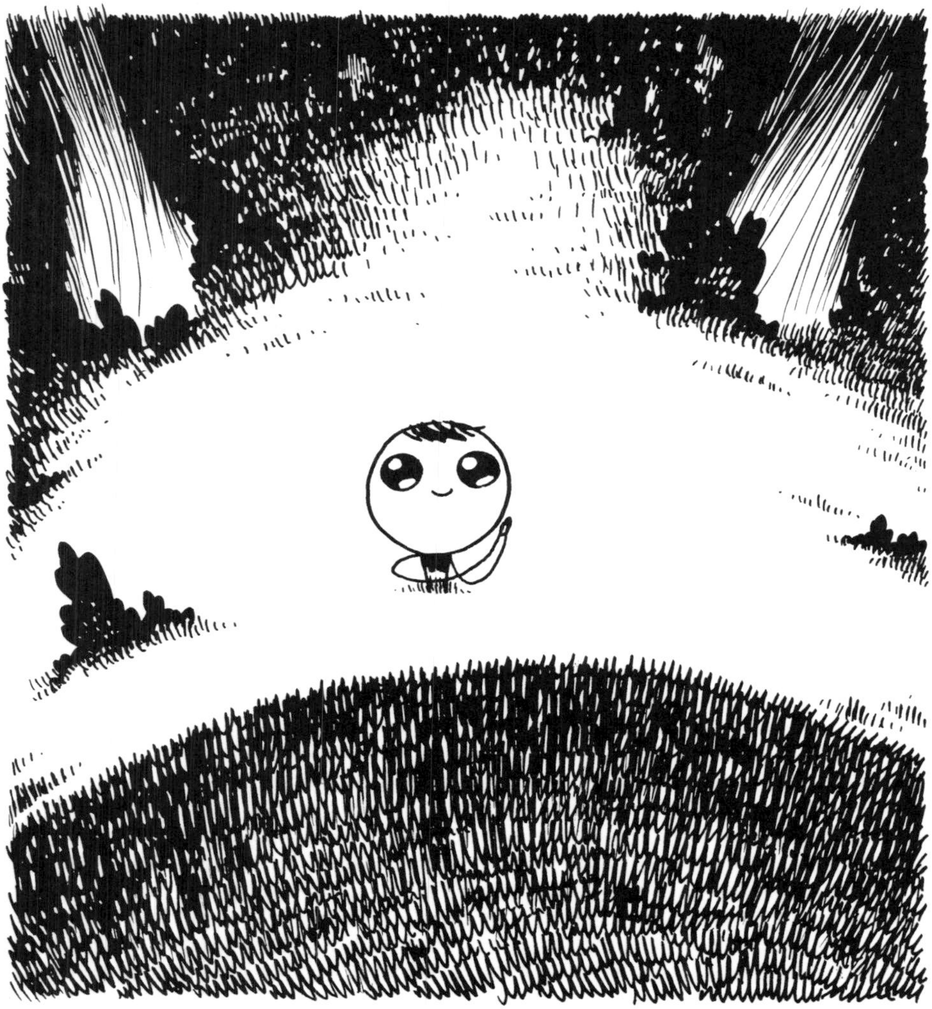

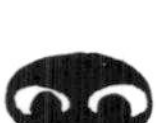

"Listen to me. I can see your hopes and dreams gleaming behind your eyes. But you're all grown up now, even if you're not very big. I'm not lovable, loving, or lovely. But others will be. You'll see. I promise. I'll help you, sure. That's something we can do together."

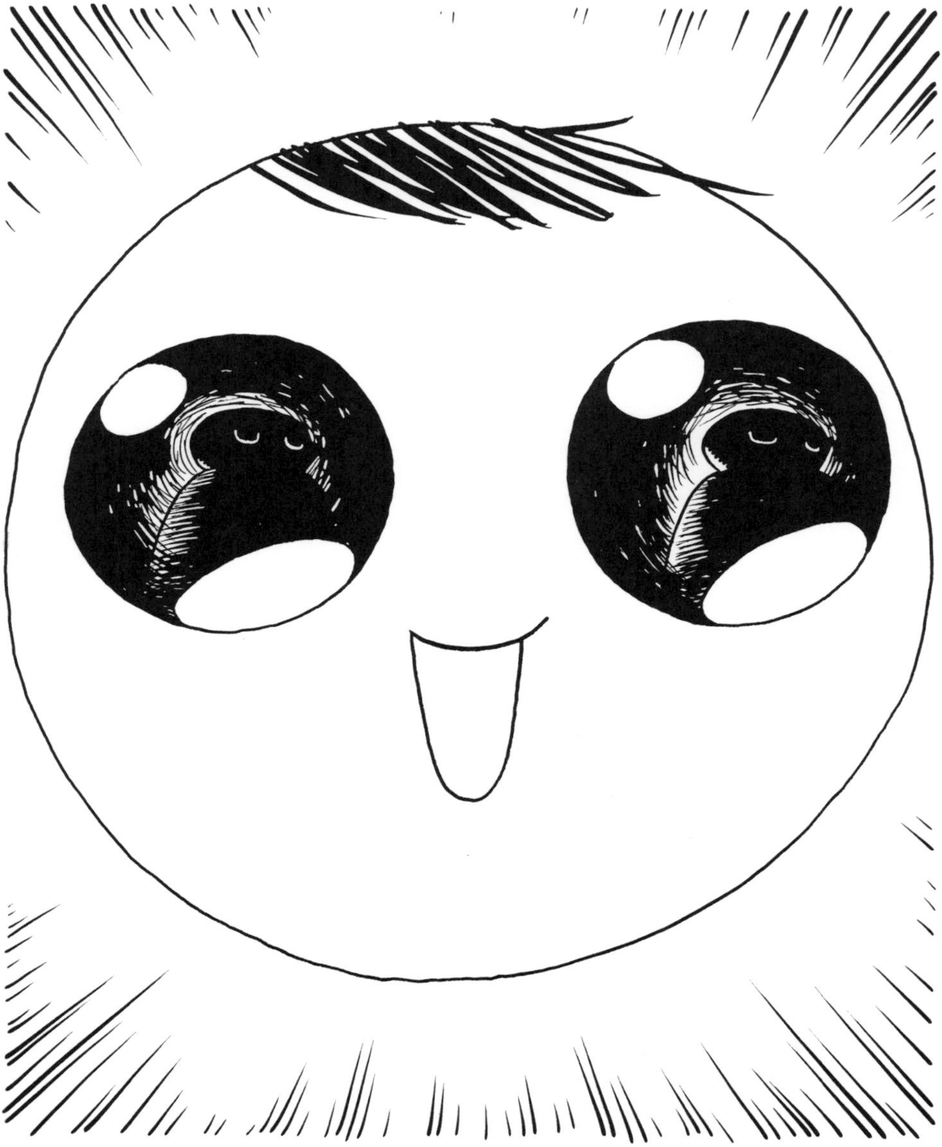

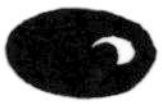 "Come on. Don't just stand there all starry-eyed."

KnickKnack SHOP
OPEN Noon to 2PM

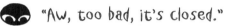

"Aw, too bad, it's closed."

"That's because it's four o'clock."

"Well, we'll have to figure something else out."

"What are you doing?"

"Growing a sign."

"What for?"

The Big Man wrote letters on the sign with care.

Alphonse watched with wonder.

Suddenly, the Big Man spun the sign around proudly.

 "Here. The solution to your loneliness. Now you can leave me the heck alone."

MOST WANTED ★ ☆ ★ ☆ ★ CONTEST

 "You're crazy, Big Man! There's no prize!"

 "Yeah, but people still like winning. Trust me, you've got nothing to lose."

 "It still seems crazy."

 "(sigh) Look, now it's your turn. You have to come up with something for them to do, to test them. I remember this one story where a girl had to kiss a slimy, green thing and ta-daa! It turned into a prince."

 "Okay! I'm on it!"

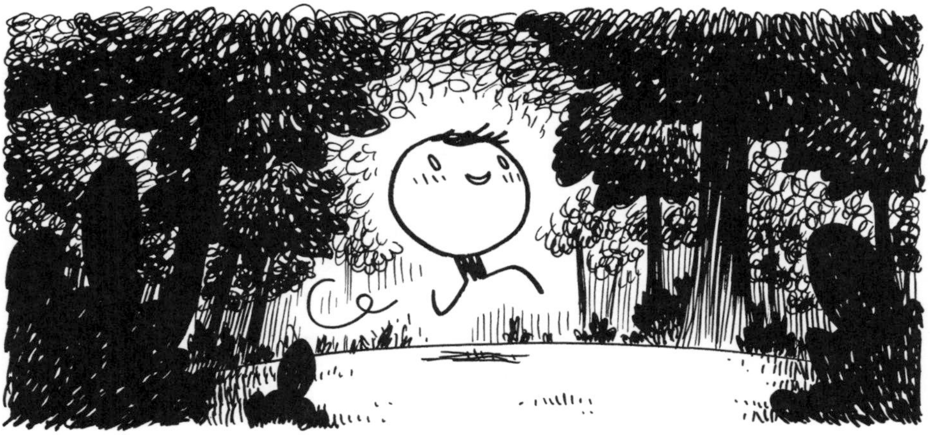

"I want a princess of my own!"

"Hey! Open up!"

Bam! Bam! Bam!

"Pleeease!"

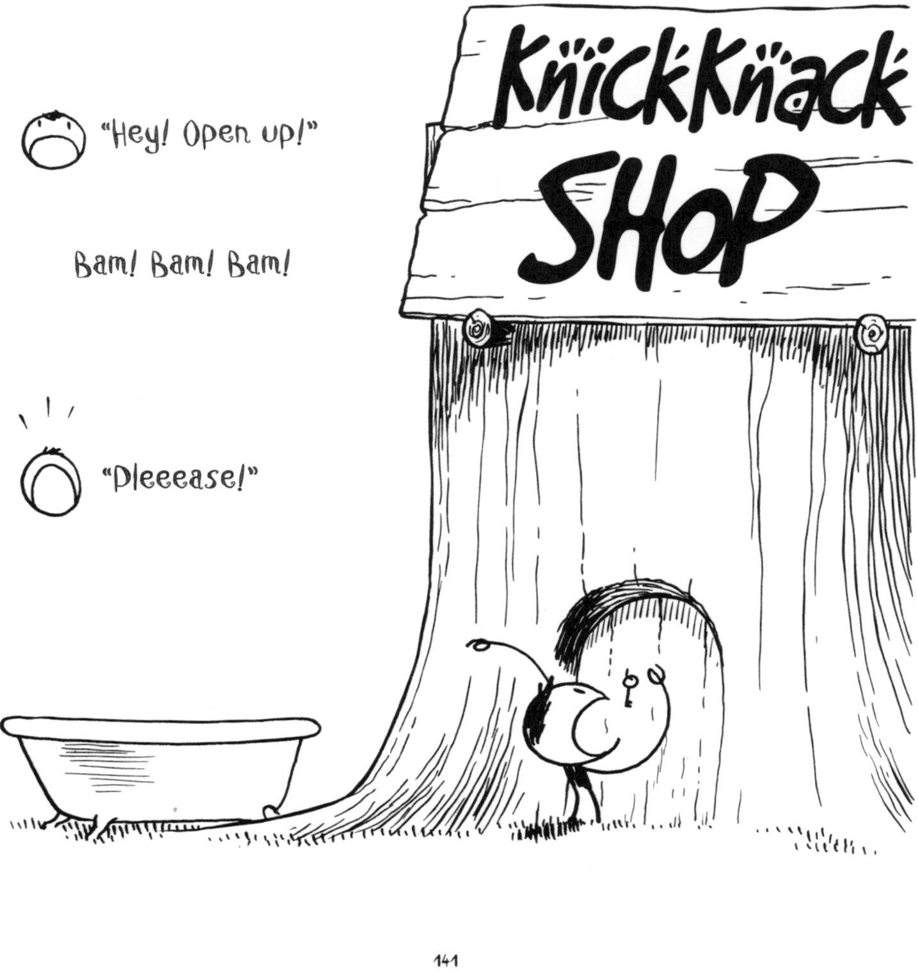
KnickKnack
SHOP

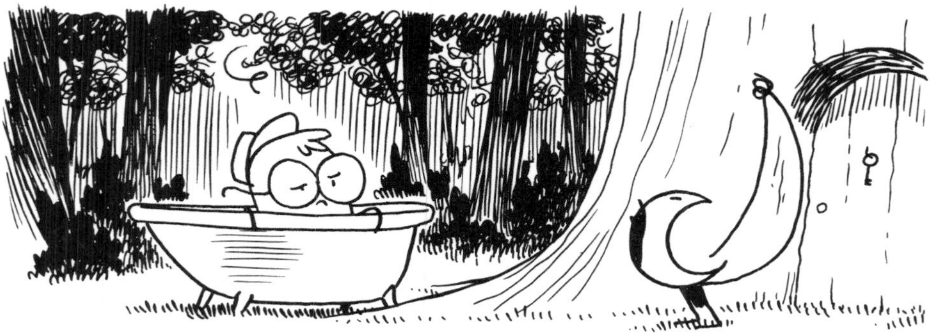

"What?! What do you want?"

"It's me! Alphonse!
Please open your store!"

"What do you need?"

"Something green! It's an experiment!"

"Here's the key. If you need the wheelbarrow,
ask Spud."

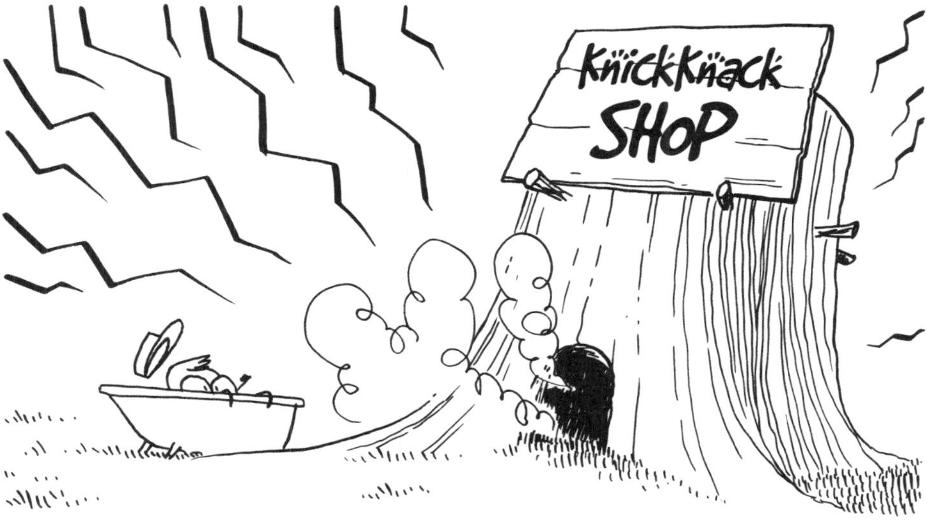
KnickKnack
SHOP

Alphonse searched the store high and low.

He brought back all kinds of things:

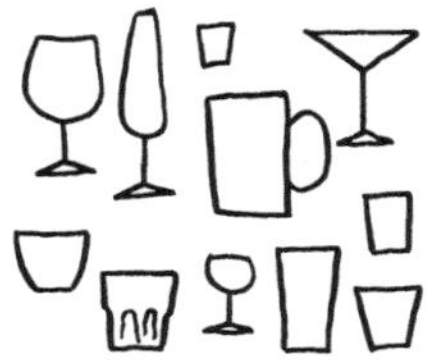
Green glasses

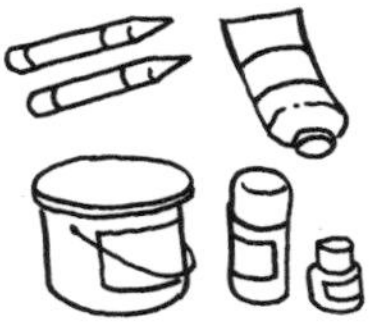
Green paint

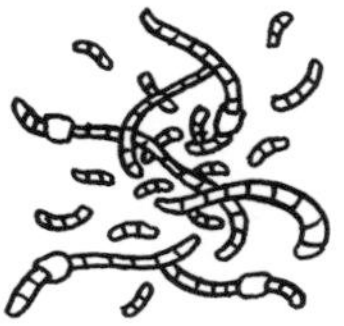
Green worms

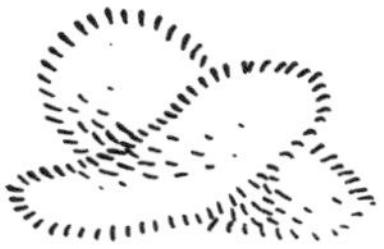
Green slippers

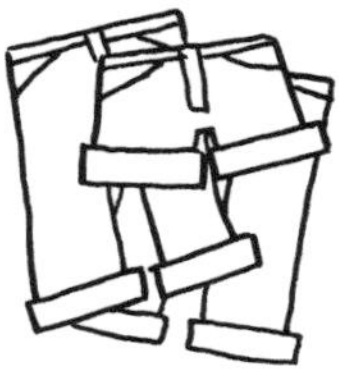
Green jeans

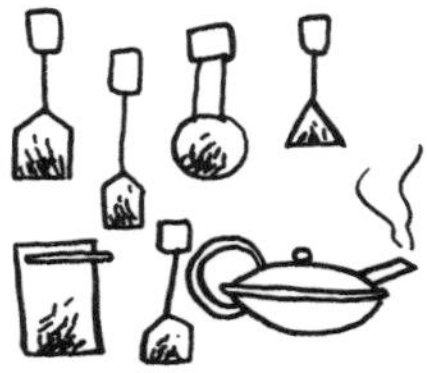
Green tea

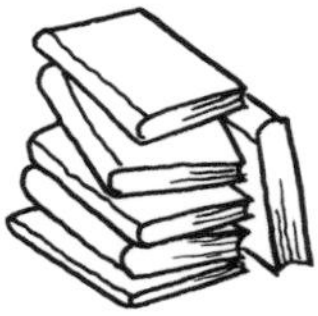
Green books

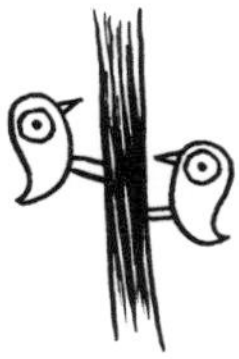
Green woodpeckers

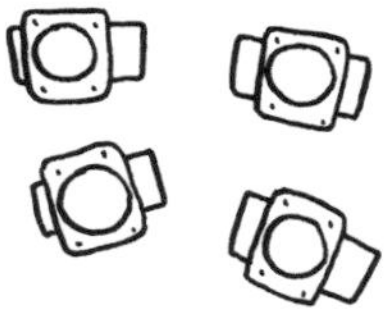
Green doorknobs

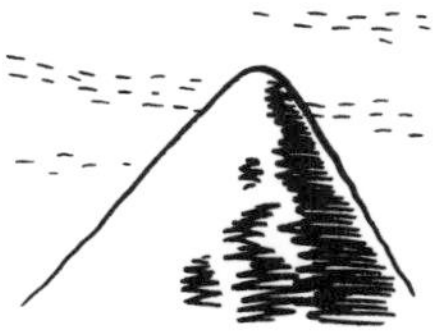
A green hill

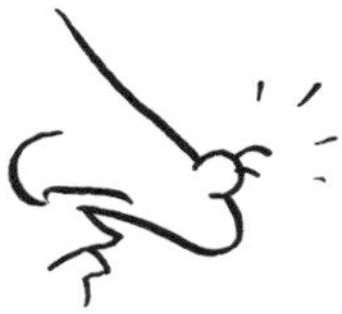
A green wart

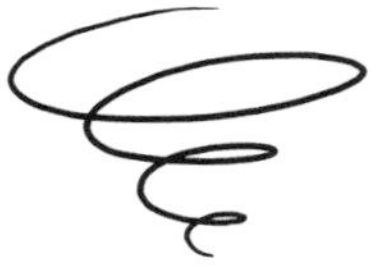
A green feeling

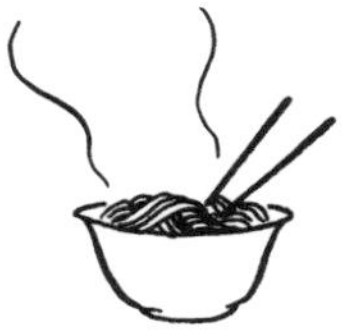
Green noodles

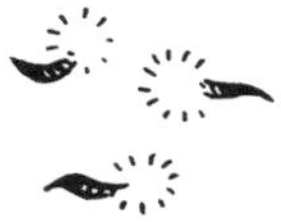
Green fireflies

Green yarn

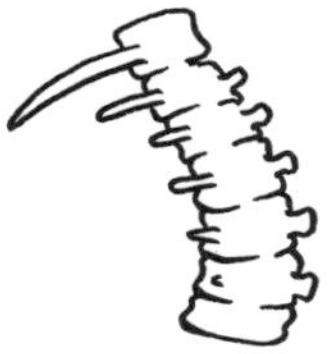
A green spine

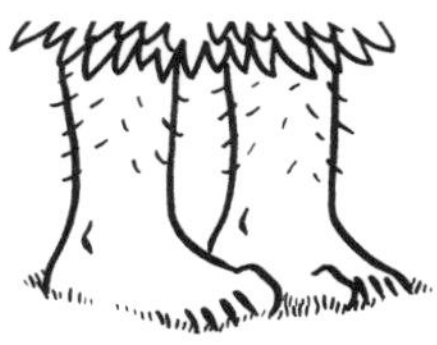
A green giant

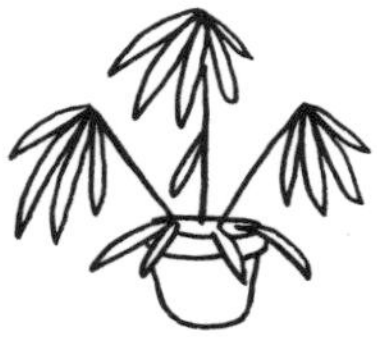
A green plant

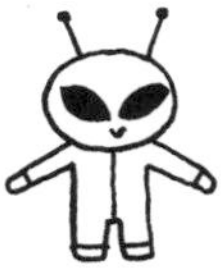
A little green man

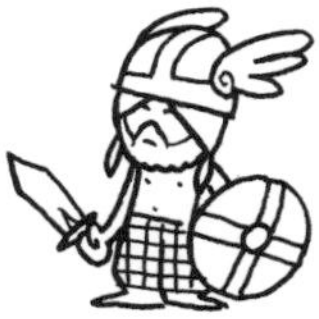
A green viking

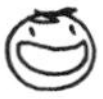 "Ta-daaaaaa!"

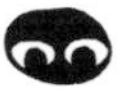 "That's quite a grab bag."

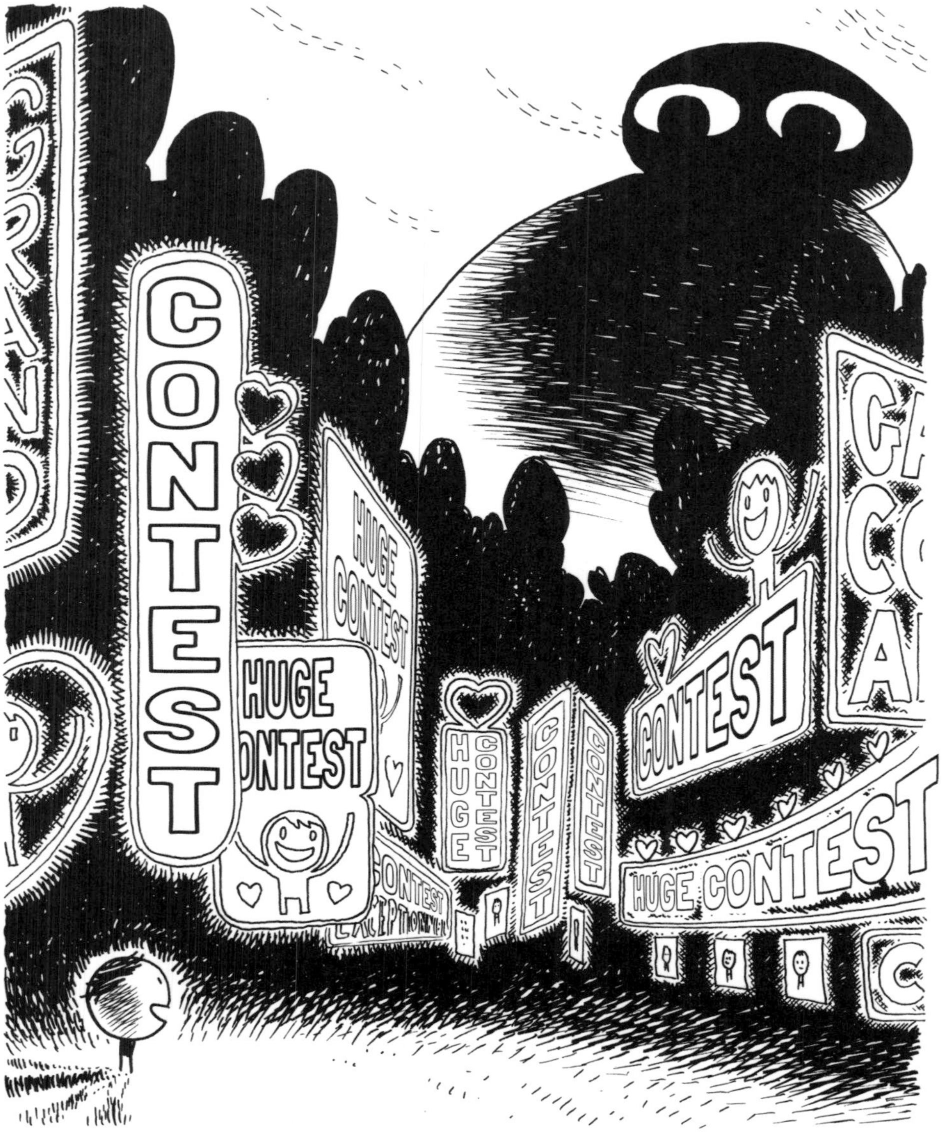
CONTEST
HUGE CONTEST
HUGE CONTEST
HUGE CONTEST
CONTEST
CONTEST
CONTEST
HUGE CONTEST

"Meanwhile, I put up more signs."

Indeed, the forest was winking and blinking.
A lot.

"Penelope would have loved this."

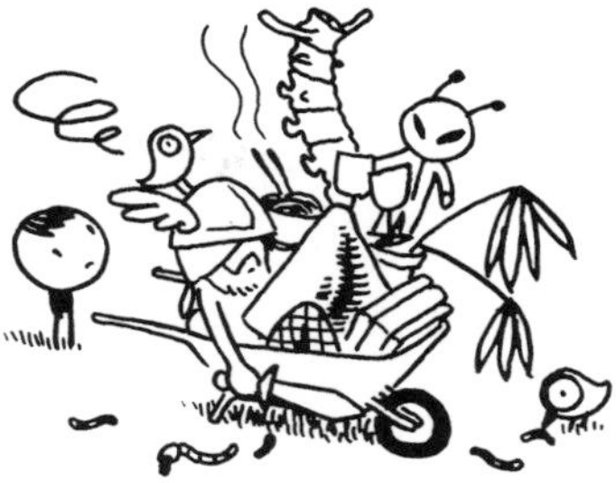

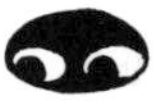

"Yeah, but... something tells me that stuff won't cut it."

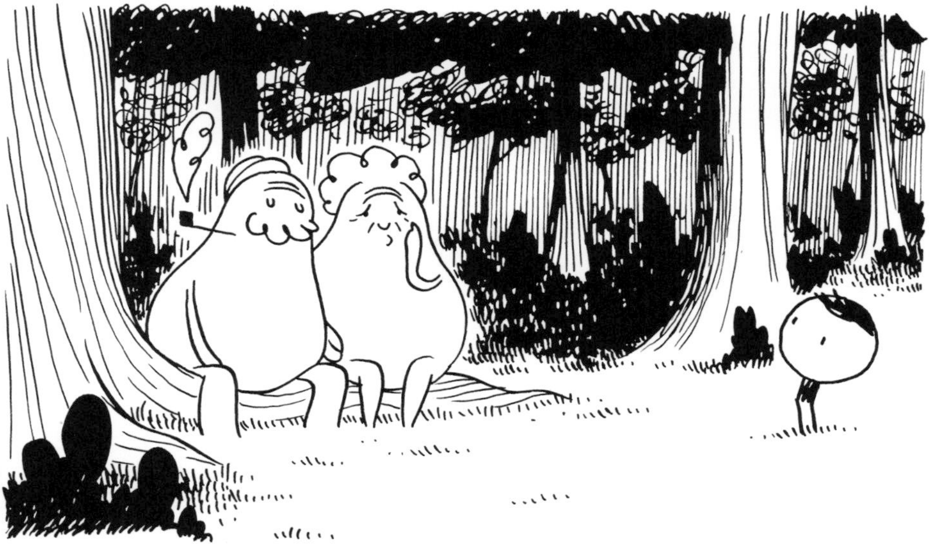

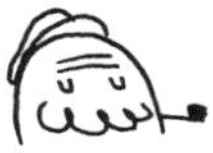

"Well, there were slippers and enchanted rings in the fairy tales, weren't there?"

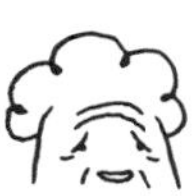

"If you ask me, sweetie, it's not the feet or fingers that make for a happy marriage."

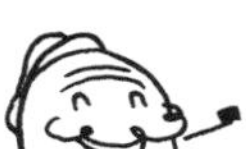

"Oh, like you'd know anything about that!"

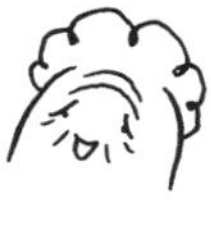

"Haw haw (snort)! Aw, cut it out, you!"

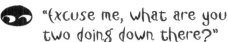 "Excuse me, what are you two doing down there?"

 "My bunions were hurting."

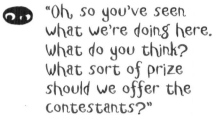 "So we sat down here and sorta took root."

 "Oh, so you've seen what we're doing here. What do you think? What sort of prize should we offer the contestants?"

"Dear boy, I think you're straying from the point of this exercise!"

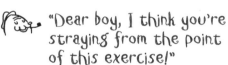 "Please don't confuse him with riddles."

"It's not about finding the right thing for someone, it's about finding the right someone for someone."

"Now you're confusing me..."

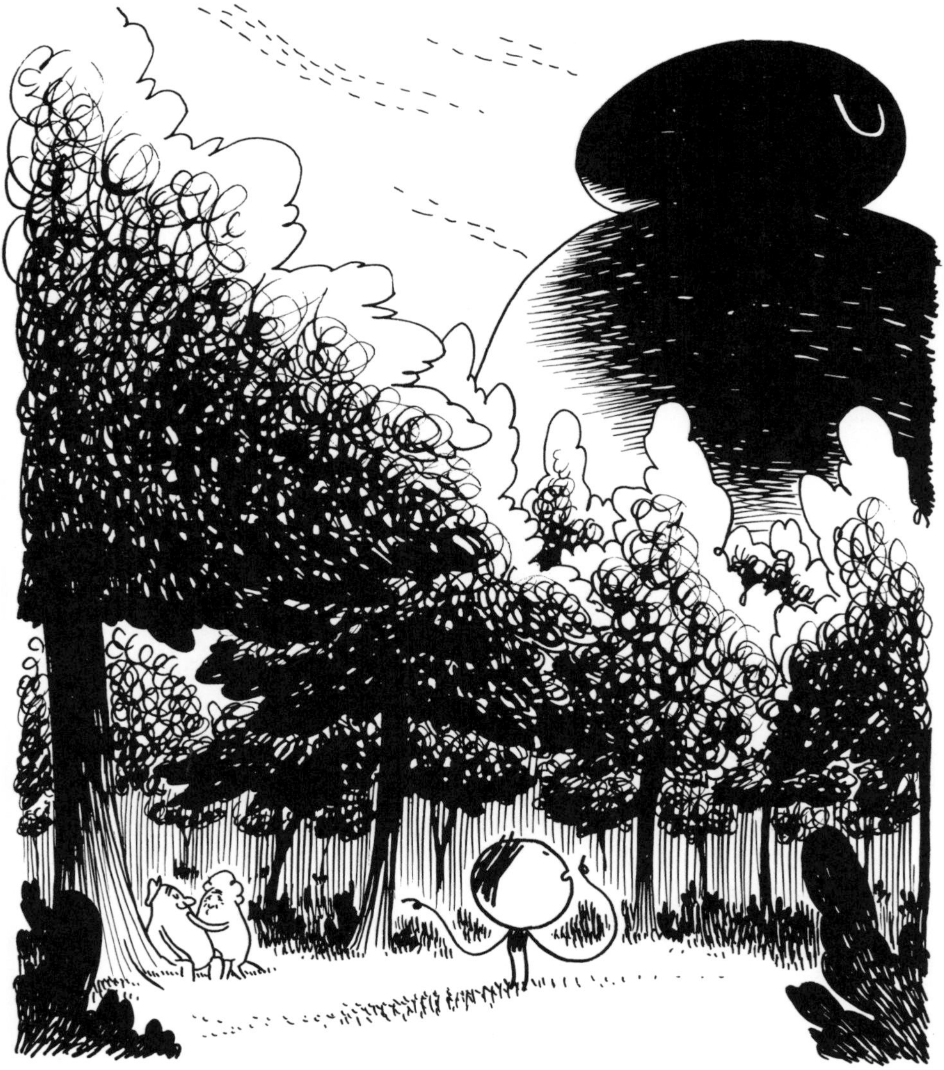

"Y'know, Big Man, that sappy old man might be right."

"What is this? A mutiny?"

"No! I just wonder what they mean, that's all."

"Fine, figure it out..."

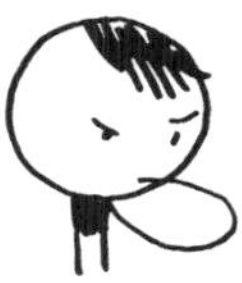

"This is getting complicated."

"C'mon over here, kid."

Alphonse sat down beside the sappy man and woman and looked them in the eye.

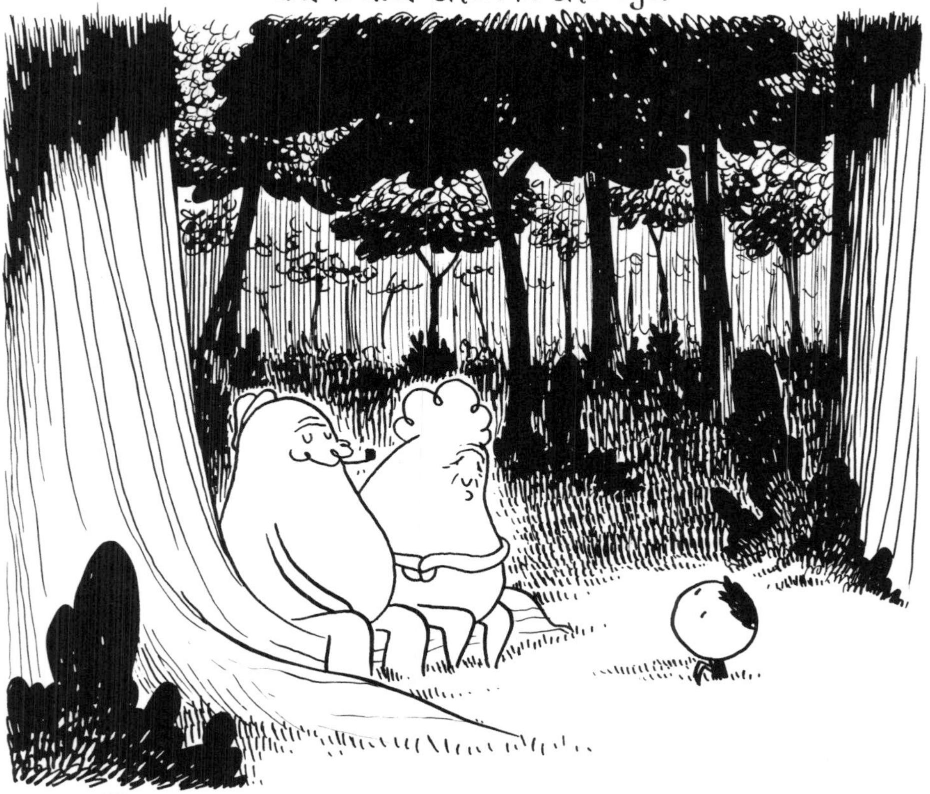

"We love each other, see?"

"And I love endives!"

"Ha ha, that's funny. Endives are gross."

"Hush! I'm talking!"

 "He and I are in love!"

 "Right. And I love endives."

 "No, my dear. You're not listening."

 "At best, you can love endives like a friend. But you can't be IN LOVE with them."

 "You're going to confuse him, dear."

 "You might like endives a lot but with your stomach. But you love PEOPLE with your HEART!"

 "You mean like when you get off a roller coaster and your heart is pounding?"

 "Yes! I mean... no!"

 "Don't worry, boy. You'll find someone to brighten your days."

 "I hope I don't go blind looking..."

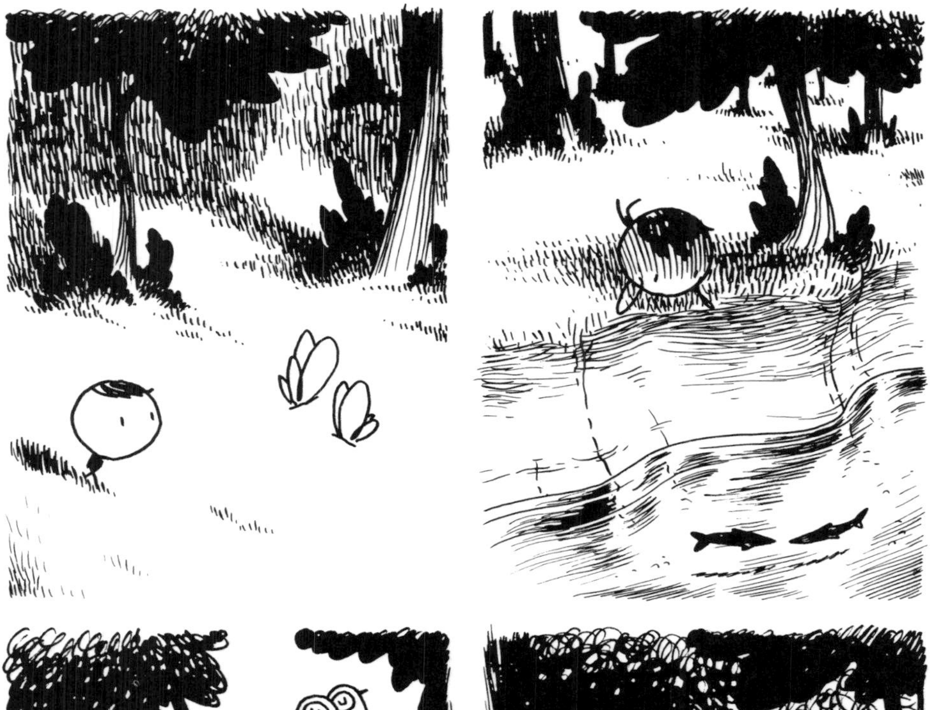

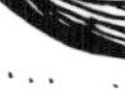 "What am I doing wrong?"

But the two old roots had twisted into a knot.

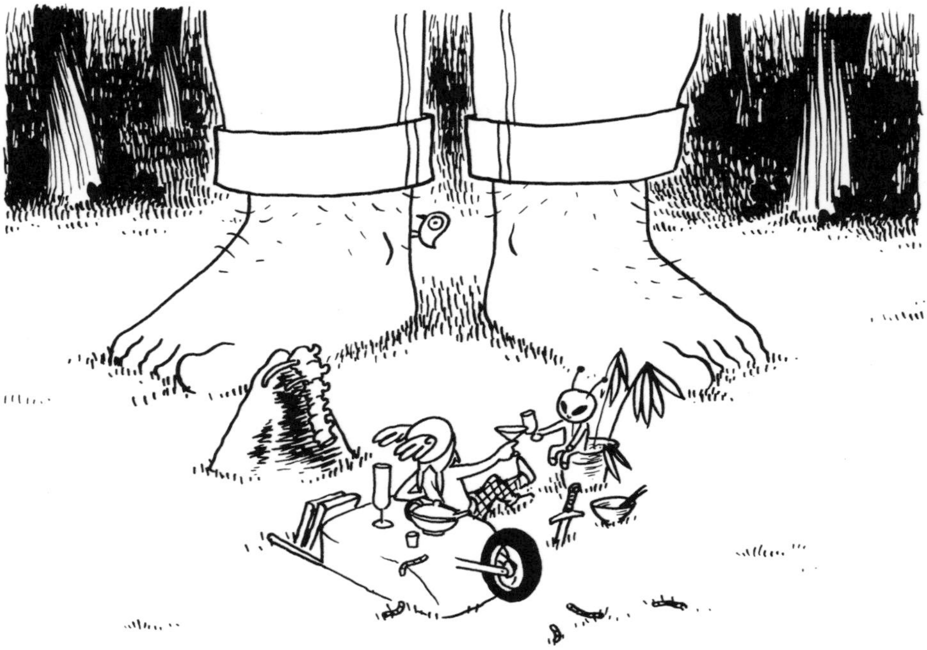

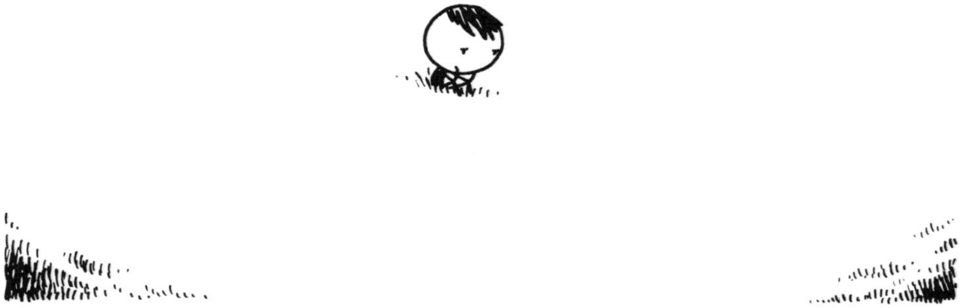

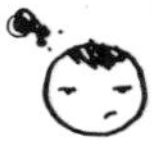 "(sigh)..."

At that moment, a tiny voice emerged behind him.

"Um... excuse me. Is this the right place for the contest?"

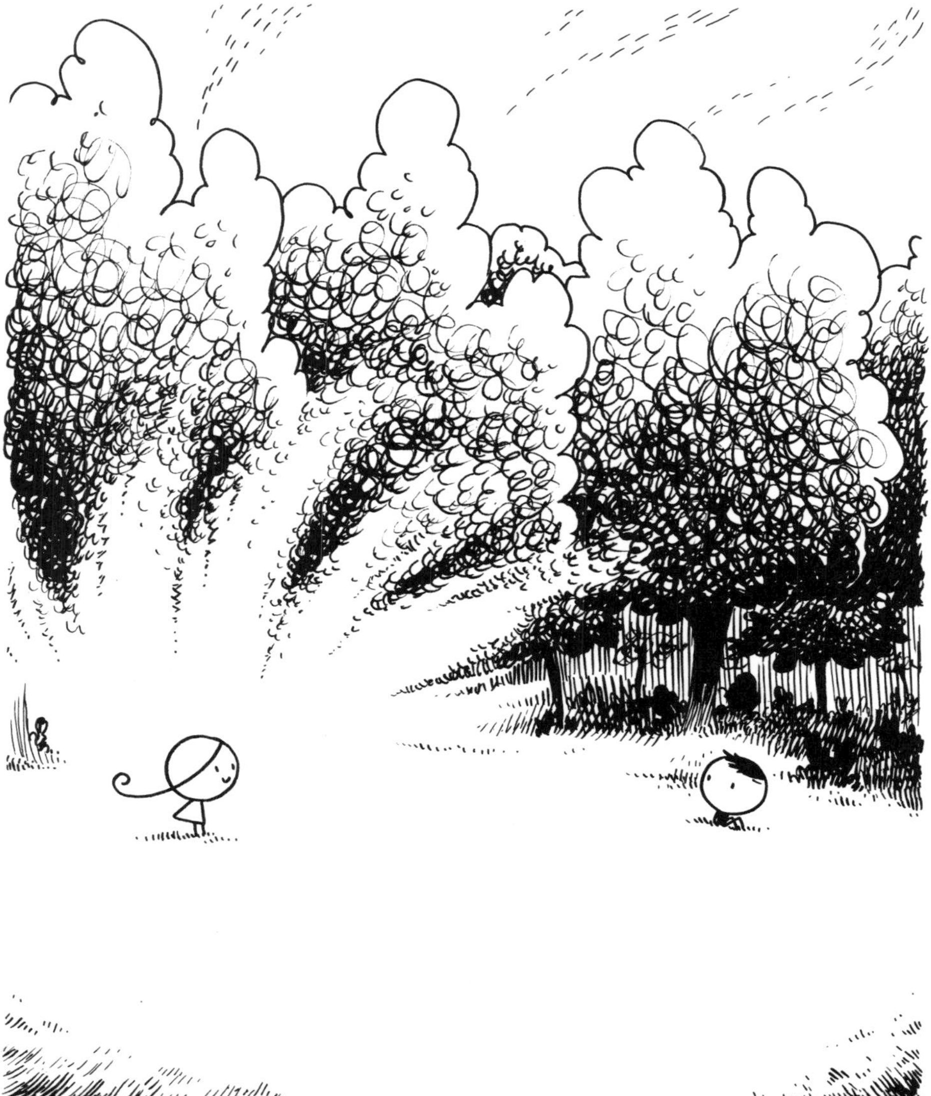

"I... you... we... uh..."

"Yeah, I think so, too."

"You remind me of an endive."

 "Ooo, that's my favorite! Can I try out for the contest?"

 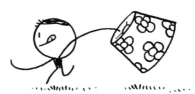

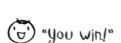 "You win!"

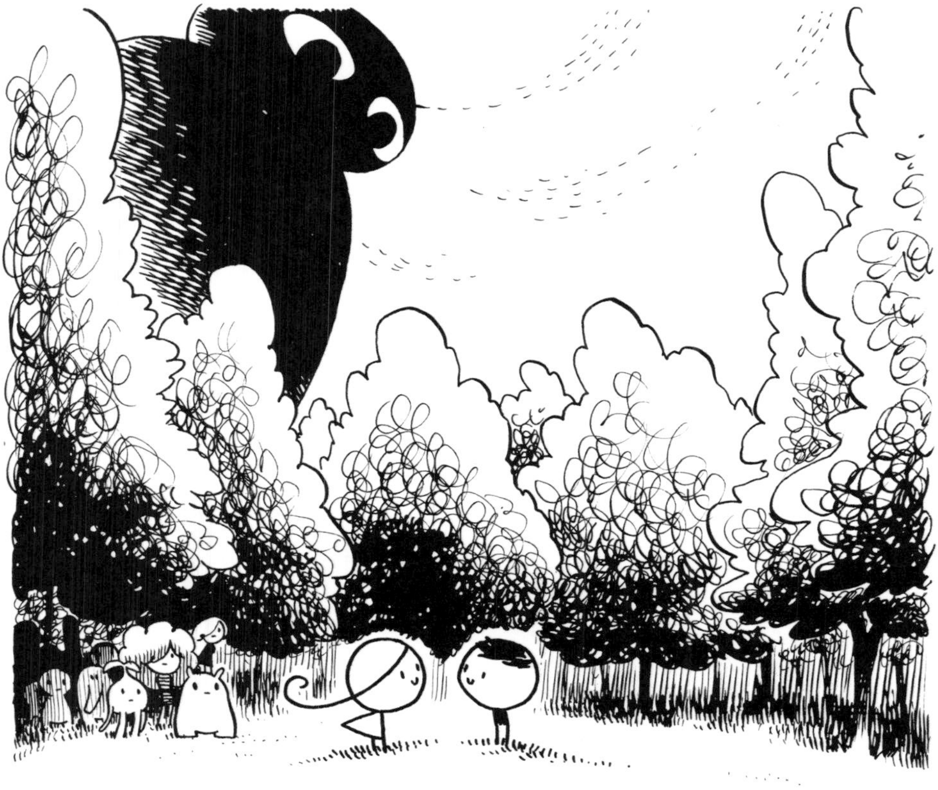

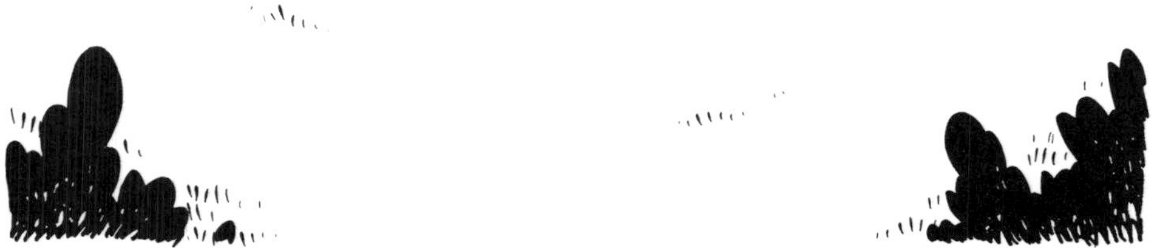

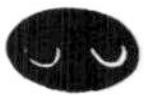 "Hey, peewee! Look what I found!"

But no one was listening.

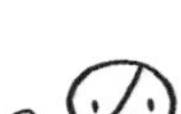 "My name is Lilili Chabadibada."

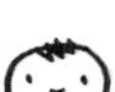 "I'm Alphonse Tabouret."

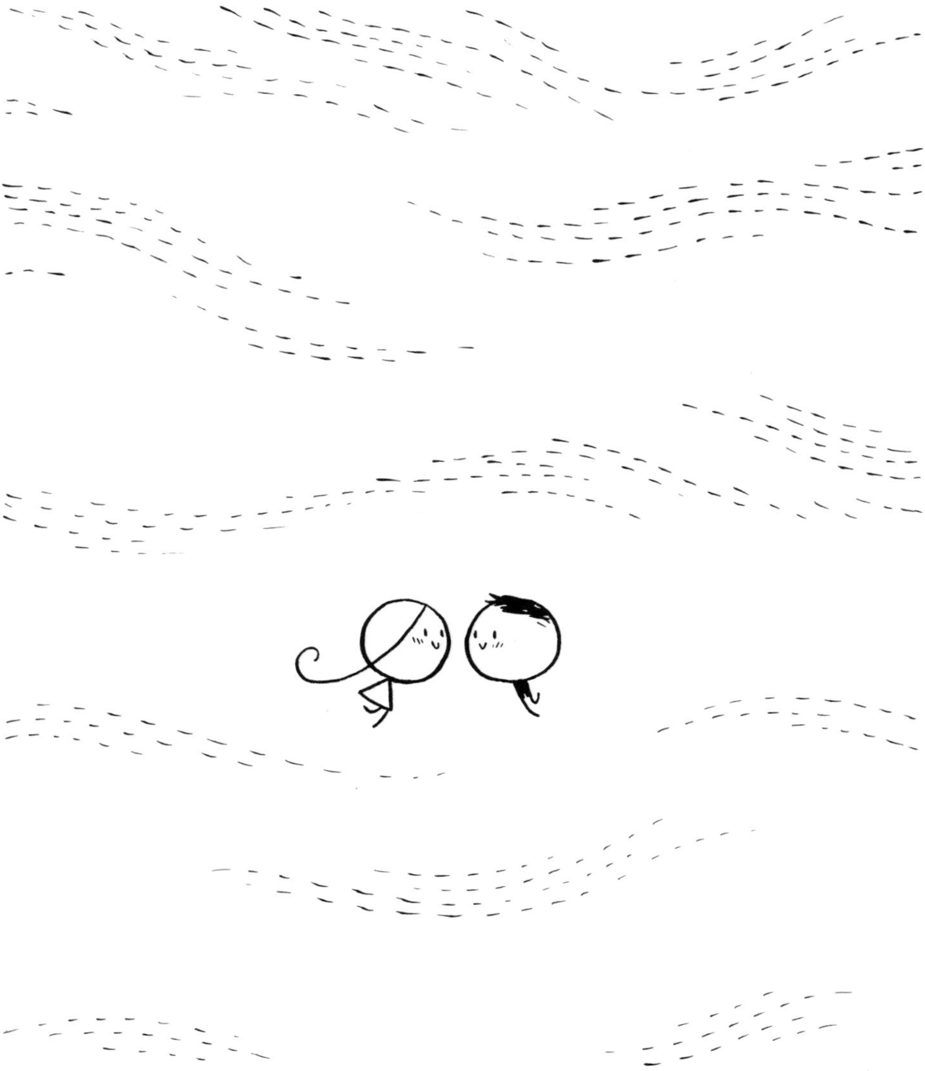

Swept up in a waft of perfection, Lilili and Alphonse told each other their life stories.

The rest of the world disappeared, for at long last, neither of them needed anything anymore.

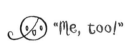 "Me, too!"

 "Me, too!"

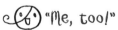 "Me, too!"

 "Me, too!"

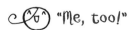 "Me, too!"

"Me, too!"

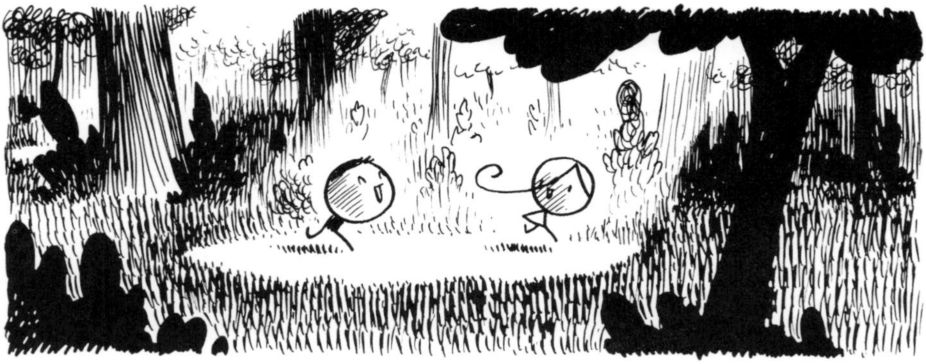

They reflected each other's dreams...

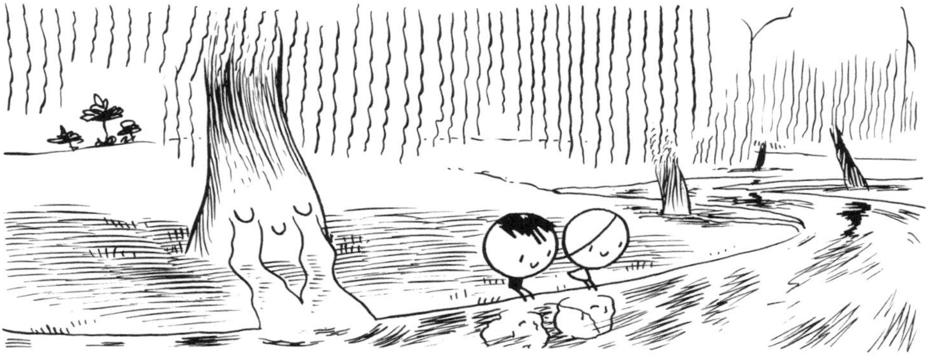

...rang each other's bell to turn the page...

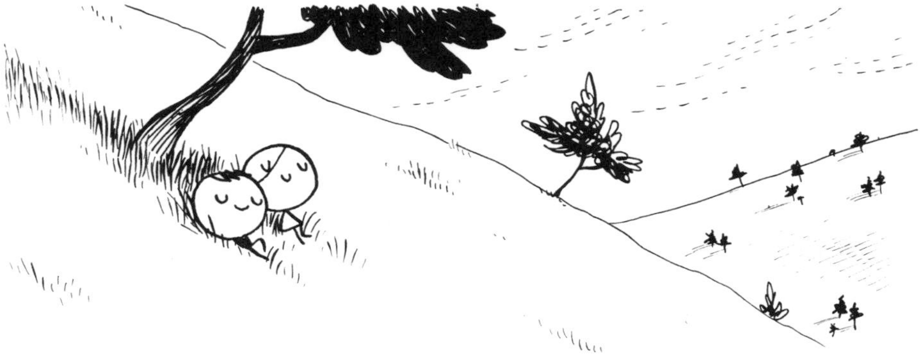

...and opened each other's skylight so they could count the stars together.

 "I love you."

 "I've missed you."

 "We only just met this morning."

 "And I... I love you, too."

 "Are you sure?"

 "Yes. You said it first."

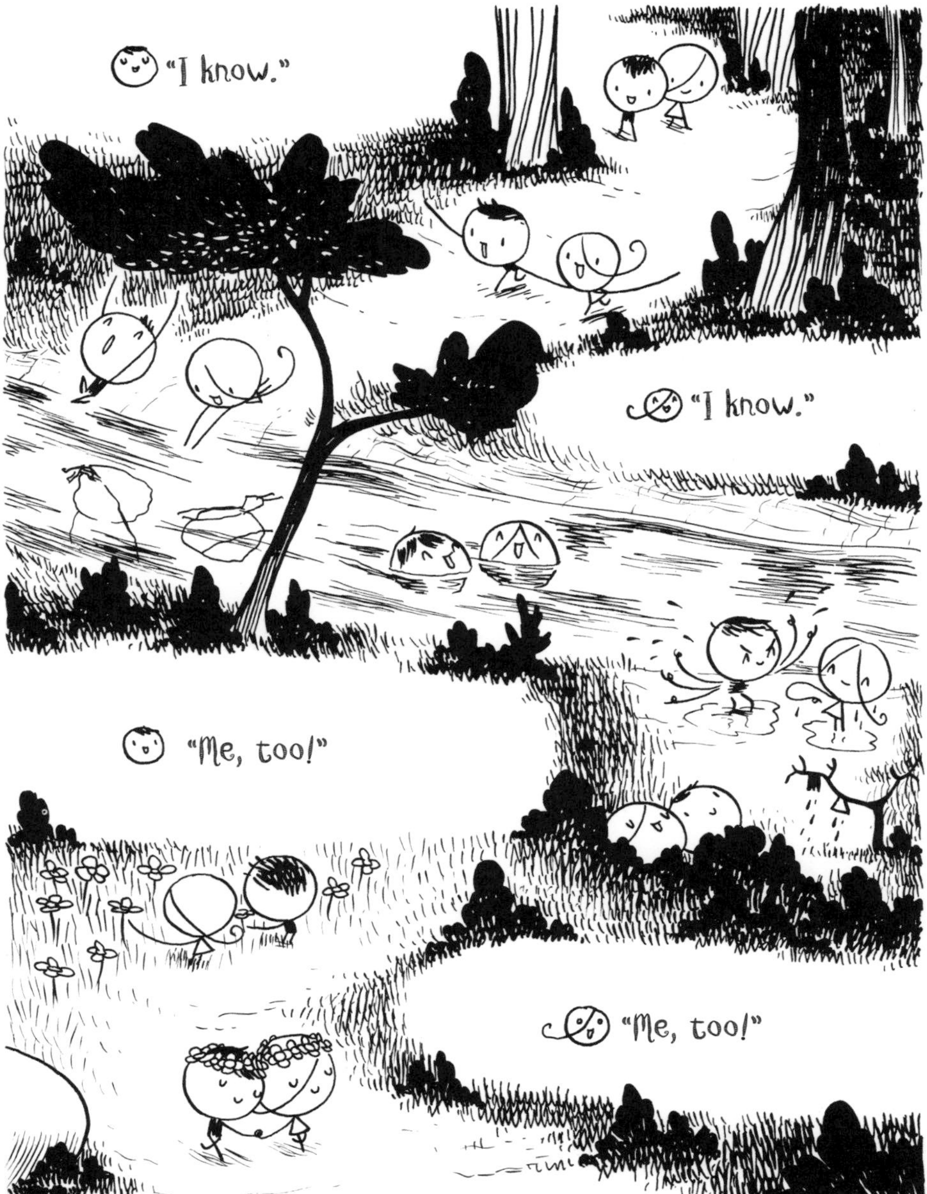
"I know."
"I know."
"Me, too!"
"Me, too!"

They frolicked through their todays
toward their tomorrows,
and all was well.

And yet, over the course of this perfect love,
boredom set in.

Plus, it was almost noon.

"I'm hungry."

"Me, too!"

"Is that all you know how to say?"

"You remind me of someone else..."

"Oh yeah? That's pretty rude!"

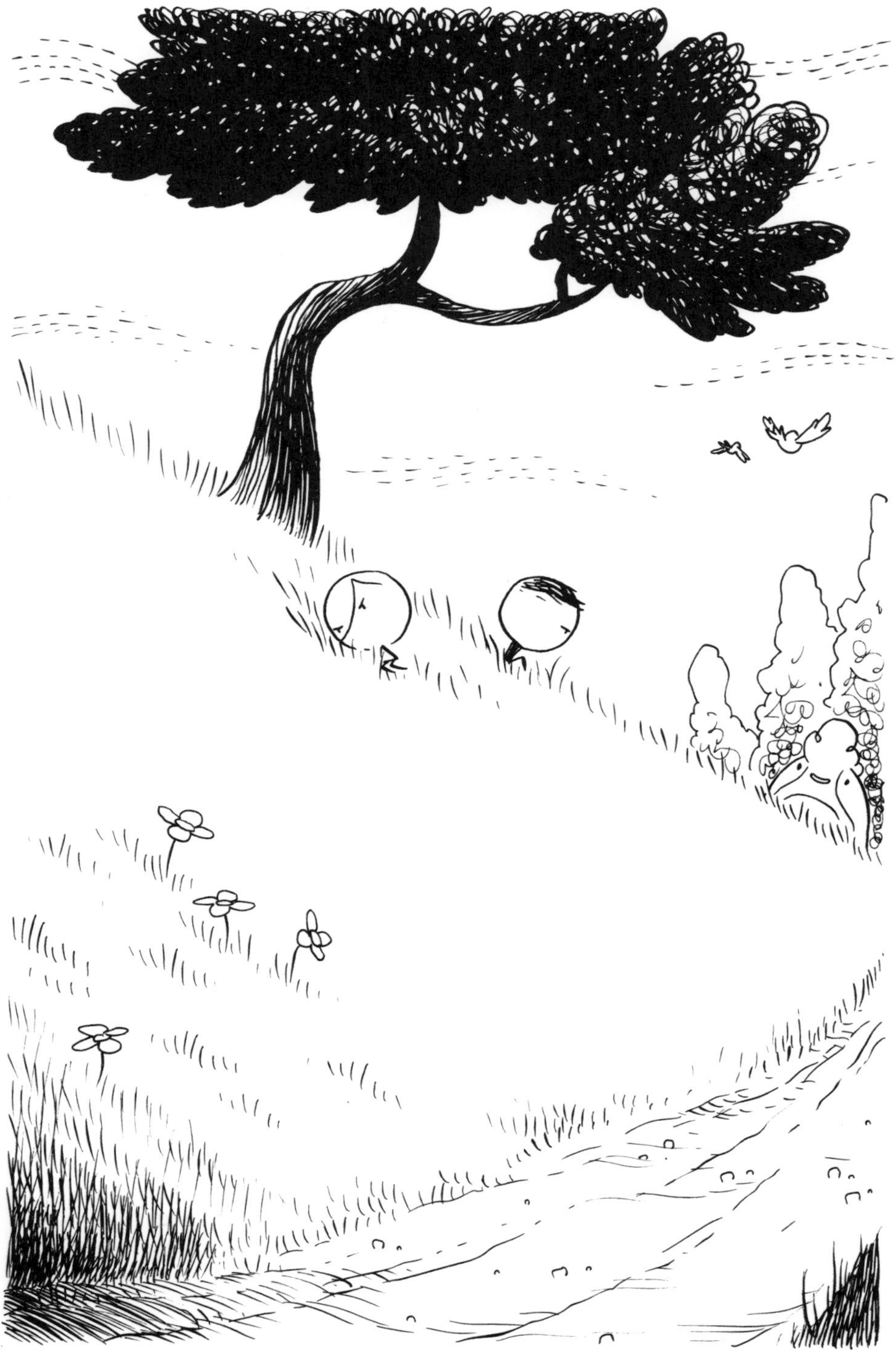

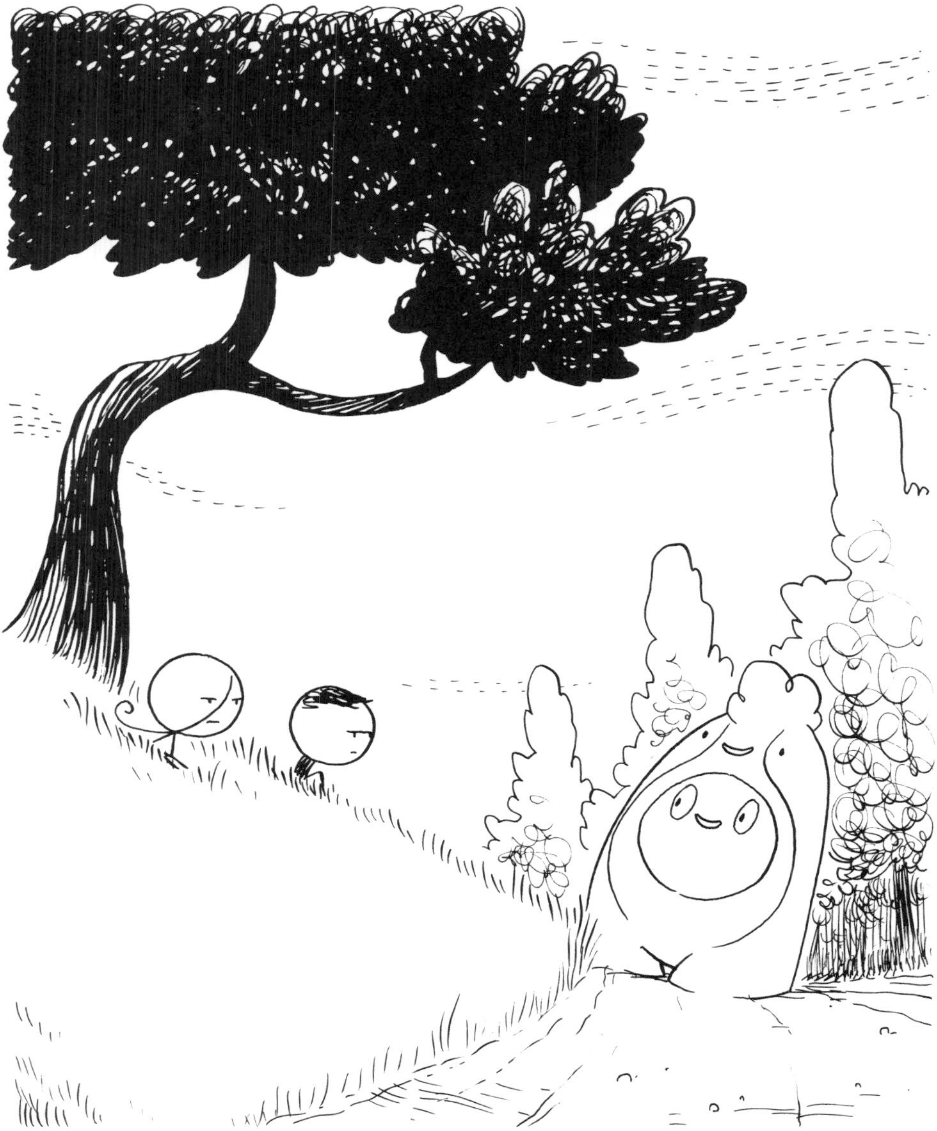

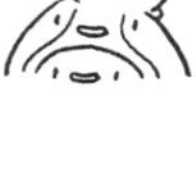

"Tut-tut, young lovers! What's the matter? Having a little spat?"

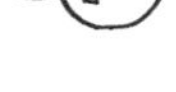

"No! We never fight!"

 "Well, we sure do sometimes!
We don't always agree on what to have for
dinner and get mad at each other. We'll get
all worked up and then sulk, like you two.
But we make up. That's the important part."

 "I just told you we never fight!"

 "Sure, I see. But it's normal. Everybody
disagrees every now and then. You have to
be different to complete each other."

 "We never get angry!"

 "You sound just like the last time
we got angry. It was crazy!
Don't worry, everything will
turn out fine."

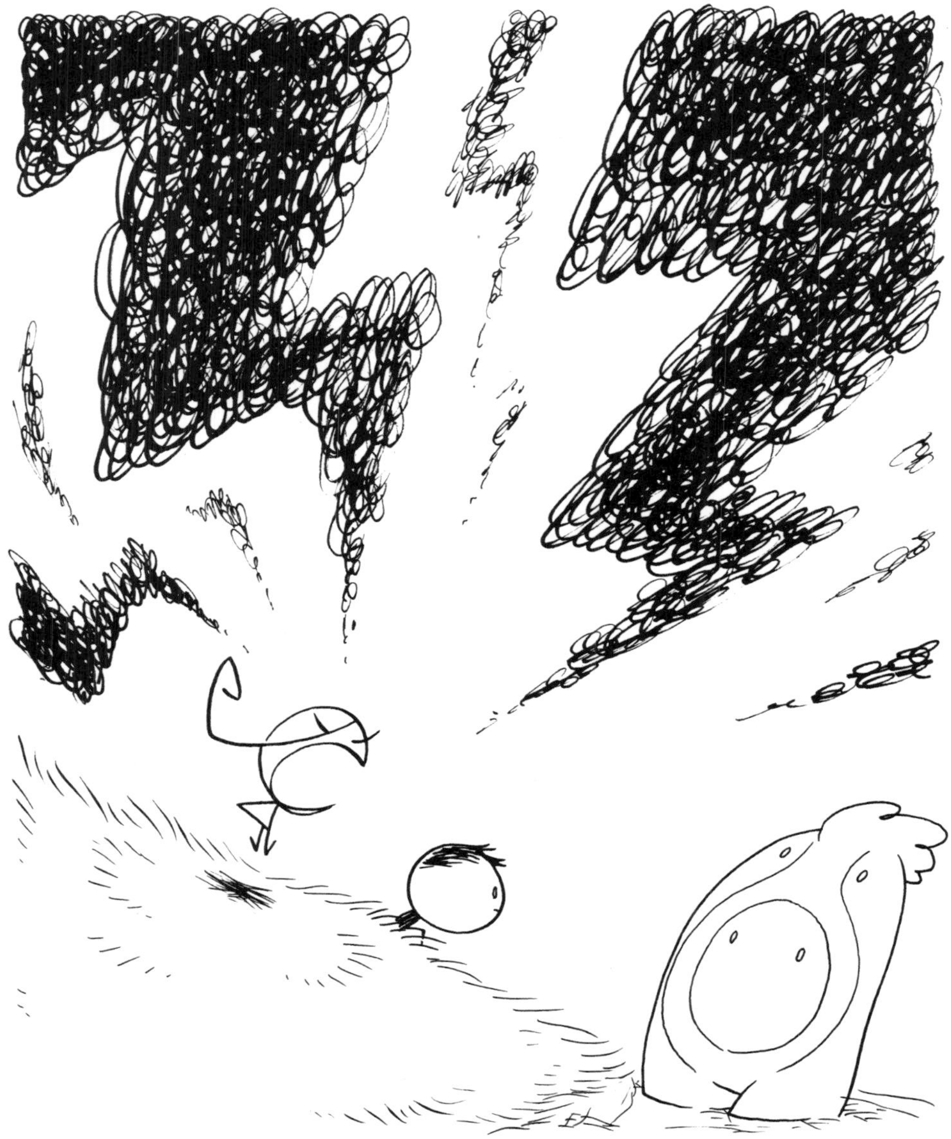

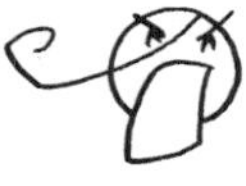 "I said we never get angry!"

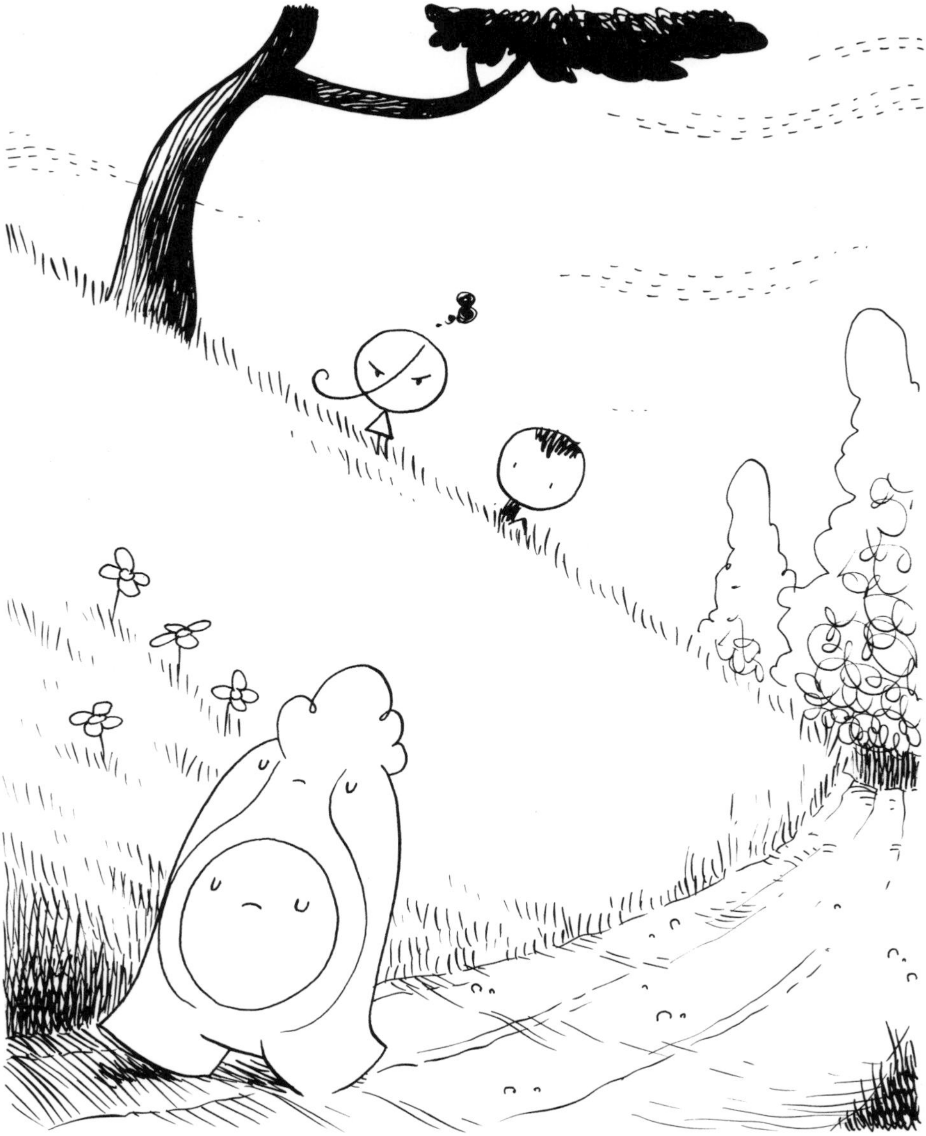

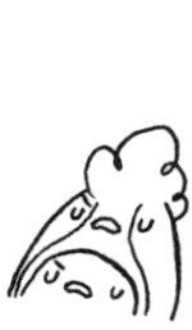

"Wow, no wonder you're so angry, with a temper like that!"

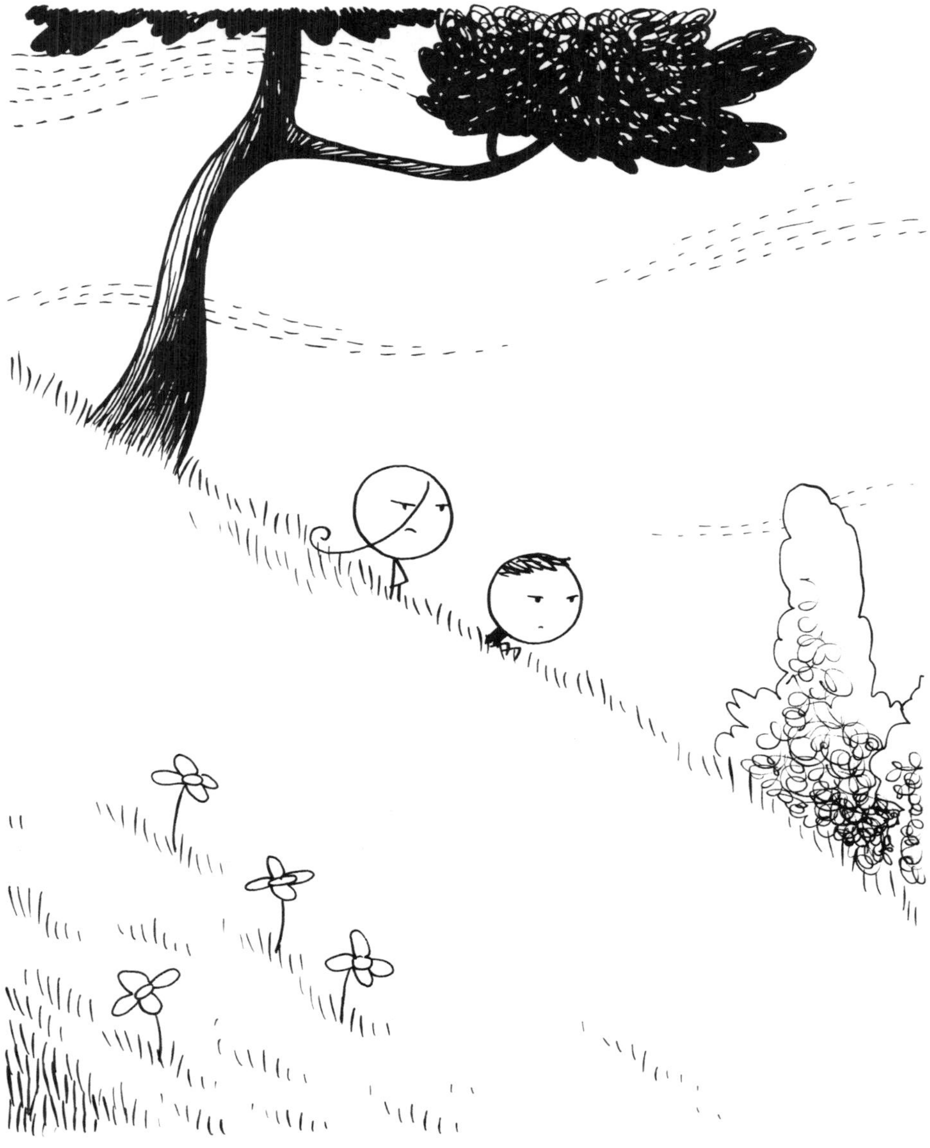

"I can't even tell you how annoying those two are."

"Totally."

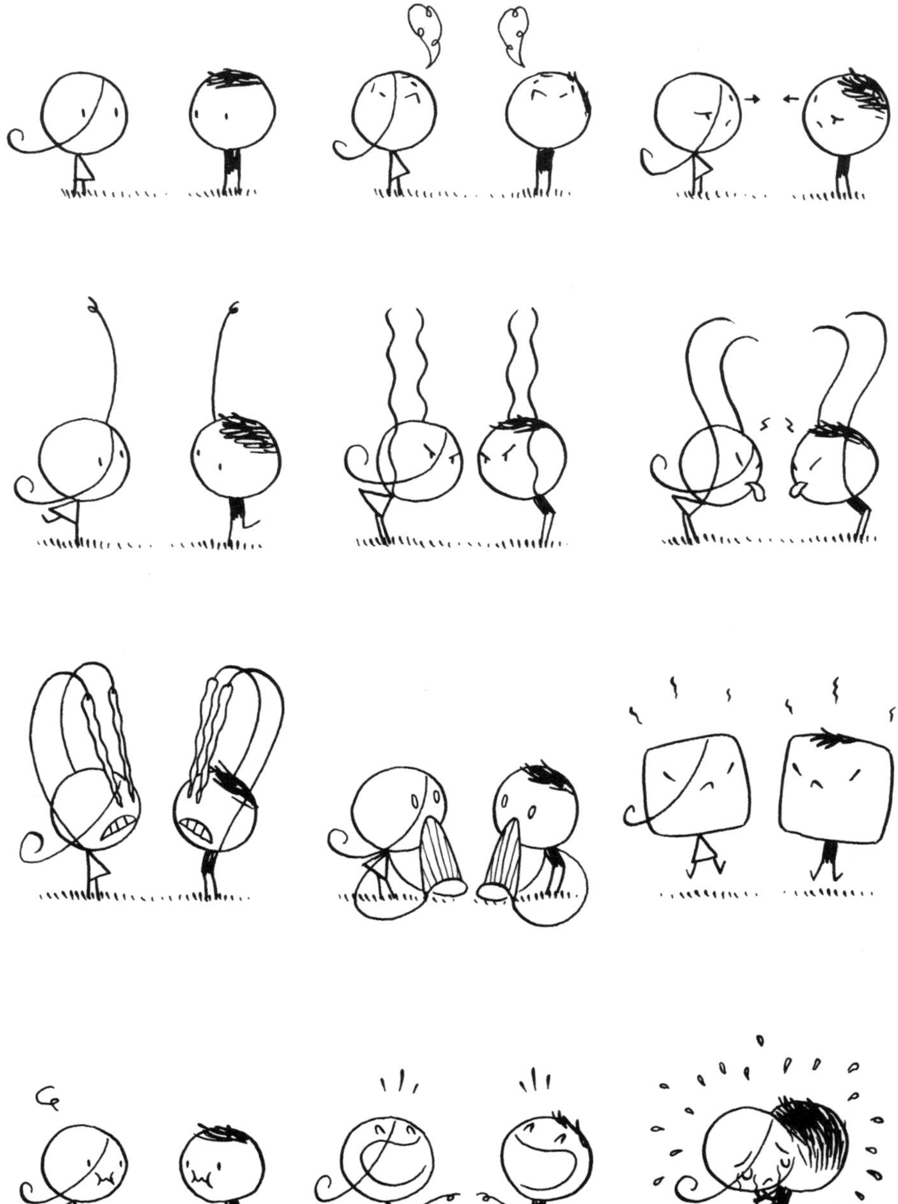

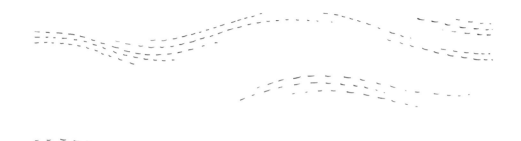

 "I don't want you to be bored. I don't want tomorrow to be like yesterday and all the boring days before it."

"Me neither, 'cause then I won't make you laugh anymore. I love you, y'know."

"Oh, you said it first!"

"I'm gonna go for a walk, okay?"

"Sure, I'll be here."

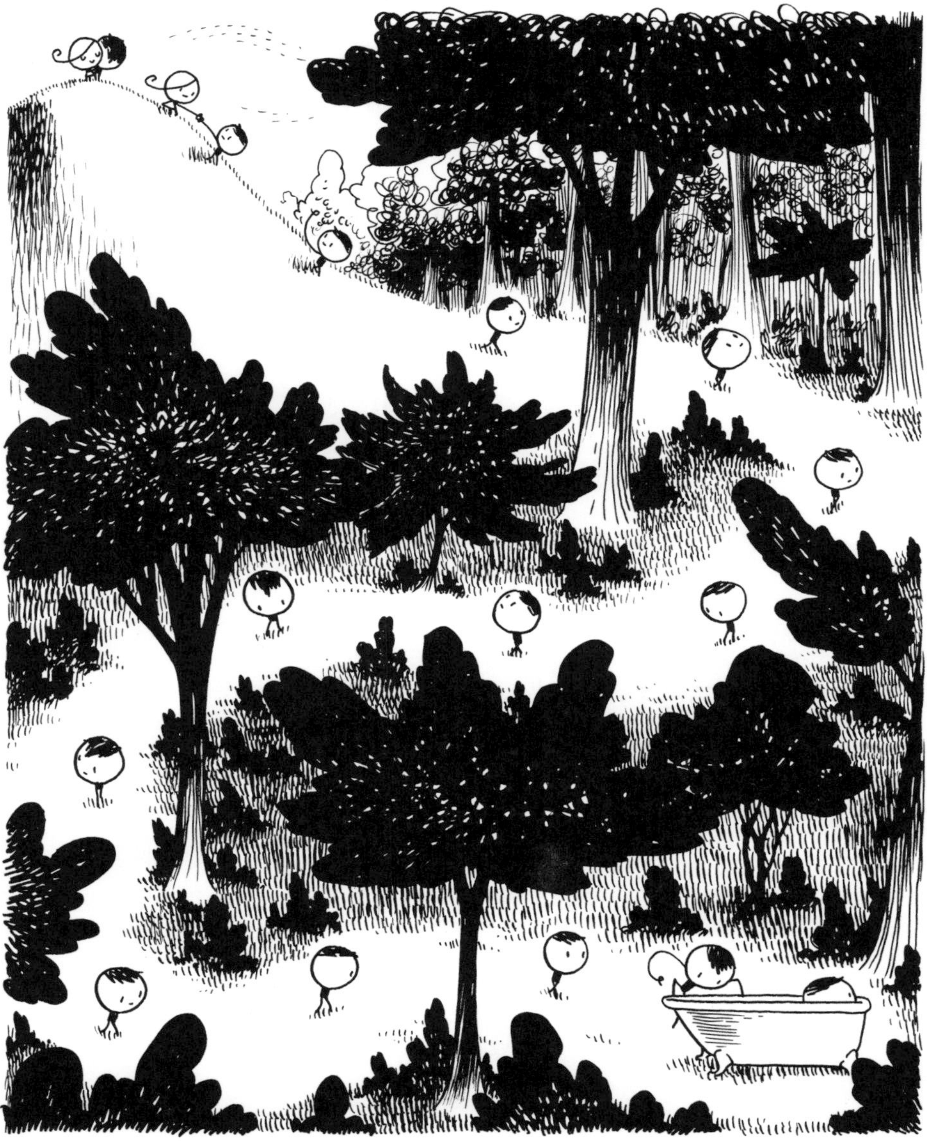

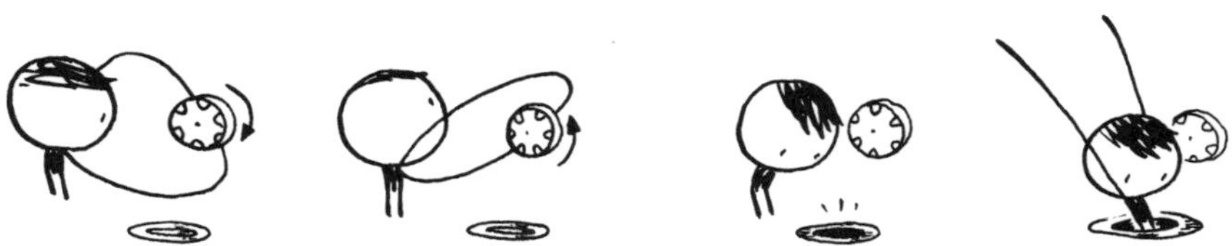

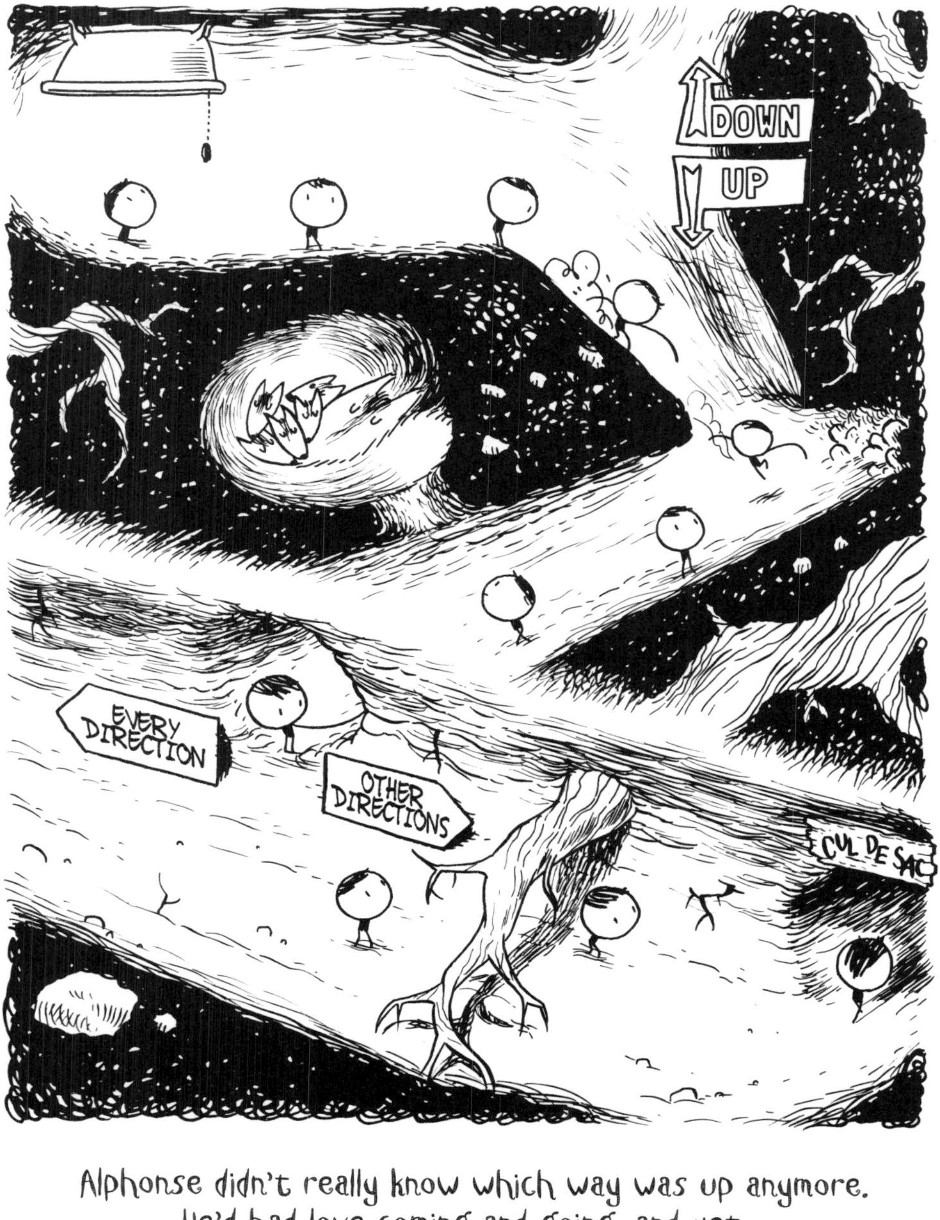
DOWN
UP
EVERY DIRECTION
OTHER DIRECTIONS
CUL DE SAC

Alphonse didn't really know which way was up anymore.
He'd had love coming and going, and yet...

...he wished someone would explain why love wasn't enough to make him perfectly happy.

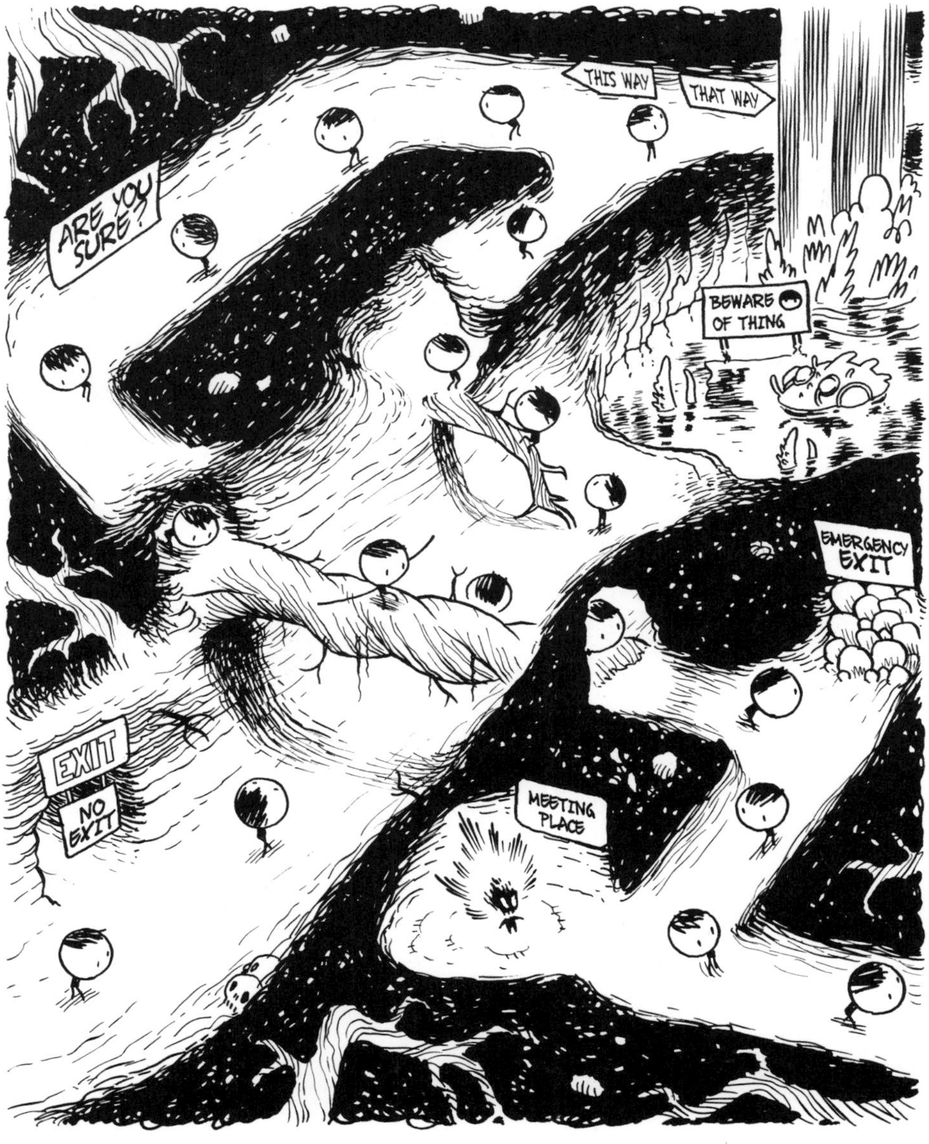
THIS WAY
THAT WAY
ARE YOU SURE?
BEWARE OF THING
EMERGENCY EXIT
EXIT
NO EXIT
MEETING PLACE

Maybe love was just too complicated.

Maybe knitting would be a better use of his time.

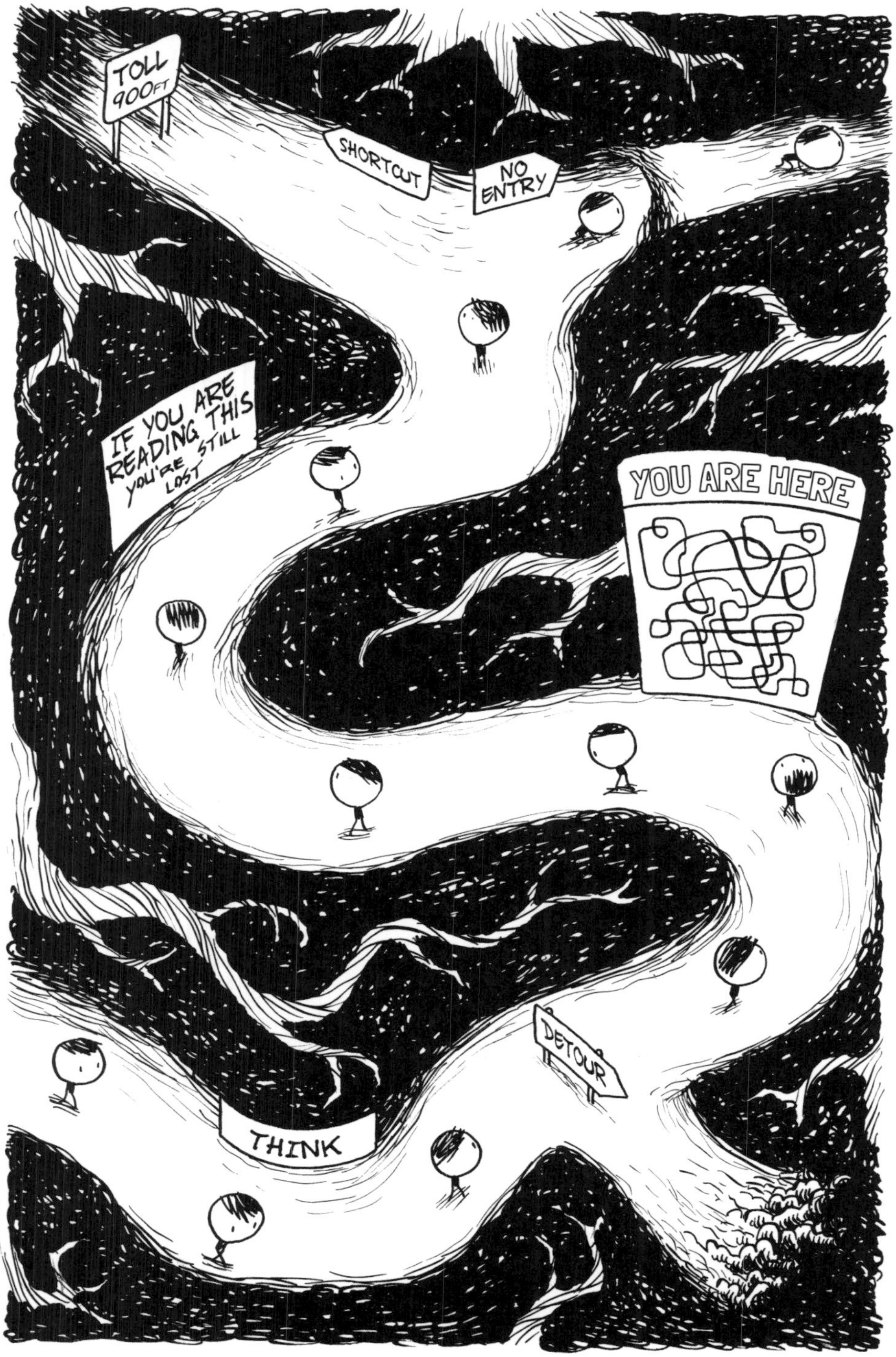
TOLL 900FT
SHORTCUT
NO ENTRY
IF YOU ARE READING THIS YOU'RE STILL LOST
YOU ARE HERE
DETOUR
THINK

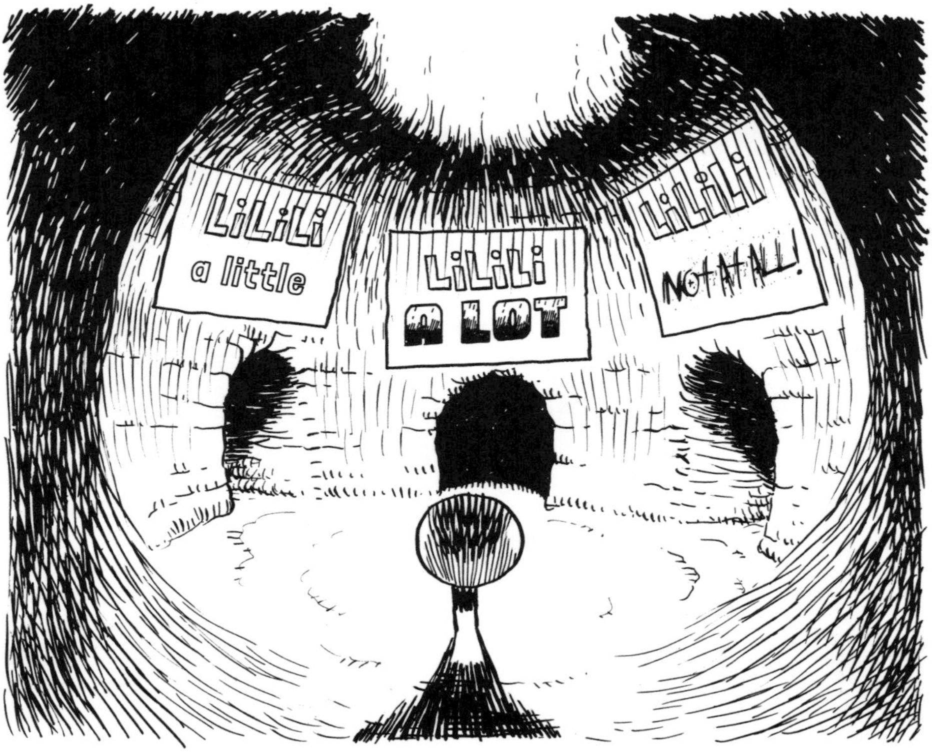
LiLiLi
a little
LiLiLi
A LOT
LiLiLi
NOT AT ALL!

Alphonse hesitated a little...

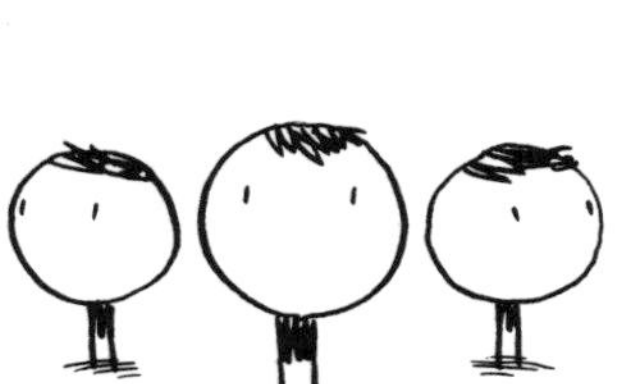

...then a lot...

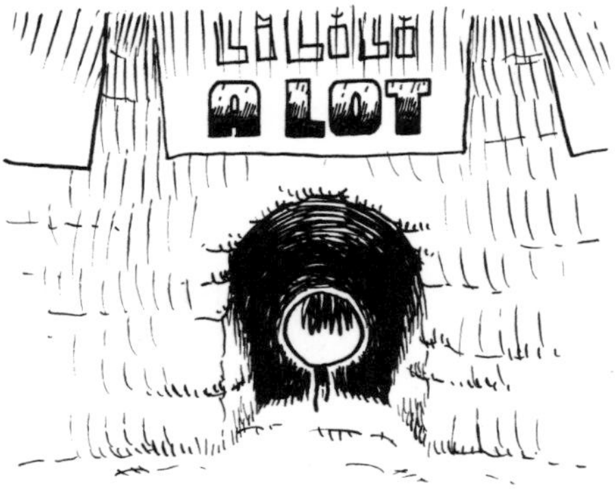
A LOT

...and then not at all.

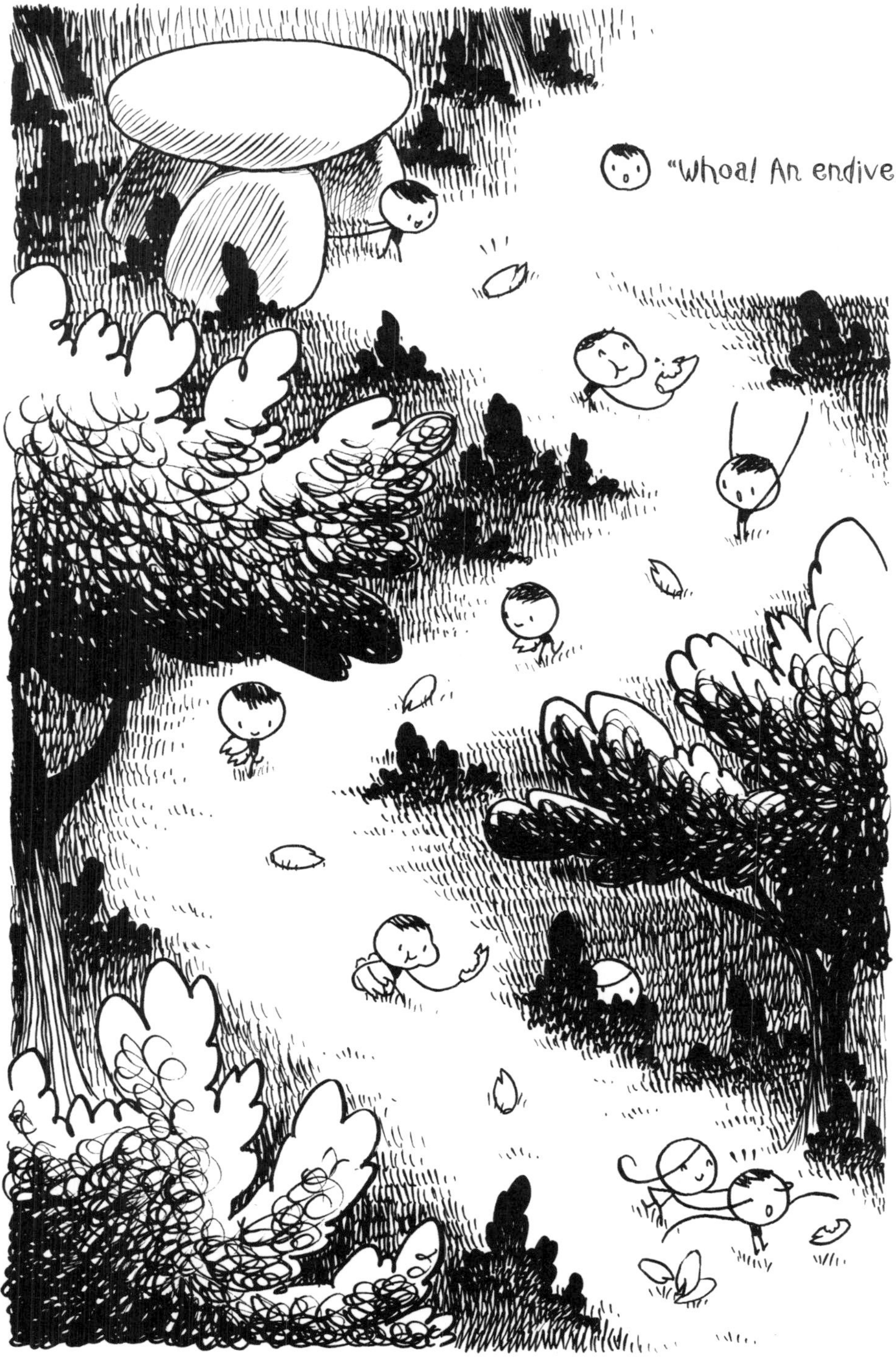
"Whoa! An endive!"

 "You made the right choice!"

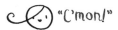 "C'mon!"

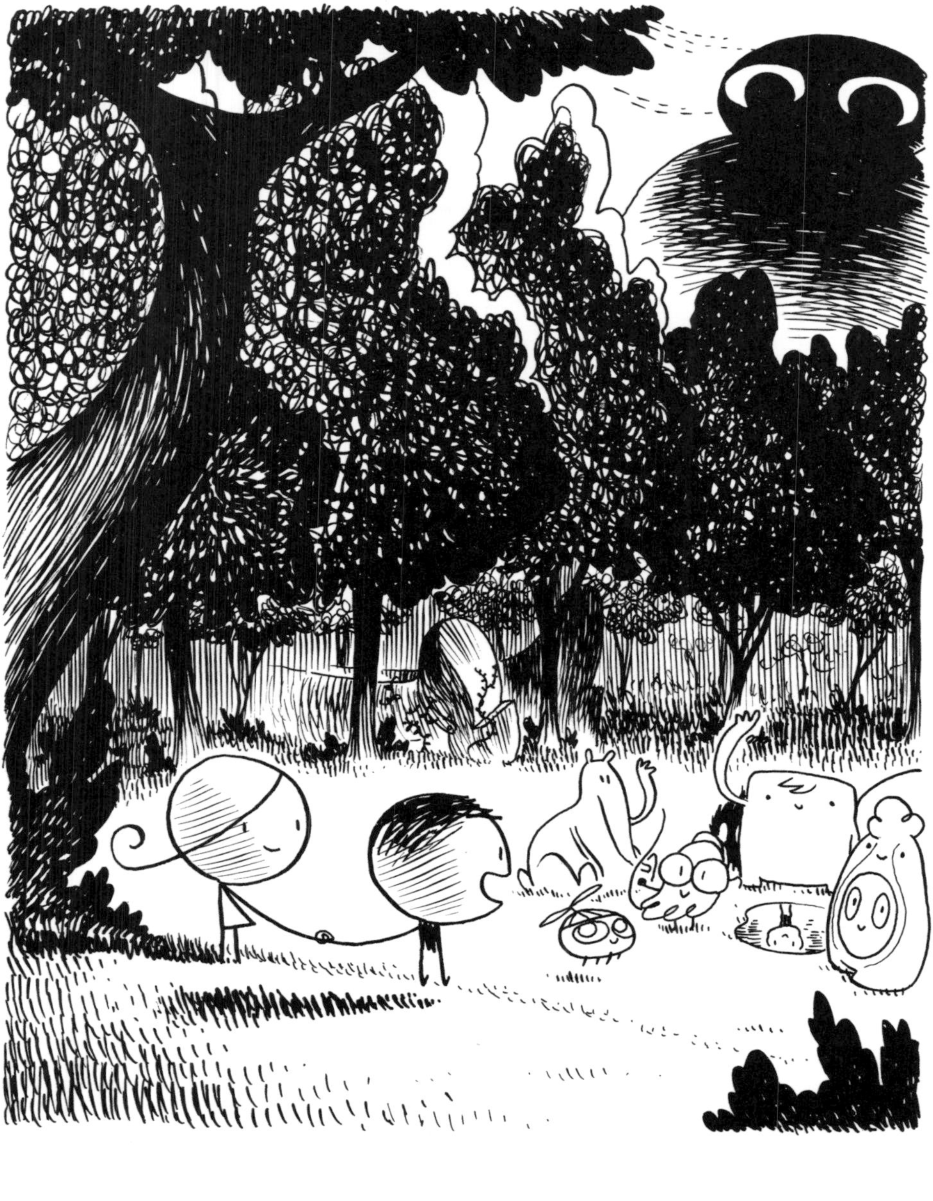

“They all helped. We made noodles with smackers and shiny skewers. There’s yesterday’s salad and bubble drinks. You wanna dance?”

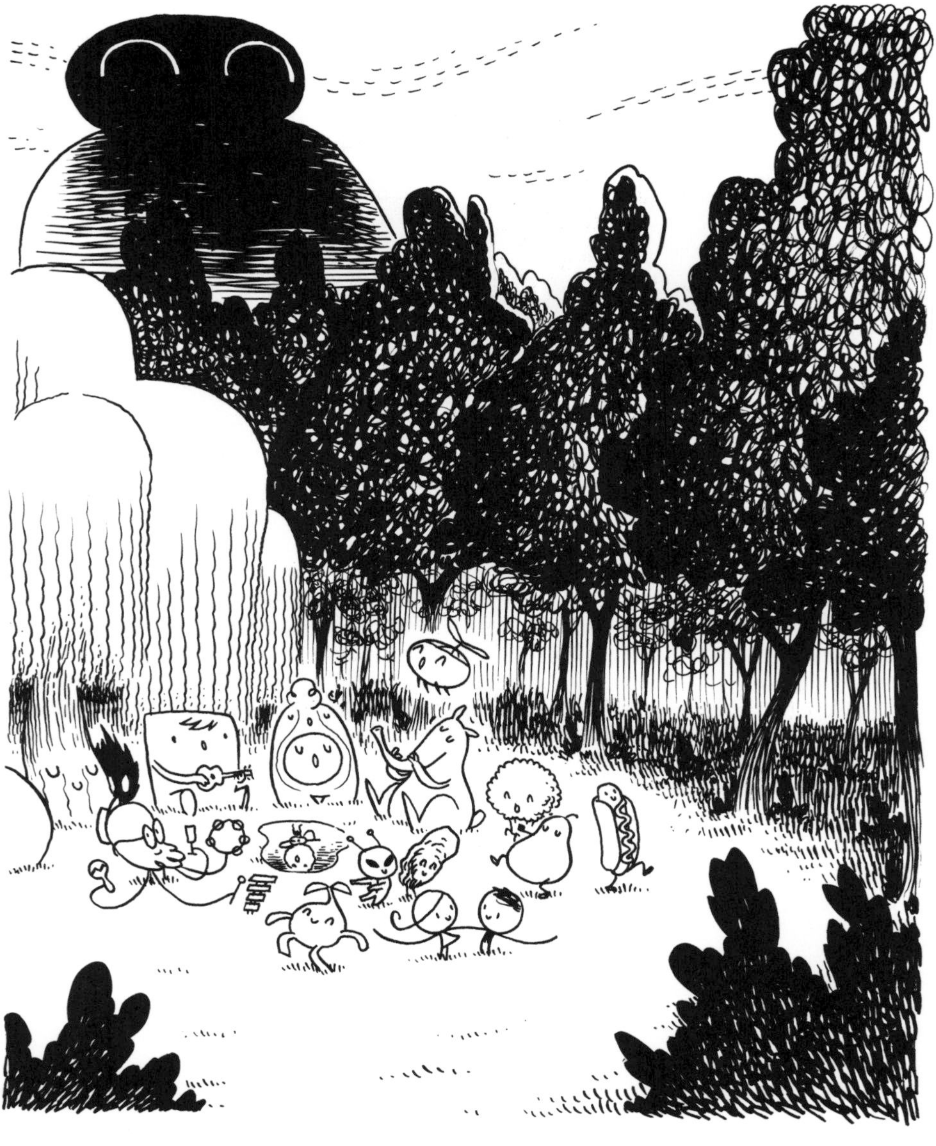

“We have a surprise for you!”

“Another one?”

"You have to go on another journey. But I know you'll come back if you miss me and you want to. You'll be able to have adventures so you can tell me all about them. You can bring me back surprises... maybe that'll even become your specialty."

 "Maybe you'll never come back.
But I hope you do."

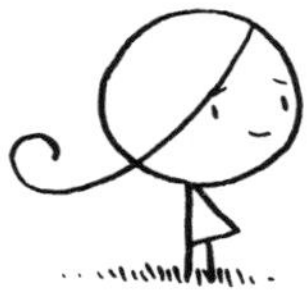

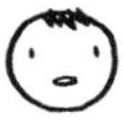 "But... aren't you coming?"

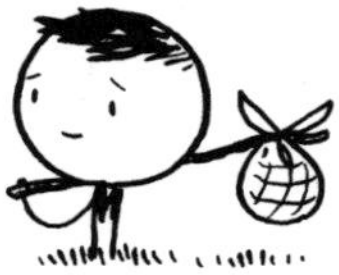

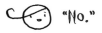

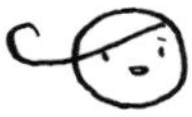 "No."

After a whole bunch of hugs and sloppy kisses,
the party came to an end.

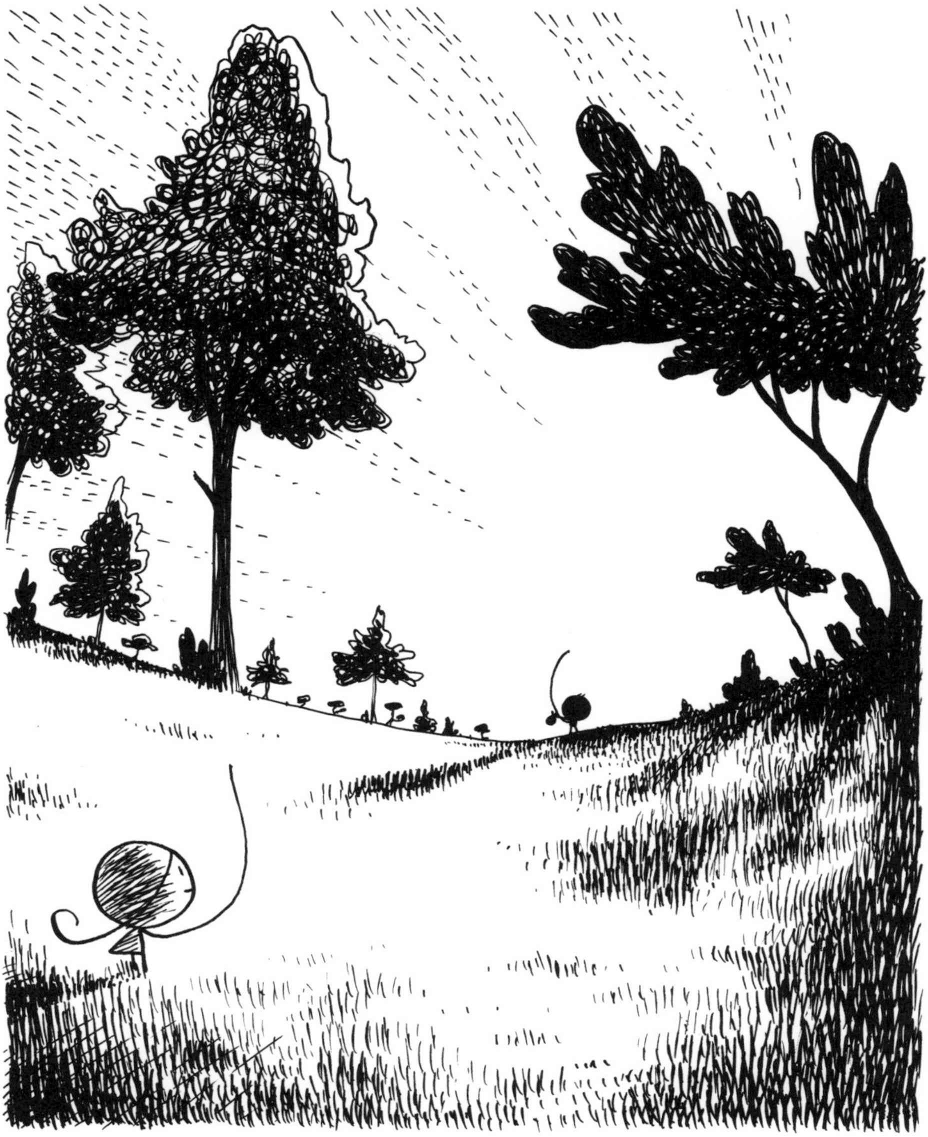

And Alphonse set out on his journey.

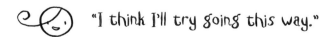 "I think I'll try going this way."

fin

Sibylline, Capucine & Jérôme   May 2010

As we explored our forest of a story,
we encountered Bastien Vivès, Anouk Richard,
Vince, Alfred, Natacha Sicaud, Kness, Capucine,
Domitille Collardey, and Libon, each of whom
drew Alphonse in their own way.

A big thank-you to all of them!

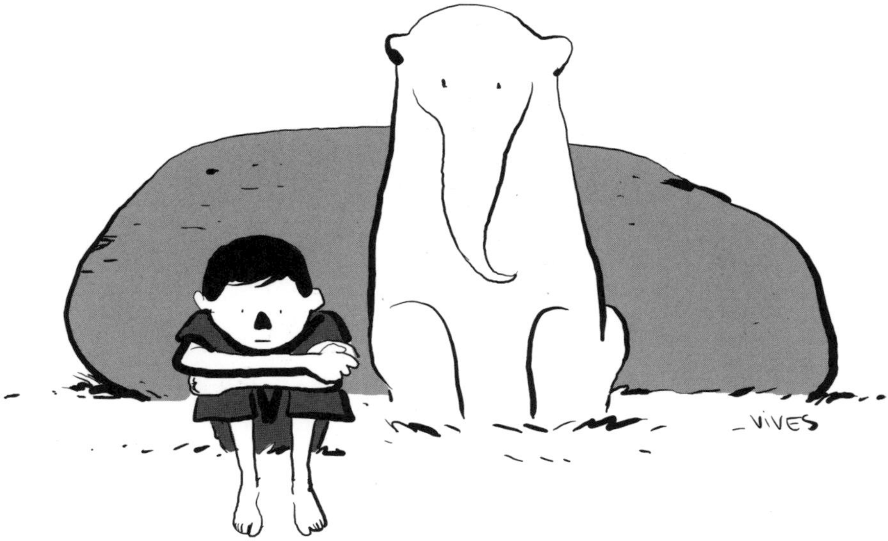
VIVES

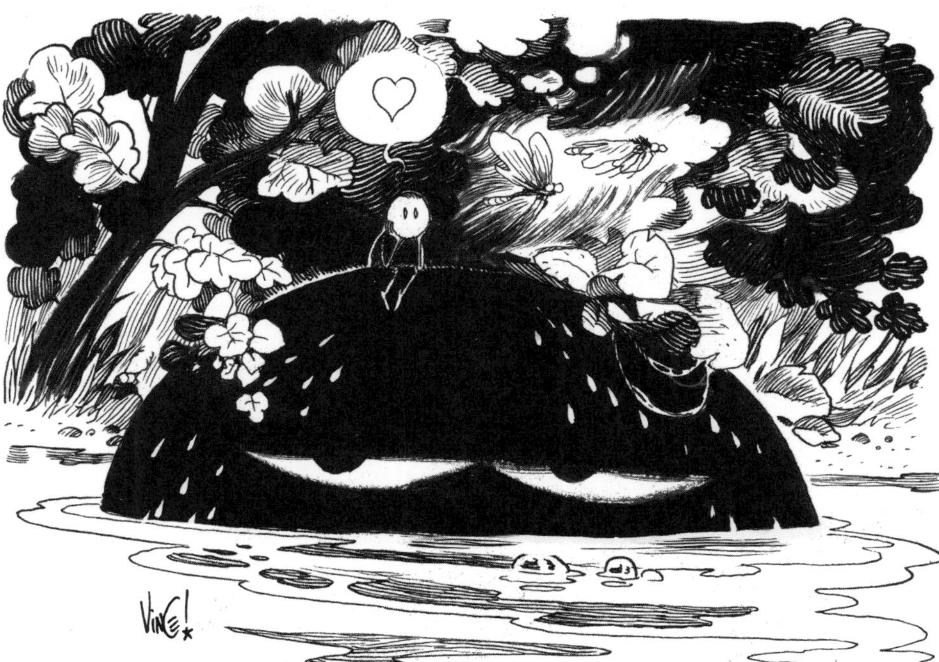

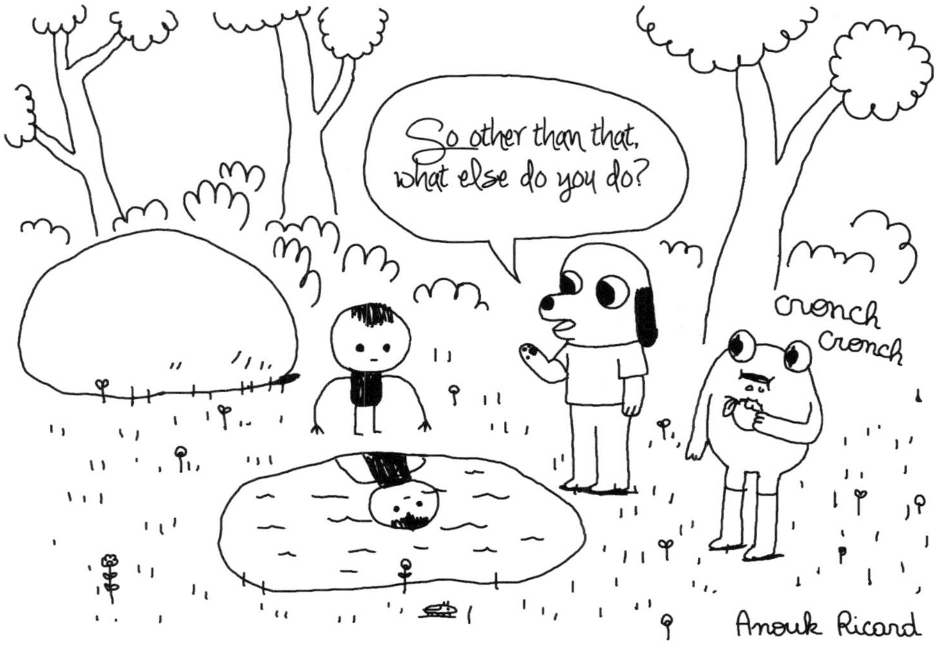
So other than that, what else do you do?
cronch cronch
Anouk Ricard

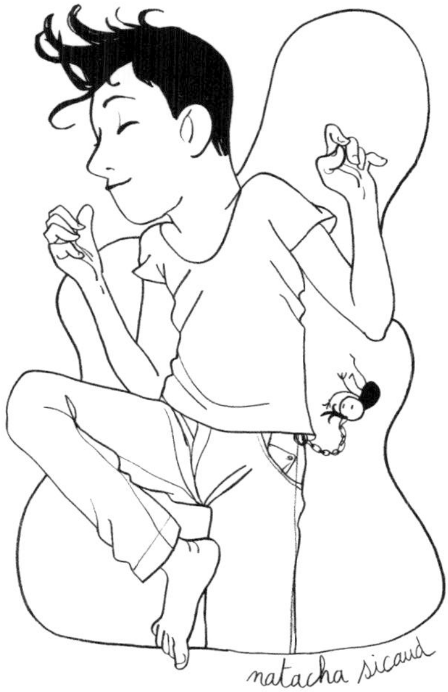
natacha sicaud

fig. 57

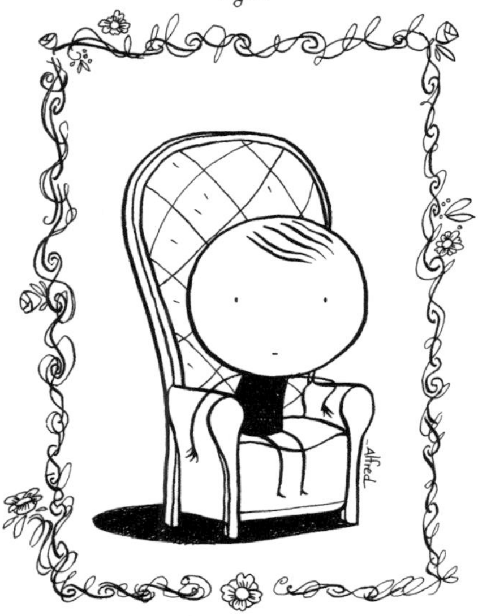
Alfred

Portrait of Alphonse in an armchair

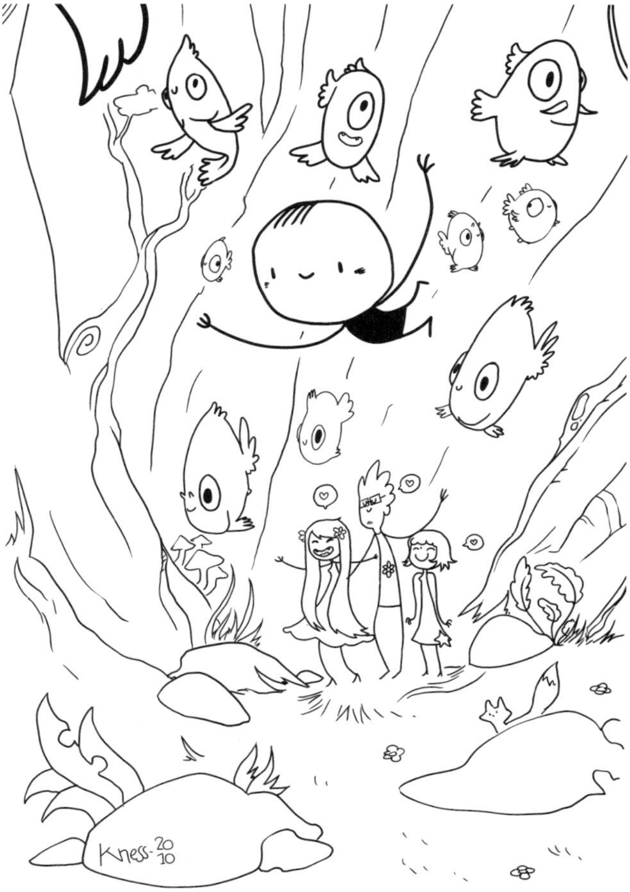
Kness-2010

Capucine.

Libon.

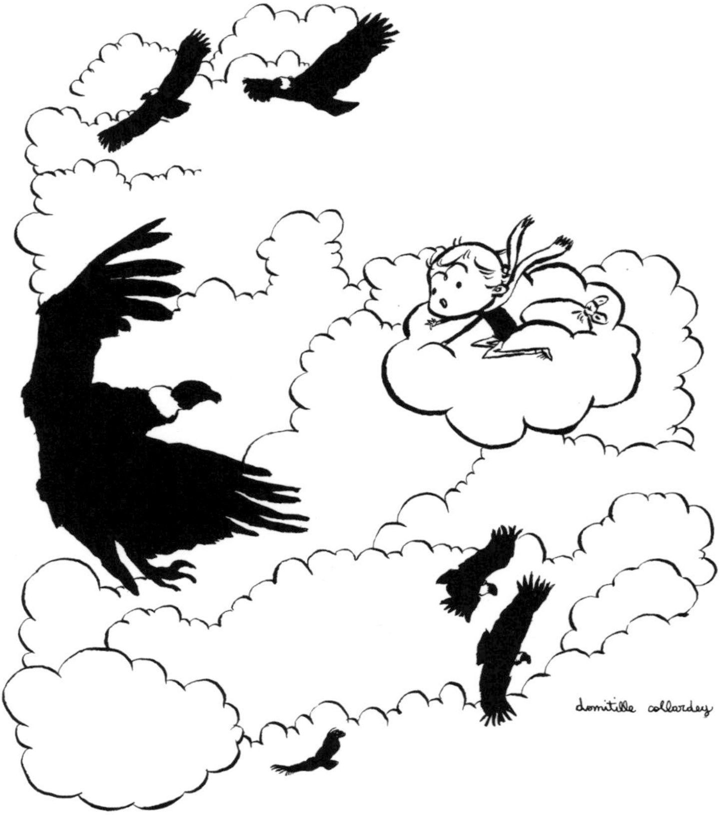
domitille collardey

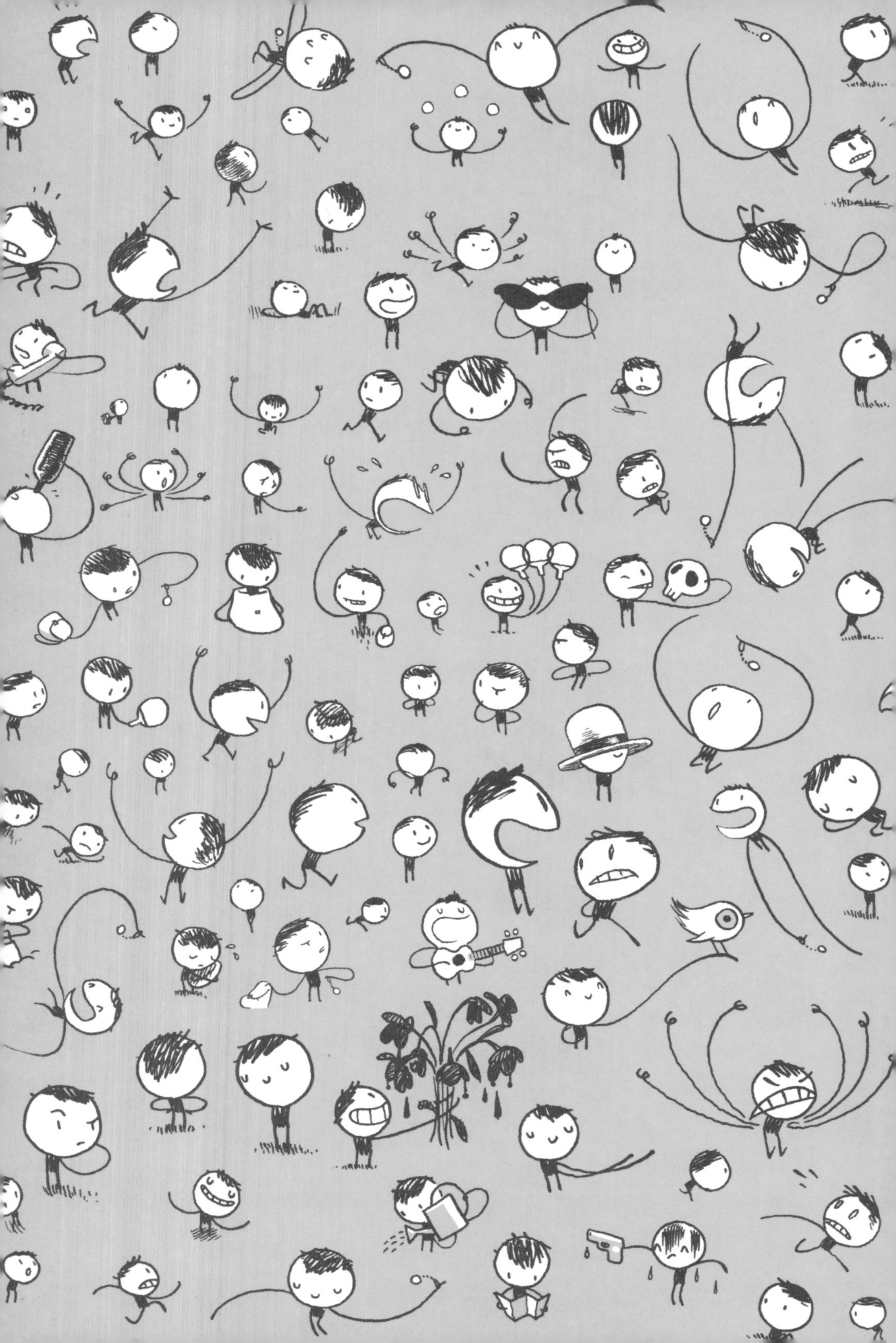